I ESDRAS
From Origin to Translation

SOCIETY OF BIBLICAL LITERATURE
SEPTUAGINT AND COGNATE STUDIES SERIES

Series Editor
Bernard A. Taylor

Editorial Advisory Committee

N. Fernández Marcos, Madrid
I. Soisalon - Soininen, Helsinki
E. Tov, Jerusalem

Number 47

I ESDRAS
From Origin to Translation

by
Zipora Talshir

I ESDRAS
From Origin to Translation

by

Zipora Talshir

Society of Biblical Literature
Atlanta, Georgia

I ESDRAS
From Origin to Translation

by
Zipora Talshir

Library of Congress Cataloging-in-Publication Data
Talshir, Zipora.
    I. Esdras : from origin to translation / by Zipora Talshir.
        p.   cm. — (Society of Biblical Literature septuagint and
    cognate studies series ; no. 47)
        Includes bibliographical references and index.
        ISBN 0-88414-006-7 (cloth : alk. paper)
        1. Bible. O.T. Apocrypha. Esdras, 1st—Criticism, Textual.
    2. Bible. O.T. Apocrypha. Esdras, 1st—Criticism, interpretation,
    etc. I. Title. II. Title: First Esdras. III. Title: One Esdras.
    IV. Series: Septuagint and cognate sutdies series ; no. 47.
    BS1715.2.T35   1999
    229'. 106—dc21   99-38500
                                            CIP

            08 07 06 05 04 03 02 01 00 99   5 4 3 2 1

Printed in the United States of America
on acid-free paper

TABLE OF CONTENTS

Contents vii

CHAPTER TWO: I ESDRAS' *VORLAGE* COMPARED WITH
2 CHR 35-36, EZRA 1-10 AND NEH 8

FOREWORD

My acquaintance and fascination with the Book of I Esdras started years ago in a course held by my mentor in Biblical studies, the late Prof. I.L. Seeligmann. He then initiated and coached my dissertation on the book, which was approved at the Hebrew University of Jerusalem in 1984, after his death. I am indebted to him for his insistence to pass on to his students his method and dedication to lucid philology.

The Book of I Esdras has survived in Greek as one of the books of the Apocrypha.[1] The title 'I Esdras, or sometimes 'Apocryphal Esdras', distinguishes it from the other books named after Ezra, first and foremost the canonical book of Ezr-Neh, for which there is a continuous, consistent translation in the corpus of the LXX, known as 'Second Esdras' (= II Esdras).[2]

A special feature of I Esd is its intermediate position between canonical literature and the Apocrypha. A large part of the book (the seven chapters I Esd 1-2 and 5-9) parallels, with some changes, material to be found in 2 Chr 35-36, Ezr and Neh 8. The two chapters I Esd 3-4, however, are non-canonical: they tell the Story of Three Youths. The relationship between I Esd and Chr-Ezr-Neh is therefore somewhat similar to the relationship between the canonical books of Daniel and Esther, on the one hand, and their LXX versions, on the other.

---

[1] The Church, too, has not granted I Esd a definite status; Jerome is largely responsible for this inferior position. See Pohlmann (1895); Denter (1962).

[2] 'First Esdras' is the title of the book in the main Greek tradition; Lucian calls it 'Second Esdras' (Ezr-Neh being 'First Esdras' in his canon), and the Latin tradition calls it 'Third Esdras' (after Ezr = I Esdras, and Neh = II Esdras). Interestingly enough, MSS 46-52 call II Esd 'The Third Book of Chr'.

This volume deals with the formation of I Esd. The issue is approached from three different angles. First, the **composition** of the book is discussed, considering its make-up and structure in comparison with Chr-Ezr-Neh, in attempt to establish its *raison d'être*. The second issue is anchored mainly in textual criticism, tracing in detail the ***Vorlage*** of I Esd in the chapters parallel to the MT in order to determine how the discrepancies between the texts emerged. Finally, we turn to the translator, analyzing his **translation** technique and philosophy and trying to outline the milieu in which he worked.

This general threefold study of I Esd's formation is the result of a detailed text-critical commentary on the book to be published in a forthcoming volume. The texts mentioned in this volume in brief will be discussed at length in the commentary *ad locum*.

I Esd is cited according to the Göttingen edition of the book prepared by R. Hanhart.[3]

---

[3] I thank David Luvitsh, Ann Brenner and Marc Turnage for the English version of this volume.

CHAPTER ONE

THE COMPOSITION OF I ESDRAS

Introduction: I Esdras' *raison d'être* – the Story of the Youths

A comparison between I Esd and the parallel material in the canonical books of Chr-Ezr-Neh reveals the following main differences:

1. I Esd contains only the last two chapters of Chr (2 Chr 35-36 = I Esd 1), opening, therefore, with Josiah's celebration of the Passover.

2. The direct continuation of 2 Chr 36 in I Esd is Ezr 1.[1]

3. In I Esd the letter of complaint to Artaxerxes (Ezr 4:6-24 = I Esd 2:15-25) is inserted immediately after Cyrus' edict (Ezr 1 = I Esd 2:1-14), while the parallel to Ezr 2:1-4:5 is shifted to just after the Story of the Youths.

4. The Story of the Youths (I Esd 3:1-5:6) is the most unique feature of I Esd, having no parallel whatever in the canonical literature.

5. The direct continuation of Ezr 10 in I Esd is Neh 8.

6. There is no trace in I Esd of Neh 1-7 (except for the last verse of Neh 7).

7. I Esd breaks off in the middle of Neh 8:13.

The following table shows the different arrangement of the material. The division into units is dictated by the comparison and may therefore be arbitrary in regard to extent and content.

---

[1] So that the identical passages 2 Chr 36:22-23 and Ezr 1:1-3a are automatically merged.

The signs used in the table are:

=   denotes parallel units in Chr-Ezr-Neh and I Esd.

~   denotes units which appear in the parallel text but in a different place.

- - - denotes units missing in the parallel text.

Chr-Ezr-Neh		**I Esd**
[A] 2 Chr 35-36 From Josiah's Passover to the Destruction	=	[A] I Esd 1
[B] Ezr 1 Edict of Cyrus	=	[B] 2:1-14
~		[D] 2:15-25 Letter of complaint
- - -		[X] 3:1-5:6 Story of the Youths
[C] Ezr 2:1-4:5 List of returnees, building of the altar, building of the Temple begun and interrupted	=	[C] 5:7-70
[D] Ezr 4:6-24 Letter of complaint		~
[E] Ezr 5:1-6:22 Building of the Temple resumed and completed	=	[E] 6:1-7:15
[F] Ezr 7:1-10:44 Ezra's arrival and activities	=	[F] 8:1-9:36
[G] Neh 1:1-7:71(72) Nehemiah's memoirs		- - -
[H] Neh 7:72, 8:1-12 (13) Reading of the Torah	=	[H] 9:37-55
[I] Neh 8:13-13:31 Further activities of Nehemiah		- - -

I Esd differs, therefore, from the canonical books (i) in its outer limits, (ii) in the relationships among the books of Chr-Ezr-Neh, (iii) in the order of the chapters, and (iv) above all in the Story of the Youths.

These topics have fired the imagination of scholars for many generations. This is not surprising, for I Esd offers what seems like simple solutions to some of the crucial problems relating to the composition of Chr-Ezr-Neh. Pohlmann's comprehensive study (1970) dealt with these problems starting with a survey of the relevant scholarship. He grouped the scholars who had treated these problems into two categories: 1) those favoring the *Fragmenthypothese*, and 2) protagonists of the *Kompilations- hypothese*. The former consider I Esd a fragment of a larger work that included all of Chr-Ezr-Neh; they conclude, in addition, that I Esd preserves part of an earlier redaction than that in the canonical books.[2] The latter see I Esd as a compilation of different units, arguing that the author was acquainted with the canonical books and culled what he needed from them.[3] Pohlmann's survey provides a good picture of the history of scholarship in this area. Although, one would expect, on principle, to find views intermediate between the two extreme hypotheses and different conclusions regarding various problems. Indeed, Pohlmann himself proposed an eclectic view. In his opinion, I Esd is a fragment of a complete translation; however, while it is a reworked version of material identical in structure with Ezr 1-6, it testifies to a more original edition in which the books of Ezr and Neh were not combined.

---

[2] In this category Pohlmann mentions (pp. 19-26) the views of Michaelis (1783), Trendelburg (1795), Dähne (1834), Treuenfels (1950-51), A. A. Pohlmann (1859), Howorth (1893-1907), Marquart (1896), Torrey (1910), Hölscher (1923), Mowinckel (1964). Another comprehensive study worth mentioning, from the beginning of the century, is Theis (1910), and the article by Cross (1975) should also be included.

[3] Pohlmann (pp. 15-19) sums up the views of Bertholdt (1813), Bayer (1911), Walde (1913), Rudolph (1949). On p. 15 n. 6 he lists about a dozen more scholars of a similar opinion. We might add here the studies of Kaufmann (1956) and Grinz (1963), who define I Esd as 'a collection of narratives'.

Recently Dieter Böhler (1997) published a new study on I Esd, dealing mostly with two major issues: the sequence Ezr-Neh 8 and the location of the letter of complaint to Artaxerxes. In his view, I Esd, without the Story of the Youths, preserves the original edition of the book, before a later redactor introduced Nehemiah's memoirs and ensuing changes. This redactor, living in the time of the Maccabees, added to the originally Temple-Torah centered edition of I Esd the claim for political sovereignty characteristic of Ezr-Neh.[4]

The present writer believes that I Esd is neither a 'fragment' surviving from a mostly lost book, nor, strictly speaking, a compilation of chosen units from the canonical books, but rather, a section deliberately cut out from Chr-Ezr-Neh, to form a framework for the Story of the Youths. I Esd never existed without the Story of the Youths. The latter, therefore, is the *raison d'être* of the book.

I. Beginning and End of the Book

The outer limits of the current version of I Esd make it very difficult to see the book as a self-contained entity. It begins in the middle of Josiah's reign with his celebration of the Passover (in parallel to 2 Chr 35). The end of the book parallels Neh 8:13, breaking off not only in the middle of the events but quite literally in mid-sentence.

a. End of the Book

I prefer to begin with the end of the book, which as it were speaks for itself: the book quite clearly breaks off for purely technical reasons; it

---

[4] Since Böhler's work became available to the present writer after this volume was completed, we mention his concepts on these issues in general in hope to answer his opposing views more properly in due time.

ends with the words καὶ ἐπισυνήχθησαν "then they assembled" – the beginning of a sentence which is left incomplete. It is inconceivable that the author would have deliberately ended the book in this way, and it is pointless to try to reconstruct the exceptional circumstances that might have unexpectedly interrupted his work.[5] Much more plausibly, the book was damaged at some point in time and the end is lost. It seems self-evident that the truncated work was the specific version surviving in I Esd, in which the reading of the Torah (Neh 8) follows the divorce of the 'foreign women' (Ezr 10).[6] Moreover, the damage most probably took place in the Greek translation, as the translator of I Esd would probably not have perpetuated a defective ending in the original work.[7]

---

[5] Some scholars have argued notwithstanding that this is indeed the original end of the book; see Cook (1913), pp. 1-2, though the examples he cites of similar endings are entirely irrelevant, as the verb in our case does not flow from the previous text but begins something new. Van der Kooij's suggestion (1990) is likewise unconvincing: καὶ ἐπισυνήχθησαν hardly rounds off the ὅτι clause in Greek, let alone in a Hebrew *Vorlage*. See also the proposal of Rudolph (1949), p. xv, who suggests that καὶ ἐπισυνήχθησαν is a gloss meaning: for the sequel see Neh 8:13 ff. In spite of the close of Chr, which is a kind of pointer to the sequel in Ezr, this idea of Rudolph remains unconvincing.

[6] I Esd also possessed its distinctive details, as well, when it was broken off: Neh 8:13 opens with the words ...וביום השני נאספו "on the second day... gathered". In I Esd, on the other hand, the text breaks off after the words καὶ ἐπισυνήχθησαν. We may assume that the text parallel to ביום השני followed immediately. In other words, the verb and its modifier changed places. It is a typical feature of I Esd, in contrast to the MT, that the verb is brought forward before other parts of the sentence (see pp. 223ff). We cannot determine whether the changed word-order was the work of the translator or already present in the translator's source; even so, the MT is superior because the point of interest here is the day, not the gathering; cf. vv. 1-2: ויאספו כל העם... ביום אחד לחדש השביעי "And all the people gathered... on the first day of the seventh month..."; and cf. Neh 8:18-9:1.

[7] See the completions in Lucian's version and in some MSS of the Latin translation of I Esd.

The content of the lost part of the book is another question. As our text includes the first part of Neh 8:13, the sequel most probably included the celebration of the feast of Booths (vv. 13-18). Josephus, who obviously made use of I Esd here,[8] goes on after the reading of the Torah to describe the whole celebration of the feast of Booths.[9] Nevertheless, his testimony should be treated with some caution, for Josephus frequently 'tied loose ends together' as he saw fit.[10] Moreover, though he surely used I Esd and not the canonical Ezr (or a parallel Greek version), he went back to the canon for the story of Nehemiah (but severed it, in contrast to the canonical books, from the story of Ezra).[11] At any rate, one cannot conclude from Josephus' version that I Esd, too, went on to give an account of the celebration of the feast of Booths after describing the reading of the Torah and, presumably, the rest of Nehemiah's activities.[12] Later I shall suggest

---

[8] See Pohlmann (1970), pp. 74ff. He is right in his conclusion (p. 113) that Josephus relies on I Esd in respect of content, sequence of events and even certain points of linguistic usage; but one should still not discount the logical possibility that the canonical books, too, were at his disposal and that he indeed used them on occasion. And see the criticism of In der Smitten (1971), pp. 381-382; Williamson (1977), pp. 22-24.

[9] Ant. XI 157.

[10] Thus, for example, he describes the deaths, at a ripe old age, of both Ezra (*ibid.* §157) and Nehemiah (*ibid.* §158).

[11] He follows Neh 1:1-7:4; it would seem that he was familiar with Neh 9-13, but he only hints at this material, and even then very briefly; see Williamson (1977), p. 25. Treuenfels (1850), pp. 774-777, asserted, on the basis of Josephus, that I Esd also included Nehemiah's memoirs.

[12] It is worth mention that, in contrast to Neh 8:9, the parallel passage in I Esd 9:49 does not identify 'the governor' (התרשתא) as Nehemiah, perhaps indicating that the author of I Esd wished to ignore Nehemiah. Nevertheless, the omission may result from a different reason: even if Nehemiah's memoirs were available to the editor, he would presumably have been wary of mentioning him here, before the proper time. Moreover, perhaps I Esd testifies to the original text, in which the governor was anonymous, as in Ezr 2:63. Surprisingly, the name Nehemiah is added in the latter's parallel in I Esd 5:40. This addition must be secondary since Nehemiah is entierly out of place in this context which deals with the return in the days of Darius.

that the author of I Esd indeed suppressed the story of Nehemiah instead
assigning a major role to Zerubbabel.

b. Beginning of the Book

The book begins, as it ends, abruptly, in the middle of Josiah's reign
(in parallel to the beginning of 2 Chr 35), and one is again faced with the
question: was the opening section of the book lost, and, if so, how long
was it? Here, however, in contrast to the end of the book, which breaks off
in mid-sentence, the explanation of physical damage is not applicable; for
the beginning relates, after all, to the beginning of a well-defined episode
in Josiah's reign – his celebration of Passover.

1. Can it be Proved that I Esd is Part of a Complete Translation of Chr-Ezr-Neh?

The arguments that I Esd did not originally begin with Josiah's Passover
celebration are mainly indirect. For example: it is not plausible that the
author would open with the words καὶ ἤγαγεν; it is not plausible that the
author would begin his account in the middle of a king's reign, when he
could have described the entire reign; the celebration of Passover does not
seem to have a particular significance in the book's general design; and,
generally speaking, the layout of the book as it is today does not seem to
be based on a well-defined plan. It was therefore suggested that the book
originally opened no later than the beginning of Josiah's reign, in parallel
with 2 Chr 34, or that I Esd had originally contained the entire Book of
Chr. The present book, then, would be a mere fragment of a rather large
work.[13]

---

[13] Pohlmann (1970), pp. 32-33.

The only concrete proof that I Esd originally contained the whole Book of Chr is the quotation of 2 Chr 2:11-13 by Eupolimos, a 2nd century Greek historian, as cited by Eusebius.[14] Torrey[15] argued that the Greek of this quotation is similar to that of I Esd, implying that there once existed a complete translation of the Chronicler's work, of which I Esd is but a fragment. Does the passage by Eupolimos indeed testify to the original form of I Esd?

The parallel texts in 2 Chr 2:11-13, LXX and Eupolimos are as follows:

2 Chr 2:11-13

ברוך ה' אלהי ישראל אשר עשה את השמים ואת הארץ אשר נתן לדויד המלך בן חכם
יודע שכל ובינה... ועתה שלחתי איש חכם יודע בינה לחורם אבי בן אשה מן בנות דן
ואביו איש צרי...

Blessed be the Lord God of Israel, who made heaven and earth, who has given King David a wise son, endued with discretion and understanding... Now I have sent a skilled man, endued with understanding, Huram-abi, the son of a woman of the daughters of Dan, and his father was a man of Tyre.

LXX

11 Εὐλογητὸς κύριος ὁ θεὸς ᾿Ισραὴλ ὃς ἐποίησεν τὸν οὐρανὸν καὶ τὴν γῆν ὃς ἔδωκεν τῷ Δαυὶδ τῷ βασιλεῖ υἱὸν σοφὸν καὶ ἐπιστάμενον σύνεσιν καὶ ἐπιστήμην... 12 καὶ νῦν ἀπέσταλκά σοι ἄνδρα σοφὸν καὶ εἰδότα σύνεσιν τὸν Χιράμ τὸν πατέρα μου 13 ἡ μήτηρ αὐτοῦ ἀπὸ θυγατέρων Δάν καὶ ὁ πατὴρ αὐτοῦ ἀνὴρ Τύριος...

Eupolimos:

Εὐλογητὸς ὁ θεὸς ὃς τὸν οὐρανὸν καὶ τὴν γῆν ἔκτισεν ὃς εἵλετο ἄνθρωπον χρηστὸν ἐκ χρηστοῦ ἀνδρός. καὶ ἀρχιτέκτονά σοι ἀπέσταλκα ἄνθρωπον Τύριον ἐκ μητρὸς ᾿Ιουδαίας ἐκ τῆς φυλῆς Δαβίδ...

Examination of the two Greek texts indeed reveals a considerable difference between the wording of the LXX and that of the quotation in

---

[14] Praepar. evangelica IX 34:1-2; see Holladay (1983), p. 122.

[15] Torrey (1910), p. 82.

Eupolimos' work. Is this difference indeed due to Eupolimos' use of a different translation, such as that of I Esd? The only evidence of the connection between I Esd and the language of the quotation is the equivalent of the verb עשה, 'to make', in the phrase 'who made heaven and earth'. In the LXX, as usual, עשה is rendered by ποιεῖν, whereas Eupolimos uses the verb κτίζειν. The translator of I Esd uses the same verb in the same phrase in 6:12 (Ezr 5:11) ἡμεῖς ἐσμεν παῖδες τοῦ κυρίου τοῦ κτίσαντος τὸν οὐρανὸν καὶ τὴν γῆν.[16] Nevertheless, this 'proof' is easily refuted. Linguistically speaking, one expects a greater similarity between the flowing language of I Esd and the living Greek of the historians. Moreover, it is difficult to trace the vestigial modes of expression of the anonymous translator in a passage that has been entirely recast: after all, the original Greek translation was transmitted first by Eupolimos, and later also by Eusebius. The distance in language and content between the biblical text and its parallel as cited by the historians is so considerable as to be unattributable to the translator – not even to the translator of I Esd.[17] There are no characteristic discrepancies of this order between the text of I Esd and the parallels in Chr-Ezr-Neh.

In sum, despite the temptation, one cannot see the passage in Eupolimos-Eusebius as a quotation from a translation, a fragment of which has survived in I Esd.

A further remark: if such a comprehensive translation existed, Josephus made no use of it. And if there had been such a translation, one would

---

[16] The parallel MT does not read the verb: אנחנא המו עבדוהי די אלה שמיא וארעא "we are the servants of the God of heaven and earth", but one may assume that the translator's *Vorlage* read עבד, the Aramaic equivalent of עשה.

[17] Thus, ὃς εἵλετο ἄνθρωπον χρηστὸν ἐκ χρηστοῦ ἀνδρός conveys only the general idea of אשר נתן לדויד המלך בן חכם יודע שכל ובינה. Farther on in the Eusebius-Eupolimos version Solomon conducts a correspondence, similar to that with the king of Tyre, with the king of Egypt, without any basis in the biblical text. And there are many more such expansions, abbreviations and changes, which hardly return to a variant text or translation.

have expected him to use it, in view of his adherence to I Esd in his account of the Restoration. That he did not use a translation related to I Esd for the whole Book of Chr we learn from his account of the last kings of Judah, from Josiah's Passover and on – a period documented in I Esd. Josephus bases his history here not only on the Book of Kings but also on Chr, but not the version preserved in I Esd.[18] He has recourse to I Esd only for the period of the Restoration; he probably knew the book as one devoted mainly to that period. It is most unlikely that he would have proceeded in this way if he had at his disposal a comprehensive, continuous work covering the whole period of Chr-Ezr-Neh.[19]

Finally, one can perhaps draw conclusions from Josephus as to Eupolimos' procedure: Josephus, too, like Eupolimos, did not use an unknown translation of Chr, despite his constant use of independent language and content. It is unlikely that three translations of Chr existed, and even the existence of two translations to a large-scale work like Chr, is rather improbable.[20] If the LXX versions of Chr and Ezr-Neh were very late translations, it might be justified to suggest the existence of an older Greek translation, part of which has come down to us in I Esd, but this thesis is no longer commonly held, and especially not in relation to LXX-Chr, which is what concerns us at this moment.[21]

There is, therefore, no real evidence that the translation surviving in I Esd was ever part of a translation of the whole of Chr.

---

[18] Thus, he relies for Josiah's Passover and his encounter with Pharaoh Neco not on the very brief version of the Book of Kings but on Chr, but not in the typical guise of I Esd. For example, Josephus writes (Ant. X, §76) that Josiah did not heed Neco's warning, as in 2 Chr 35:22, both MT and LXX; while I Esd states (1:26) that he did not heed the words of the prophet Jeremiah. A further example: Josephus relates (*ibid.* §77) that the king was wounded on the battlefield, as in 2 Chr 35:23, while I Esd says nothing of the king's being struck by warriors (1:27).

[19] Neither would one have expected him to insert various events, taken mainly from the books of Jeremiah and Daniel, between the periods of the monarchy and the Restoration.

[20] Williamson (1977), pp. 14-16.

[21] Allen (1974), I, pp. 6-17.

2. Is there any Evidence that I Esd Originally Began with Josiah's Passover?

Besides the question of a complete translation of Chr-Ezr-Neh in the version preserved in I Esd, scholars have debated whether the lost material at the beginning of the book included just one episode – the first chapter of Josiah's reign (2 Chr 34). Had I Esd indeed opened in parallel to 2 Chr 34, at the inception of Josiah's reign, no-one would have doubted that this was the original intention of the author.

It is rather difficult to draw any conclusions from the details of the text as to the work as a whole; some details seem to embody references to the opening chapter of Josiah's reign (2 Chr 34), while others seem deliberately to ignore it.

On the one hand, the final verse of Josiah's reign, 1:31 (2 Chr 35:26), being as it is part of the concluding formula, sums up the entire reign and not just part of it. That in itself does not necessarily imply that I Esd originally covered the whole reign. Nevertheless, it is striking that I Esd's version of the verse reveals ties with 2 Chr 34 which are not in the MT. As against the MT: ויתר דברי יאשיהו וחסדיו ככתוב בתורת ה' "Now the rest of the acts of Josiah, and his good deeds according to what is written in the law of the Lord", I Esd reads: καὶ τῆς συνέσεως αὐτοῦ ἐν τῷ νόμῳ κυρίου, possibly for ובינתו בתורת ה' "and his understanding of the law of the Lord". This reading seems to refer more specifically to the reading of the 'Book of the Law' that had been found during Josiah's reign, and the reforms that he instituted on that basis (2 Chr 34), and, therefore, it may well be the original text. In I Esd, which does not relate the specific event of the finding of the scroll, the expression may have been interpreted as a general reference to Josiah's piety.[22]

---

[22] It is doubtful whether the translation of yet another verse distinguishes those of Josiah's activities recounted in I Esd from those that are not. As against 2 Chr 35:27 דבריו הראשנים והאחרנים "his acts, first and last", we read in I Esd 1:31 τά τε προπραχθέντα ὑπ' αὐτοῦ καὶ τὰ νῦν. If we understand the Greek as translated by Cook (1913): "and the things that he had done before and the things recited now", it

On the other hand, another passage in the text lends credence to the hypothesis that the author's awareness of the extent of his book agrees with its present opening. As against 2 Chr 35:20 אחרי כל זאת אשר הכין יאשיהו את הבית "After all this, when Josiah had prepared the temple", the parallel passage in I Esd 1:23 reads: Καὶ μετὰ πᾶσαν τὴν πρᾶξιν ταύτην᾽Ἰωσίου, note, there is no direct reference to the Temple (the words את הבית are not rendered). In other words, in contrast to the MT, which explicitly refers to Josiah's activities in the Temple as described in 2 Chr 34, the summary in I Esd is concerned with Josiah's activities in general, as the apocryphal book contains no parallel to 2 Chr 34.[23] If it could be argued that this change was deliberate, it might constitute an indication of the original form of the book; however, the circumstances in which the verse in question received its present form are unknown.[24] The verse stands at a transitional point in the book, and, therefore, may have been subject to alteration; thus, the LXX-Chr omits these connecting words

would follow that the translator distinguished Josiah's first actions, not referred to in the book he was translating, and those told here and now. However, the verb 'recited' is superimposed on the Greek text but not actually in it: προπραχθέντα refers to things that are being done, not recited or written (νῦν is the opposite of προ..., and the complete opposition is: τά προπραχθέντα ὑπ᾽ αὐτοῦ # τὰ νῦν πραχθέντα ὑπ᾽ αὐτοῦ). Τὰ νῦν is a legitimate, though unusual, equivalent to אחרונים 'last' (cf. the phrase דורות אחרונים 'the present generations' in Qumran and Rabbinical Hebrew). It is worth noting, with due caution, that the specific translation adopted here for the final formula (and for its other occurrences in the sequel) supports the thesis that there was at the time no complete translation to Chr; if the translator had already dealt with this formula innumerably many times, throughout Chr, he would hardly have varied his rendering several times toward the end of the book; see 1:32-33 (2 Chr 36:1-3).

[23] Talshir (1984), pp. 13-14; van der Kooij (1991*), p. 250.

[24] The omission of the words את הבית may be simply a slip of the pen. Alternatively, the translator may have been responsible: after beginning to translate as he did, with a noun replacing the verbal combination, the direct object was left hanging and he simply omitted it.

altogether, after previously adding material culled from the parallel passage in the Book of Kings (see below). I Esd, too, has an additional passage at this point (1:21-22, unparalleled anywhere). Possibly, therefore, the different wording of the text, which does not confine Josiah's activities to the Temple, is due to the added material, which constitutes a general summary of Josiah's activities.

The current text, then, seems to convey contradictory implications for the question of whether the present start of the book is accidental or deliberate. The author did not leave us a clue to this perennial problem.

3. The Evidence of I Esd 1:21-22

The two verses added in I Esd 1:21-22, warmly praising Josiah, perhaps, hint at one thing quite clearly: our author indeed chose to begin his book with Josiah. After the parallel to 2 Chr 35:19 one reads the following added text:

21 καὶ ὠρθώθη τὰ ἔργα Ἰωσίου ἐνώπιον τοῦ κυρίου αὐτοῦ ἐν καρδίᾳ πλήρει εὐσεβείας. 22 καὶ τὰ κατ᾽ αὐτὸν δὲ ἀναγέγραπται ἐν τοῖς ἔμπροσθεν χρόνοις, περὶ τῶν ἡμαρτηκότων καὶ ἠσεβηκότων εἰς τὸν κύριον παρὰ πᾶν ἔθνος καὶ βασιλείαν, καὶ ἃ ἐλύπησαν αὐτὸν ἐν αἰσθήσει, καὶ οἱ λόγοι τοῦ κυρίου ἀνέστησαν ἐπὶ Ἰσραήλ.

And the deeds of Josiah were upright in the sight of his Lord, for his heart was full of godliness. The events of his reign have been recorded in the past concerning those who sinned and acted wickedly toward the Lord beyond any other people or kingdom, and how they grieved the Lord deeply, so that the words of the Lord rose up [were fulfilled] against Israel.

Now, as we have already stated, the LXX, too, like I Esd, adds material after 2 Chr 35:19. Except for the position in the text, there is no connection between the two additions.[25] The added text in the LXX is a

---

[25] Thus Nestle, p. 27, arguing against the view (current in his day) that I Esd is a reworking of the LXX; similarly Hanhart (1974*), p. 13.

translation of a text borrowed from 2 Kgs 23:24-27. The translator does
not copy the LXX to that passage (at least, not the currently extant version
of the LXX); he translates from a Hebrew text, probably from a version of
Chr in which the addition was already present. This expanded version is
probably secondary, as the theodicy expressed in it – clearly representative
of the doctrine of cumulative punishment typical of the Book of Kings – is
at variance with the spirit of the Chronicler, who consistently favors
immediate, inflexible punishment.[26] At any rate, this text cannot possibly
be considered as a source for I Esd, even if one assumes that the translator
has produced a very free, paraphrastic version.

Like the addition in the LXX, the added verses in I Esd are also a
late addition – and again, not by the translator. Underlying the Greek text
is a Hebrew source. This is evident in regard to almost every constituent,
from a routine phrase like ἐνώπιον τοῦ κυρίου to an idiomatic expression
such as καὶ οἱ λόγοι τοῦ κυρίου ἀνέστησαν ἐπὶ Ἰσραήλ. We suggest
that it goes back to a text such as the following conjectured *Vorlage*:

ותכון מלאכת יאשיהו לפני אלהיו בלבב שלם וביראה. ודבריו הנם כתובים על הימים
הראשונים על החוטאים והפושעים בה׳ מכל גוי וממלכה ואשר הכעיסוהו בדעת
(/ברעתם) ודברי ה׳ קמו על ישראל.

But this source was not part of the original text of Chr.[27] Its style is
quite distinctive, and its message, however one interprets the addition,
does not fit well into the frame of Chr.

Unfortunately, the meaning of the added verses in I Esd is far from
clear. Some scholars have understood the references to 'sinners' as applying
to Josiah as well. Since this clashes with the 'righteous king' conception
of I Esd, they are forced to explain the passage as an addition to the

---

[26] Bickermann (1962), pp. 24-27.

[27] Torrey (1910), p. 88, sees this passage as an original fragment of Chr, intended to
replace the similarly positioned passage of Kings and to provide its own explanation
as to why Josiah's actions did not alter the national fate; the text, he argues, is
defective and its meaning was therefore obscured.

original I Esd.[28] But the real meaning seems to be different. The verses make a distinction between the righteous king and the sinners. The first verse refers to Josiah, saying that he acted reverently and wholeheartedly (v. 21). The second verse, however, refers to those who sinned against the Lord. This part is difficult to explain: what actions are being condemned? what are the 'early [lit.: first] days' in which these actions took place? who are the sinners against the Lord? and, finally, what were the words or things that "were fulfilled concerning Israel"?

The text offers no explicit answers. The most attractive solution, proposed repeatedly over many decades of scholarship,[29] is that the passage is referring to 2 Kgs 23:15-18 (not echoed in 2 Chr 34). It closes the circle begun in the prophecy of the man of God concerning Josiah's destruction of the altar that Jeroboam built at Bethel: הנה בן נולד לבית דוד יאשיהו שמו וזבח עליך את כהני הבמות המקטירים עליך ועצמות אדם ישרפו עליך "Behold, a son shall be born to the house of David, Josiah by name; and he shall sacrifice upon you the priests of the high places who burn incense upon you, and men's bones shall be burned upon you" (1 Kgs 13:1-3). While the Chronicler omitted any reference to this prophecy, the author of I Esd returned to it. Like the author of Kings, he considered it a mark in Josiah's favor that his actions had been foreseen in those 'early days', and the prophecy had indeed been "fulfilled concerning Israel" in his time. The meaning of the passage would then be as follows: Josiah's actions were foretold long ago, in the early days, in the book that told the history of the sinners against the Lord (the sins of Jeroboam); and God's words had indeed come true in Josiah's day. I believe this is still the most plausible interpretation of the passage.

---

[28] Walde (1913), pp. 88-89. Myers, too, persists in the view that the original passage was omitted because it lumped Josiah together with the evil kings; Myers (1974), p. 28.

[29] Fritsche (1851), p. 16; Torrey (1945), p. 405; Rudolph (1955), p. 331; Hanhart (1974*), p. 13.

Van der Kooij reexamined the problem proposing a different solution for the many difficulties raised by this passage; his solution, moreover, led him to a certain theory concerning the beginning of the book.[30] To his mind, the text intends to distinguish between Josiah, the righteous king, and his subjects, sinners and evildoers who grieve Josiah by their actions. I Esd 1:22 is based on 2 Kgs 22 and on its parallel in 2 Chr 34. However, the account of Josiah's reform in those chapters does not accord with the verdict delivered by the author of I Esd on the sinning people, since the people, too, take part in the reforms (see, especially, 2 Chr 34:33). Here, then, argues van der Kooij, is the reason that the author of I Esd did not include 2 Chr 34 in his work.

Although van der Kooij's distinction between Josiah and the people is logical and well rooted in later traditions,[31] his solution ignores the time definition: "the early days".[32] These words belie his explanation that the text is referring to the misdeeds of Josiah's own subjects, or even the time of his father Manasseh.

As to the general conclusion about the book's beginning, if vv. 21-22 are indeed referring to the sins of the people in Josiah's time, hence implying an ideology different from that of 2 Chr 34, and especially v. 33, the author could have omitted this last verse, just as he added vv. 21-22. This is not a sufficient reason for such a far-reaching literary decision as excluding 2 Chr 34 and beginning the book in the middle of Josiah's reign.

---

[30] Van der Kooij (1991*).

[31] He specifically cites Ben Sira, but the same is true of the Talmudic sages; see below.

[32] The text speaks of 'early/first days' and not of 'first books', as van der Kooij intimates in an effort to circumvent the problem: "Der Text von I Esr 1, 22 nimmt Bezug auf ein bestimmte Passage in den 'früheren' Büchern der Könige und der Chronik" (p. 246). There are no grounds for the assumption that the author of I Esd considered his work as a new book based on early books.

In our view, the added verses do not constitute proof that I Esd originally began as it does today, with Josiah's celebration of Passover; but they may support the thesis that the book did begin, and deliberately so, with Josiah. If the book did indeed open with Josiah's celebration of Passover, this was most probably the result of a largely redactional decision, the redactor being primarily interested in the sequel and less in the starting point. A similar device was adopted by another redactor whose work has reached us, namely, the Chronicler. Indeed, the Chronicler opens the narrative-part of his book with the last chapter of Saul's reign (the battle on Mount Gilboa, 1 Sam 31 = 1 Chr 10).[33] Perhaps this was not an uncommon device among authors of those times.

Of all the differences between our text and its parallel in the MT, the addition in I Esd 1:21-22 is the most salient in both length and content, except for the major departures due to the inclusion of the Story of the Three Youths and the structure of the book. The particular reference to Josiah's reign must indicate the author's special attitude to that king.[34] Indeed, the author of I Esd, in his special attitude to Josiah, is adding his voice to a persistent trend, stressing Josiah's outstanding qualities. Josiah enjoyed a unique status among the kings of Judah and Israel, both in biblical and later literature.

The Book of Kings highlights his position by the prophecy to Jeroboam (1 Kgs 13), already mentioned above, which arouses expectations for his reign and his activities. Furthermore, we read in 2 Kgs 23:25 that וכמהו לא

---

[33] I first learned of this comparison from Prof. S. Talmon.

[34] The author of the current text of I Esd may, indeed, have done Josiah a last kindness in his treatment of that king's tragic end. Josiah's death is described in three different ways: in the Book of Kings he dies at Megiddo and his slaves carry his corpse to Jerusalem (2 Kgs 23:29-30); in Chr he is wounded at Megiddo and brought to Jerusalem, where he dies (2 Chr 35:23-24); but in I Esd he only weakens on the battlefield, whereupon he returns to Jerusalem and dies in his bed, 1:27-29; see Talshir (1996).

"Before him there was no ‏היה לפניו מלך אשר שב אל ה׳... ואחריו לא קם כמהו‏ king like him, who turned to the Lord...; nor did any like him arise after him".

Ben Sira, too, lauds him: ‏שם יאשיהו כקטרת סמים הממלח מעשה רוקח.‏ ‏בחך כדבש ימתיק זכרו וכמזמור על משתה היין. כי נחל על משובתינו וישבת תועבות‏ ‏הבל. ויתם אל אל לבו ובימי חמס עשה חסד...‏ "The memory of Josiah is like a blending of incense prepared by the art of the perfumer. It is sweet as honey to every mouth, and like music at a banquet of wine. He was led aright in converting the people, and took away the abominations of iniquity. He set his heart upon the Lord; in the days of wicked men he strengthened godliness" (Sirach 49:1-4).

The Sages of the Talmud uphold Josiah's honor,[35] and warn against ascribing any misdeed to him.[36] The Sages also considered the question of why Josiah's good deeds were not taken into account in determining the fate of the nation as a whole; their answer was to distinguish between the king and his subjects: Josiah had indeed repented sincerely and completely, but his contemporaries continued to support idolatry, which they successfully concealed from him,[37] ‏והוא אינו יודע שאין דורו דומה יפה‏ "and he did not realize, however, that his generation did not appear good enough (in the eyes of God)".[38]

---

[35] Babylonian Talmud, Sanhedrin 104a.

[36] Babylonian Talmud, Shabbat 56b: ‏כל האומר יאשיהו חטא אינו אלא טועה שנאמר: ויעש‏ ‏הישר בעיני ה׳.... אלא מה מה אני מקיים יוכמהו לא היה לפניו מלך אשר שב׳ וגו׳, שכל דין שדן מבן‏ ‏שמנה עד שמנה עשרה החזירן להן... ופליגא דרב, דאמר רב: אין לך גדול בבעלי תשובה יותר‏ ‏מיאשיהו בדורו‏ "Whosoever says, Josiah sinned! – is surely in error, for Scripture states, 'And he did what was right in the eyes of the Lord...' [2 Kgs 22:2]. But then how can one fulfill the words of Scripture, 'Before him there was no king like him, who turned etc.'? – Any judgment that he had delivered between the ages of eight and eighteen, he returned it to the litigants [i.e., he returned whatever property had changed hands as a result of his judgment, for fear that he had misjudged the case]... This is contrary to the statement of Rav, who said: There is no greater penitent than Josiah in his generation".

[37] Echa Rabba, Pisqa 1.

[38] Babylonian Talmud, Ta'anit 22b.

There can be no other meaning for the beginning of the book – if the beginning it indeed is – but the wish to start with Josiah.[39] Other explanations that have been suggested in attempts to propose a plan for the book are less than plausible. This is particularly true with regard to generalities, such as the explanation that the book was an anthology of stories from the end of the First Temple period and the beginning of the Second Temple period which opened with the feast of Passover and closed with the feast of Booths.[40] Neither can we agree with the commonly held view that I Esd intended to describe the history of the temple from its last Golden Age until the reestablishment of the cult.[41] Indeed, if that were the case, surely the very relevant chapter of Josiah's reign that relates to the Temple – 2 Chr 34 – would have been included! The whole plan of the book would have benefited had it opened with Josiah's accession to the throne and gone on to describe the discovery of the scroll of the Law and the reading of the Law, echoed finally by the reading of the Law in Ezra's time. However, as the book stands before us today, all we can say is that the author had at his disposal a comprehensive work that included Chr-Ezr-Neh in their canonical versions but strung together. The author of I Esd was moved to intervene by his desire to include the story of the three youths. This did not necessitate copying the whole work anew. All he had to do was to begin at some specific point, and he probably chose Josiah in view of the latter's special status.

II. Continuity of Chr-Ezr and Ezr-Neh

The transition between Chr-Ezr-Neh is treated differently in I Esd than in the canonical books. In the latter, Chr and Ezr-Neh are completely

---

[39] Rudolph (1949), p. XIV.

[40] Thus Kaufmann (1956), thereby stressing his contempt for I Esd as a literary work or, in his words, 'literary miscarriage'.

[41] This has long been a popular thesis; see Bertholdt (1813), p. 1011; Schürer (1986), pp. 708-717.

separate; only the repetition of the first words of Ezr at the end of Chr ties them together to create a single complex. In I Esd, however, Ezr 1 ff. follows 2 Chr 36 without any break. As to Ezr and Neh, in I Esd the passage parallel to Neh 8 is the direct continuation of the material parallel to Ezr 10. There is no trace of Nehemiah's memoirs (Neh 1-7; 9-13) in the apocryphal book.

a. Connection between Chr and Ezr-Neh

The problem of the relationship between the Books of Chr and Ezr-Neh has been discussed untiringly in the scholarly literature.[42] The field was

---

[42] It is incomprehensible to me why, even today, scholars familiar with the Hebrew language and with Talmudic literature continually hark back to the *barayta* in the Babylonian Talmud (Bava Batra 15-16) in connection with the composition of the anonymous books of the Bible, in general, or the relationship between Ezr-Neh and Chr, in particular. This is the case even in Japhet (1991), p. 1. The *barayta* is indeed concerned with the 'writing' of the books of the Bible, but there is no doubt that the sense of the root כתב there has nothing whatever to do with the composition of the books; the connotation of כתב there is the committing of the books to writing as part of the canon (for a good example of this usage of the verb in the Babylonian Talmud see Yoma 29a, where the question discussed is whether the Book of Esther may or may not be written down). Among other things, the text in Bava Batra states that King Hezekiah and his companions (based on Prov 25:1) 'wrote' Isaiah, Proverbs, the Song of Songs and Ecclesiastes; or that the men of the Great Assembly (referring to Neh 10) 'wrote' Ezekiel, the Twelve Minor Prophets, Daniel and Esther. Surely no Rabbinical authority could have attributed the composition of these books to Hezekiah etc. The meaning is: they committed the books to writing in their authoritative versions. Neither is it clear why any doubts are expressed concerning the statement of the *barayta* in regard to our books: עזרא כתב ספרו ויחס דברי הימים עד לו "Ezra wrote his book and the genealogies of Chronicles up to himself". This by no means implies that ancient tradition attributed the 'composition' of Chr to Ezra. Moreover, the text undoubtedly means that Ezra committed his book and the entire book of Chr to writing, for otherwise the barayta would not have solved the problem of who 'wrote' Chr — and it systematically lists all the books of the Bible, one by one, proposing a solution to the problem for each; it is inconceivable that Chr should be the only exception; see D. Talshir (1988*).

long dominated by the school founded by Zunz (1832), which considered these books as a single entity, the work of one author; even today this view is held by several important authorities, such as Mosis (1973), Willi (1972) and others. The contrary view, following Segal (1943), is that of the school whose chief contemporary representatives are Japhet (1968 and later) and Williamson (1977), who have tried to challenge the unanimity of previous studies by citing various linguistic, literary and ideational distinctions between these books. Their tone is decisive in the extreme, as if implying that all doubts on this question have been dispelled and there is nothing further to say.[43] I maintain, however, that their arguments do not categorically prove that the 'books' were indeed composed by different writers or, *a fortiori*, that they were not created in the same school.[44]

The linguistic discussion is currently deadlocked. On the one hand, no conclusive linguistic proofs have been adduced that one author was responsible for both works, even though the common elements are quite impressive, particularly when exclusive to both; on the other hand, the arguments in favor of linguistic differentiation cannot withstand criticism.[45]

From the literary point of view, the differentiating arguments are very weak; thus, for example, it has been argued that the author of Chr consistently describes the death of each king, while the deaths of Zerubbabel,

---

[43] A good, though somewhat biased, summary of the subject and the relevant bibliography is Japhet (1991).

[44] Japhet (1991), pp. 312-313: "...in terms of a theological 'school' the Book of Chronicles and the Book of Ezra-Nehemiah are not related... Ezra-Nehemiah and Chronicles were written by different authors, at separate – though proximate – periods in the Persian-Hellenistic period, and express varying theologies and objectives".

[45] The linguistic arguments were presented by Japhet (1968); Williamson (1977), pp. 37-59. Some of the 'proofs' have been challenged by D. Talshir (1988), specifically criticizing the validity of some of the arguments and the method adopted to prove on linguistic grounds that two different writers were concerned. For a summary see Japhet (1991), pp. 302-304.

Ezra and Nehemiah are shrouded in mystery. But this opposition of literary techniques is undermined if one notes that the Chronicler, in his account of the kingdom of Judah, faithfully follows the Books of Kings; the 'technique' here is not the Chronicler's, and consequently he does not abandon it when he comes to deal with the later leaders.[46] He is simply bound by the constraints of his sources.

Finally, from the standpoint of the author's world of ideas,[47] the strongest argument is the failure of Ezr-Neh to refer to Zerubbabel's Davidic lineage, while glorification of the Davidic line is a paramount motif of Chr. We cannot be sure as to the background for this omission. At any rate, the Chronicler lived at a time when Zerubbabel was no more than a transitory episode, no more than the leader of the returnees at a certain point in time. He did not fulfill the hopes of national resurgence; rather, he disappeared from the historical stage like other governors.

Another argument points to the different conception of the Chronicler who takes great pains to preserve the unity of 'all Israel', as against the author of Ezr-Neh who is concerned with Judah and Benjamin alone. In Ezr-Neh, it was reality that overcame utopia; but at a time of national exultation the notion 'all Israel' comes to life in that book too. Thus, in the Aramaic summary of the dedication of the Temple, we read, והקרבו "They offered at לחנכת בית אלהא דנה... על כל ישראל תרי עשר למנין שבטי ישראל the dedication of this house of God... for all Israel..., according to the number of the tribes of Israel" (Ezr 6:17). Similarly, on the occasion of Ezra's return: הבאים מהשבי בני הגולה הקריבו עלות לאלהי ישראל פרים שנים עשר "At that time those who had come from captivity, the returned על כל ישראל exiles, offered burnt offerings to the God of Israel: twelve bulls for all Israel" (Ezr 8:35). 'All (of) Israel', כל ישראל, recurs elsewhere as a

---

[46] Japhet (1991), pp. 306-308.
[47] See Williamson (1977), pp. 60-70, also (1987), *contra* Haran (1986); Japhet (1991), pp. 304-306.

designation for the population concerned (Ezr 2:70 = Neh 7:72; Ezr 8:25; 10:5; Neh 12:47). Moreover, the term 'sons/people of Israel', בני ישראל, is used quite frequently (more than ten times in different contexts, e.g., Ezr 3:1, 6:21, 7:7). In sum, in Ezr-Neh the political term 'Judah and Benjamin' is used alongside, and not in opposition to, the concept of 'all Israel'.

In general, one must allow for the inherent difference between Chr, which is an account of the distant past, and Ezr-Neh, whose attention is concentrated on times leading up to the present.[48] When writing about the kingdom of Judah, the author is not subject to the same dictates as he is when treating the satrapy of Judah, which was then under Persian rule. Little wonder, then, that the story of the kingdom of Judah is marked by the glory of its kings of old securely on their thrones, while Ezr-Neh offers little hope for a renewal of that independence.

In addition, the amount of material at our disposal to characterize the author of Ezr-Neh is severely limited. Once the lists and Nehemiah's memoirs (Neh 1-7; 11-13), the Aramaic source in Ezr (most of chapters 4; 5-6; 7) and perhaps also the story of Ezra (particularly the part couched in first person, Ezr 7-10) are excluded, not much is left to create an impression of the author's language, literary style or spiritual world. Here, perhaps, is the main difference between Chr and Ezr-Neh. The bulk of Chr bears the mark of a single, individual author, although that author copies entire chapters from his sources. In Ezr-Neh, however, the balance of material between the author and his sources is different, and the author has left much less of his personal imprint. The author is responsible for the historical construction: it was he who created – not too successfully – the composite picture of the Restoration during the reigns of Cyrus and Darius, as well as the combined treatment of the activities of Ezra and

[48] Just as Thucydides does not apply the same criteria in treating the history of the past and the present. Similarly, we do not consider Josephus equally reliable for antiquity and for his own times.

Nehemiah. Only a few passages were written by the author himself, the most obvious being the description of the building of the altar and the foundation of the Temple (Ezr 3:1-4:5). His account of the role of the Levites, particularly the class of Temple singers instituted by David (3:8-11), carries the mark of the Chronicler.[49] One cannot ignore the close affinity between the author of this passage and the Chronicler, even if the two were not identical.

Even if Ezr-Neh existed at some time as a separate work, someone made the effort to link it up with Chr. Just as someone created a continuous saga of Deuteronomistic historiography, despite the fact that the individual works it embodies differ considerably in their nature, conception and literary style, some redactor did the same for the Chronicler's work. The hand of that redactor is discernible in the inclusion of the list from Neh 11 in 1 Chr 9. He has no scruples about repeating the list of returnees of Neh 7 in Ezr 2 in order to portray the Restoration in Cyrus' reign; similarly, he uses the list of inhabitants of Jerusalem in Neh 9 to complete his ethnic-geographical introduction.[50] The redactor makes creative use of the lists to form historical constructs.

That Chr-Ezr-Neh form a continuous whole is likely given the practice of compilers of historiographical books. It is no accident that differentiation between the individual books of Deuteronomistic historiography is so difficult. A book could have been written as a sequel to an existing work, or as a chapter on the events preceding an existing history. Otherwise, a redactor could have planned the beginning of a work to continue an existing work, or reshape the end of an existing book to create a transition to

---

[49] See Talshir (1983).

[50] Compare, on a smaller scale, the use made of the list of David's officials, which appears twice as a kind of marker: first in 2 Sam 8:16-18, before the chapters of the Succession Narrative; and a second time after those chapters (20:23-26), before the incorporation of the Appendix (chapters 21-24).

another work. Admittedly, the repeated verses at the beginning of Ezr (1:1-3a), and at the end of Chr (2 Chr 36:22-23), are no proof that Chr and Ezr were originally a continuous work; however, the link is not created by those verses alone. Even without them it seems clear that the end of Chr was formulated with an eye to the sequel in Ezr: ויגל השארית מן החרב אל בבל ויהיו לו ולבניו לעבדים עד מלך מלכות פרס. למלאות דבר ה' בפי ירמיהו עד רצתה הארץ את שבתותיה כל ימי השמה שבתה למלאות שבעים שנה "He took into exile in Babylon those who had escaped from the sword, and they became servants to him and to his sons until the establishment of the kingdom of Persia, to fulfill the word of the Lord by the mouth of Jeremiah, until the land had enjoyed its sabbaths. All the days that it lay desolate it kept sabbath, to fulfill seventy years" (2 Chr 36:20-21). Like the author of the Books of Kings, who takes a step beyond the destruction to the improvement in the lot of Jehoiachin, our author, writing in the Persian period, leads the story to the threshold of the imminent Restoration, עד מלך מלכות פרס "until the establishment of the kingdom of Persia". Another motif common to the end of Chr and the beginning of Ezr is the fulfillment of Jeremiah's prophecy: למלאות דבר ה' בפי ירמיה "to fulfill the word of the Lord by the mouth of Jeremiah" (2 Chr 36:21) / לכלות דבר ה' בפי ירמיהו "that the word of the Lord by the mouth of Jeremiah might be accomplished" (Ezr 1:1). It is not only the conclusion in 2 Chr 36:21 that was formulated so as to be continued at the beginning of Ezr, for it closes an entire pericope which opened with Zedekiah's accession to the throne: ויעש הרע בעיני ה' אלהיו לא נכנע מלפני ירמיהו הנביא מפי ה' "He did what was evil in the sight of the Lord his God. He did not humble himself before Jeremiah the prophet, who spoke from the mouth of the Lord" (36:12). The smooth transition from Chr to Ezr is thus well anchored in the beginning of Zedekiah's reign with the motif of fulfillment of Jeremiah's prophecy. In sum, there is a marked inner and outer link between Chr and Ezr-Neh.

Neither can the evidence from I Esd be dismissed so summarily.[51]
There is no visible reason to argue that the author of I Esd is responsible
for the continuity of Chr-Ezr-Neh; more likely, it was part of his tradition.
The thesis that I Esd is, as it were, an anthology, as though the author took
one book (Chr) and picked from there two chapters as the prelude to his
own work, then turned to a completely different book (Ezr-Neh) which he
then reworked as a sequel, is untenable. Rather, I Esd is a continuous
segment lifted from a given, continuous work that progressed from the
history of the kingdom of Judah, as described in Chr, to its reconstitution
under the Persians. The author's prime goal was to integrate the Story of
the Youths, and the main part of his literary endeavor was to rework the
existing books to that end. This, too, indicates that he would not have
made special efforts to open his book with a passage from a work not
related *a priori* to Ezr-Neh. Just as the literary milieu of the author of Chr
was one in which the Books of Samuel and Kings formed a continuous
entity, the same is true of Chr and Ezr in the literary milieu of the author
of I Esd. Also, just as the author of Chr chose to begin with the battle of
the Gilboa, so too, taking that continuity for granted, did the author of
I Esd decide to begin his book with Josiah's celebration of the Passover.

One conjecture, of a different type, that has recently been thrust into
the debate concerning the relationship between Chr and Ezr-Neh should
be rejected out of hand – I refer to Eskenazi's theory (1986) that the
Chronicler and the author of Apocryphal Esdras were one and the same!
Eskenazi's simplistic comparison of the work of the Chronicler, forming
his own book on the basis of the Books of Samuel and Kings, to that of
the author of I Esd, forming his book on the basis of Ezr-Neh, and the
identification of those two authors, is *a priori* speculative, even before one

---

[51] Japhet (1991), p. 309: "These claims [i.e., the external indications from I Esd and
from the repetition of Ezr 1:1-3a in 2 Chr. 36:22-23] have only peripheral influence
on our debate".

checks the 'proofs' for this deduction. Neither the Chronicler nor anyone like him can possibly be credited with the authorship of the Story of the Youths, or even with its inclusion in previously existing material. The Chronicler does not write such things or use material of that type, neither would he disturb the order of events for the sole purpose of interpolating such a story.

As to the proofs themselves, they mainly point out ideas common to the Chronicler and the author of I Esd, in contrast to the author of Ezr-Neh. To this one must reply that, while essential ideological differences between books indicate that they were written by different authors, the fact that two works share certain ideas does not testify to common authorship. Eskenazi cites, for example, the 'prominence of the Davidic dynasty' as a central motif of both I Esd and Chr.[52] Both Haggai and Zechariah attach messianic hopes to Zerubbabel, but no-one suggests on that basis that there was any direct connection between them and the authors of Chr and I Esd. Moreover, the description of the author of I Esd as more receptive to foreigners, as was, *per* Eskenazi, the Chronicler, in contrast to the author of Ezr-Neh, is rather questionable. Her basis for the statement is the difficult Greek text of I Esd 5:49 καὶ ἐπισυνήχθησαν αὐτοῖς ἐκ τῶν ἄλλων ἐθνῶν τῆς γῆς... ὅτι ἐν ἔχθρᾳ ἦσαν αὐτοῖς καὶ κατίσχυσαν αὐτοὺς πάντα τὰ ἔθνη τὰ ἐπὶ τῆς γῆς, parallel to כי באיבה עליהם מעמי הארצות (Ezr 3:3). Even if I Esd implies that some of the foreign peoples were cooperating with the returnees, a similar conclusion may be drawn from Darius' decree in Ezr: ומני שים טעם למא די תעבדון עם שבי יהודיא אלך למבנא בית אלהא דך "Moreover I make a decree regarding what you shall do for these elders of the Jews [or, better: I order you to cooperate with the Jews] for the rebuilding of this house of God" (Ezr 6:8). This argument

---

[52] "The prominence of the Davidic dynasty in I Esdras is best understood as the work of the Chronicler, who shapes Ezra-Nehemiah according to the same tendencies which shaped his earlier work [i.e., Chr]" (p. 49).

is scarcely justified by the fact that, according to I Esd, Zerubbabel received permission from Darius. After all, in the canonical Book of Ezr-Neh the entire Restoration is based on decrees issued by Cyrus, Darius and Artaxerxes.[53]

The author of I Esd was active in a milieu quite different from that of the Chronicler; he has nothing whatsoever in common with the Chronistic school.

In sum: the continuity of Chr and Ezr-Neh is not a creation of the author of I Esd, but something inherent in his sources, on the background of which he composed his own work.

---

[53] Eskenazi's work evokes criticism in many other points; a philological discussion must be founded on philological method – not every argument is valid. E.g., one cannot argue that the author of I Esd omitted Nehemiah's memoirs because he esteemed the Davidic dynasty and was reluctant to include Nehemiah's derogatory reference to Solomon. If that were the case he need only have omitted a single verse (13:26) and not ten chapters. If one asserts that the author of I Esd omitted Nehemiah's memoirs because he was more liberal and open to foreigners and did not want to include Nehemiah's harsh verdict against the foreign women – how can one reconcile the fact that the same author includes Ezra's entire treatment of the problem of the foreign women (Ezr 9-10), even firmly terminating the story, unlike the canonical Ezr, with the expulsion of the women together with their sons?! One cannot say that the Chronicler omitted the story of the exile of Samaria because he wished to leave the Israelites in their homeland, while at the same time that same author relates nothing of the history of the northern kingdom so that there was no reason for him to include the chapter recounting its destruction; on the other hand, one cannot deny that the Chronicler, though omitting 2 Kgs 17, by no means disregarded the Northerners' deportation: וילכו הרצים... לאמר בני ישראל שובו אל ה'... וישב אל הפליטה הנשארת לכם מכף מלכי אשור... כי בשובכם על ה' אחיכם ובניכם לרחמים לפני שוביהם ולשוב לארץ הזאת "So couriers went... saying, O people of Israel, return to the Lord... that he may turn again to the remnant of you who have escaped from the hand of the kings of Assyria.... For if you return to the Lord, your brethren and your children will find compassion with their captors, and return to this land" (2 Chr 30:6-9).

b. Continuity of Ezr-Neh

Any scholar dealing with the Book of Ezr-Neh would dearly love to find literary evidence for what seems obvious: a text in which the material centering on Ezra is not part of the account of Nehemiah's activities but takes its logical place in the story of Ezra. Indeed, after the author has described Ezra's first year of activity (Ezr 7-10), he clears the stage entirely for Nehemiah (Neh 1-7), unexpectedly bringing Ezra back for the reading of the Law (Neh 8). The introduction of the whole episode of the reading is palpably artificial. In Chap. 7, Nehemiah describes his attempt to repopulate the empty city of Jerusalem and tells of finding the genealogical register of the first returnees, which is then cited in full. The list ends with the assertion that the newcomers 'lived in their towns'. Immediately following is the episode of the reading of the Law forming an awkward sequel to something that occurred decades before: the returnees settle in their respective towns – at the beginning of the Restoration period, and, when the seventh month comes, they assemble to read the Law – with וישבו הכהנים... וכל ישראל בעריהם ויגע החדש השביעי ובני ישראל בעריהם :Ezra ויאספו כל העם כאיש אחד... ויאמרו לעזרא.. "So the priests... and all Israel, lived in their towns. And when the seventh month had come, the children of Israel were in their towns. And all the people gathered as one man..., and they told Ezra the scribe..." (Neh 7:72-8:1). This makes no sense at all!

Moreover, the reading of the Law seriously disturbs Nehemiah's story. Nehemiah is faced with a difficult situation: והעיר רחבת ידיים והעם מעט בתוכה ואין בתים בנוים "The city was wide and large, but the people within it were few and no houses had been built" (Neh 7:4-5). Accordingly, he decides on a συνοικισμός, that is, a redistribution of population in order to settle Jerusalem, and to that end makes use of the list of immigrants (7:6-72a). However, the text, after quoting the entire list *verbatim*, goes off on a completely different course: the reading of the Torah, the prayer of the Levites, the covenant – a long episode, spanning Chapters 8-10, having nothing to do with the repopulating of Jerusalem. Only in 11:1 is the previous topic resumed: וישבו שרי העם בירשלם, ושאר העם הפילו גורלות להביא אחד מן העשרה לשבת בירושלם עיר הקדש ותשע הידות בערים "Now the leaders of the people lived in Jerusalem; and the rest of the people cast lots to bring one out of ten live in Jerusalem, the holy city, while nine tenths remained in the other towns".

These problems have stimulated scholars to try to place the reading of the Torah in context within the story of Ezra; many of them hold that it should come between Ezr chapters 8 and 9: Ezra arrives in Judah, and the first thing he does is to read the Torah to the people. This leads naturally to the divorce of the foreign wives in Ezr 9-10. Such an order of events is implied by the parallel episode in Neh 13:1-3 ...ביום ההוא נקרא בספר משה ונמצא כתוב בו אשר לא יבוא עמני ומאבי בקהל האלהים עד עולם... ויהי כשמעם את התורה ויבדילו כל ערב מישראל "On that day they read from the book of Moses... and it was found written that no Ammonite or Moabite should ever enter the assembly of God... When the people heard the law, they separated from Israel all those of foreign descent". The text of I Esd, however, does not help in properly locating the reading of the Torah, i.e., before the 'separation'. The whole episode in 9:37-55 (Neh 8) appears just after the separation from the foreign wives, 8:88-9:36 (Ezr 10). Does, then, I Esd possibly testify to an original different layout?

I Esd's starting point indicates that that is not the case. I Esd does not begin its account of the reading of the Torah with a parallel to Neh 8:1, but with a parallel to 7:72 וישבו הכהנים והלוים... ויגע החדש השביעי ובני ישראל בעריהם "So the priests, the Levites... And when the seventh month had come, the children of Israel were in their towns", I Esd 9:37. Now the first part of Neh 7:72 summarizes the list of returnees in that chapter, echoing the opening of the list in v. 6:

(6) אלה בני המדינה העלים... וישובו לירושלם וליהודה איש לעירו...

(72) וישבו הכהנים והלוים... וכל ישראל בעריהם...

(6) These were the people of the province who came up out of the captivity of those exiles... and they returned to Jerusalem and Judah, each to his town... (72) the priests and the Levites... settled in Jerusalem... and all Israel were in their towns.

The structure of the verse also testifies to its role in context: the first part – וישבו הכהנים "So the priests... settled..." – ends the list, while the second – ...ויגע החדש "And when the seventh month had come..." – leads into the sequel, also repeating the concluding words וכל ישראל בעריהם "and all Israel were in their towns". One can hardly deny the role of Neh 7:72 as a transition from the list of returnees, who scatter around the country, each settling in his own town, to the events in Jerusalem that dictate assembling the people from their respective homes. If so, what role can one assign to this verse in an entirely different context – between the story of the separation and that of the reading of the Torah, which are juxtaposed in I Esd?

The possible explanations for the processes through which the texts took shape indicate that, at this point, I Esd is probably secondary. For if one postulates that I Esd represents the original order, i.e., Neh 7:72 ff. originally occurred after Ezr 10, then, of necessity, the first contact between Neh 7:72 and the list of returnees preceding it in the Book of Nehemiah was formed when the story of the reading of the Torah was transferred to the text of Nehemiah. Only in the next stage could someone have transferred the list together with its termination v. 72 to Ezr 2, yet I Esd also includes Ezr 2 together with its final verse! It is inconceivable that I Esd represents a redaction prior to the transferal of the reading of the Torah to the story of Nehemiah, and at the same time a redaction two stages later when the list together with its final verse were relocated to Ezr 2.

Thus, I Esd cannot testify in any way to the position of the reading of the Torah in the context of Ezra's activities.[54] Moreover, the situation readily proves that I Esd is a reworked version of a redaction resembling that in the canonical book, which reproduced the list of immigrants twice (hence the duplication of the conclusion of the list in I Esd), and which included both Ezra and Nehemiah. The author of the reworked version brought together the Book of Ezr and the reading of the Torah by Ezra; but he began too early with the verse that sums up the list of immigrants, thus leaving us a key to the formation of the Book of I Esd.[55] The background might be purely technical: if we take the division of the text in the MT as proof of an ancient tradition, it might be important to note that while Ezr 7:72 is positioned directly before 8:1 ff. without any interval, 7:72 is separated from the previous verse by a sectional division (*parashah petuhah*).

To summarize the interrelationship between the Books of Chr-Ezr-Neh: (1) it seems probable that Chr and Ezr-Neh formed a single, continuous entity before the author of I Esd set out to use them for his work; (2) but the link between Ezr and Neh 8 was his own invention.

---

[54] See Bertholet (1902), pp. xvi-xvii; Kaufmann (1956), p. 105; Rudolph (1949), pp. xiii-xiv.

[55] Various hypotheses have been advanced in the scholarly literature to account for the presence of this verse in I Esd, in order to confirm I Esd as evidence of the original edition, linking Neh 8 with Ezr. Mowinckel (1964), pp. 21-25, suggested that it is a gloss, pointing to stylistic differences between the translation of the verse and its parallel in 5:45, 46 (Ezr 2:70, 3:1). These are shaky grounds, however, because one cannot rely on secondary stylistic differences in the work of a translator who is anything but stylistically uniform – his inconsistencies crop up not only in passages several chapters apart, but even in the same chapter and the same verse. In any case, a solution involving the argument of late accretions is not attractive. Another problem is, why was it considered necessary to patch the text together with this intermediate verse. The argument of Pohlmann (1970), pp. 69-71 that 9:37 is not to be associated at all with Neh 7:72 has little in its favor. Böhler (1997), pp. 86-92, has recently adopted this view and discussed it in detail.

III. The Position of the Letter of Complaint to Artaxerxes

a. The Sequence of Events

Ezr 4:6-23 interrupts the chronological sequence of events in Ezr 1-6, because it interpolates Xerxes and Artaxerxes between Cyrus and Darius, although both reigned after Darius. The explanation is well known: this is not a historical sequence but a literary one, and the author/redactor has provided a sure indication at the point where the historical sequence proper is resumed: v. 24 is an obvious *Wiederaufnahme* to v. 5. The first passage of Ezr 4 tells about the adversaries of Judah and Benjamin trying to dishearten the builders כל ימי כורש מלך פרס ועד מלכות דריוש מלך פרס "all the days of Cyrus king of Persia, even until the reign of Darius king of Persia" (v. 5). This is echoed in v. 24: באדין בטלת עבידת בית אלהא די בירושלם והות בטלא עד שנת תרתין למלכות דריוש מלך פרס "Then the work on the house of God which is in Jerusalem stopped; and it ceased until the second year of the reign of Darius king of Persia".

In addition, the function in context of v. 24 is clear from its content: it cannot be a summary or an outcome of the measures described in the letter to Artaxerxes. It refers to an interruption in the building of 'the House of God', while the entire passage 4:6-23 contains no hint, let alone explicit mention, of the house of God. In their complaint, the writers inform the king that the returnees are קריתא מרדתא ובאישתא בנין ושוריא שכללו ואשיא יחיטו "rebuilding that rebellious and wicked city; they are finishing the walls and repairing the foundations" (v. 12); the king's interests will be damaged הן קריתא דך תתבנא ושוריה ישתכללון "if this city is rebuilt and the walls finished" (v. 13), and he will lose his hegemony over the province Beyond the River הן קריתא תתבנא ושוריה ישתכללון "if this city is rebuilt and its walls finished" (v. 16). The king indeed decides to halt the work: כען שימו טעם ... קריתא דך לא תתבנא "Therefore make a decree that... this city be not rebuilt" (v. 21). There is no mention of the House of God either in the complaint nor in the response. A correspondence concerning one subject – the rebuilding of the city and the walls – cannot be summed up by referring to something else – the construction of the Temple.

The role of v. 24 as a *Wiederaufnahme* is thus confirmed, and Ezr 4:6-24 is clearly out of context.[56] It turns out that I Esd provides us, as it were, with first-hand evidence of the extraneous nature of the passage: Ezr 4:6-23 has disappeared from its 'inconvenient' position in the MT. In I Esd, the direct continuation of 5:70 (Ezr 4:5) is in 6:1 (Ezr 5:1), as it should be. But what has happened to Ezr 4:6-24? The passage has not disappeared but merely changed places: it may now be found as 2:15-25, i.e., immediately after the material parallel to Ezr 1. What is the relationship between the two redactions?

b. Preamble to the Correspondence: 2:15-16 (Ezr 4:6-11)

Ezr 4:6-11 is a rather complex text, including several preambles to letters, only one of which is actually quoted (the parts obviously not represented in I Esd are set in brackets):

6 [ובמלכות אחשורוש בתחלת מלכותו כתבו שטנה] על ישבי יהודה וירושלם. 7 ובימי ארתחששתא כתב בשלם מתרדת טבאל ושאר כנותיו על ארתחששתא מלך פרס [וכתב הנשתון כתוב ארמית ומתרגם ארמית]. 8 רחום בעל טעם ושמשי ספרא [כתבו אגרה חדה על ירושלם לארתחששתא מלכא כנמא. 9 אדין] רחום בעל טעם ושמשי ספרא ושאר כנותהון דיניא [ואפרסתכיא טרפליא אפרסיא ארכויא בבליא שושנכיא דהיא עלמיא. 10 ושאר אמיא די הגלי אסנפר רבא ויקירא] והותב המו בקריה די שמרין ושאר עבר נהרה וכענת. 11 דנה פרשגן אגרתא די שלחו עלוהי על ארתחששתא מלכא עבדך אנש עבר נהרה וכענת.

(6) [And in the reign of Ahasuerus, in the beginning of his reign, they wrote an accusation] against the inhabitants of Judah and Jerusalem.

(7) And in the days of Artaxerxes, Bishlam and Mithredath and Tabeel

---

[56] Talmon (1976), p. 322, points out that this literary device is used in Ezr-Neh as a technique for the insertion of an independent unit into a given context and cites further examples. Some authors reject this explanation of the passage's position in context; see Liver (1965).

and the rest of their associates wrote to Artaxerxes king of Persia; [the letter was written in Aramaic and translated]. (8) Rehum the commander and Shimshai the scribe wrote a letter against Jerusalem to Artaxerxes the king as follows – (9) Then wrote Rehum the commander, Shimshai the scribe, and the rest of their associates, the judges, [the governors, the officials, the Persians, the men of Erech, the Babylonians, the men of Susa, that is, the Elamites, (10) and the rest of the nations whom the great and noble Osnappar deported] and settled in the cities of Samaria and in the rest of the province Beyond the River, and now (11) this is a copy of the letter that they sent: To Artaxerxes the king: Your servants, the men of the province Beyond the River, send greeting.

The whole passage is summed up in I Esd 2:15-16 as a single, clearly phrased preamble, the retroversion of which yields the following text:

ובימי ארתחששתא מלך פרס כתב עליו על ישבי יהודה וירושלם בשלם ומתרדת וטבאל
ורחום בעל טעם ושמשי ספרא ושאר כנותהון די יתבין בשמרין ושאר ואתריא? דנה
פרשגן אגרתא: על מראנא מלכא ארתחששתא עבדך רחום בעל טעם ושמשי ספרא ושאר
כנותהון ודיניא אנש עבר נהרה.

And in the days of Artaxerxes, king of Persia, there wrote to him against the inhabitants of Judah and Jerusalem Bishlam, Mithredath, Tabeel, Rehum the commander, Shimshai the scribe, the rest of their associates who live in Samaria and the rest of the places. This is a copy of the letter. To our master, Artaxerxes the king: Your servants Rehum the commander, Shimshai the scribe, and the rest of their associates and the judges, people of Beyond the River.

Does I Esd represent a shorter, more authentic text than the MT? One cannot easily state that the entire text of the MT was available to the author of I Esd, but it can be proven that I Esd is a reworked version that abbreviated the source in order to simplify the text: As only one letter is quoted, I Esd presents only one preamble. Xerxes (Ahasuerus) has completely disappeared (though על יושבי יהודה וירושלם "against the inhabitants of Judah and Jerusalem" has been transplanted to the letter to Artaxerxes); and the two preambles to the letter to Artaxerxes, one revolving around Bishlam, Mithredath and Tabeel (Ezr 4:7) and the other around Rehum and Shimshai (v. 8), are combined in I Esd with the various writers being listed as the writers of the letter that is subsequently quoted. This combination of the two groups of names is artificial, for the king's response is addressed exclusively to Rehum and Shimshai, both in I Esd 2:21 and in Ezr 4:17, and it is they who carry out the royal decree in I Esd 2:25 and Ezr 4:23. Moreover, it is doubtful whether I Esd points to the existence of an earlier stage of the text without the list of nations (Ezr 4:9-10), as it includes part of v. 9 and a remnant of the list – דיניא, understood as 'the judges', I Esd 2:16. Thus, the text of I Esd represents a thorough reworking of a version similar to the MT. The reworking was presumably done by whomever transplanted the whole passage to its new position.

c. The Final Verse 2:25 (Ezr 4:24) and the Chronological Sequence

In I Esd, the letter of complaint to Artaxerxes, 2:15-25, occurs just after Cyrus' edict and the first stages of its realization, i.e., just after the material parallel to Ezr 1. Chronologically speaking, therefore, the sequence here is no improvement on the MT: Artaxerxes, who reigned after Darius, is interposed squarely between Cyrus and Darius.[57] Even if we emend the king's name to Cambyses, in accord with historical truth – as indeed was done by Josephus (Ant. XI, §21) – the letter of complaint is still out of context: it is not attached to any event; we have not been told that the exiles have arrived back or begun to build – but the complaint has been submitted, and moreover to another king! There is nothing in I Esd that might alleviate this chronological difficulty and bridge the discrepancy in content since the verse parallel to Ezr 4:24 – I Esd 2:25 – loses its role as a *Wiederaufnahme* in its new position.[58] Thus, the extraneous episode

---

[57] Note the mention of Ἀρταξέρξης ὁ τῶν Μήδων in the LXX to Dan 6:1.

[58] The material in I Esd parallel to Ezr 2:1-4:5, i.e., the list of returnees, the building of the altar, the laying of the temple's foundations and the complaint of the adversaries, comes only later, after the Story of the Youths. Consequently, the verse 2:25 is merely part of a continuous sequence in I Esd.

from Artaxerxes' reign has not changed place alone – the verse that was supposed to point up its extraneous nature has gone with it, in fact becoming a part of it.

Possibly, as it has been assigned a new role, the formulation of the verse has been modified, smoothing over the elements that implied a pause in the account: instead of the MT's ...באדין בטלת עבידת בית אלהא עד... והות בטלא "Then the work on the house of God... stopped; and it ceased until...", the text of I Esd presumably read ובטלת עבידת בית אלהא די בירושלם עד... "And the work on the house of God which is in Jerusalem ceased until...". Finally, in I Esd, too, this verse is concerned with the interruption of work on the Temple, and as such, it is not a fitting summary for a correspondence about the rebuilding of the whole city. Nevertheless, in I Esd, unlike the MT, the 'house of God' has a certain part in the correspondence.

d. The Insertion of the Temple into the Letter

In contrast to the situation in the MT, the Temple has found its way into the letter to Artaxerxes as it appears in I Esd.

1. In 2:17 (Ezr 4:12), instead of the MT's ואשיא יחיטו, "and repairing the foundations", the Greek I Esd reads καὶ ναὸν ὑποβάλλονται, that is, "and laying the foundations of the Temple". Possibly the translator had a different source, reading, say, ואשי היכלא יחיטו. Such a reading could have derived from a variant ואשיה (with *he* instead of *alef*), understanding the *he* as a possessive pronominal suffix (cf. καὶ θεμελίους αὐτῆς ἀνύψωσαν in the LXX); the pronoun was then replaced by its antecedent – the foundations of the temple.[59] Alternatively, this might be merely the translator's own interpretation.

---

[59] Compare 8:78 (Ezr 9:9) לרומם את בית אלהינו ולהעמיד את חרבתיו "to set up the house of our God, to repair its ruins", καὶ δοξάσαι τὸ ἱερὸν τοῦ κυρίου ἡμῶν καὶ ἐγεῖραι τὴν ἔρημον Σιών "the ruins of Zion"; and cf. below concerning the combined consideration of the city and the Temple in I Esd.

2. Further on, the MT's expression מלח היכלא מלחנא "we use the salt of the palace", is understood to refer to the Temple in 2:18 (Ezr 4:14). In reality, the expression signifies the writers' submission to the king; it has nothing to do with the rebuilding of the Temple. Though it may have been altered in the source, it was more likely understood by the translator as referring to the ongoing work of the temple: καὶ ἐπεὶ ἐνεργεῖται τὰ κατὰ τὸν ναόν.[60] Thus the Temple clearly figures in I Esd's version of the letter of complaint.

Whether the translator was adhering to his source or not, the Temple is clearly secondary in this document. This juxtaposition of the laying of foundations for the Temple and Artaxerxes' reign is rather puzzling. Moreover, while the foundation of the Temple is clearly highlighted in 2:17-18, it subsequently disappears from the rest of the complaint and is not mentioned at all in the king's reply. Finally, the very combination of the building of the Temple and the rebuilding of the city indicates the secondary nature of the account in I Esd. The house of God is the central pivot of the Restoration (Ezr 1-6), together with Ezra's activities (Ezr 7-10). The rebuilding of the city, its gates and walls, is Nehemiah's business. The complaint sent to Artaxerxes seems to be more pertinent to activities of Nehemiah's type, in which the foundation of the Temple has no place.[61]

However, for I Esd, in its particular structure, it was essential to bring in the foundation of the Temple at this point. Indeed, the letter of complaint is quoted immediately after the edict of Cyrus which explicitly permits the rebuilding of the Temple; it would be implausible that a complaint about the reconstruction of Jerusalem would not refer to the Temple! Moreover, the concluding verse 2:25, which refers only to the rebuilding

---

[60] Note that the Aramaic/Hebrew word for salt, מלח, is phonetically similar to the word מלאכה, 'work'.

[61] Böhler (1997), pp. 78-110, argues that the original edition preserved in I Esd attributed the rebuilding of Jerusalem to Zerubbabel and Ezra while the later edition of Ezr-Neh suppressed the references to the building of the city in order to reserve it for Nehemiah's activities.

of the Temple, would be irrelevant in I Esd if the laying of its foundations had not been mentioned.

In view of what we have demonstrated concerning the letter of complaint and its last verse in I Esd, the conclusion is inescapable: the sequence of the material in I Esd reflects a reworked version of a text structured as in the Book of Ezra.

e. Duplication of the Founding of the Temple

As we have seen, the reader learns in the letter of complaint that the foundations of the Temple are being laid, 2:17, and that the work on the Temple in general is gaining momentum, 2:18. Therefore, when one reaches I Esd 5, parallel to Ezr 3, which relates how the foundations of the Temple were laid, a certain tension may be created in the sequence of events. The translator seems to have sought to solve the problem by rendering the Hebrew root יסד 'found', 'lay foundations', which occurs several times in Ezr 3, by using general terms connected with building: οἰκοδομεῖν, οἰκοδομή, ἔγερσις, avoiding any direct reference to the laying of foundations.[62] Nevertheless, the verb θεμελιοῦν, the usual equivalent of יסד, does appear in the chapter, in a passage that has no parallel in the MT: 5:55 (an expansion of Ezr 3:8). If this passage comes from the main base of I Esd, there are only two possibilities: either the translator was varying his translation, regardless of the problem pointed out above, or he was using θεμελιοῦν in a broader sense (a sense also acquired by יסד) as evidenced by his use of the same verb as a translation for שכלל 'finish', 'complete' in 6:10 (Ezr 5:9). At any rate, elsewhere in the chapter the text is concerned with building in general, and one might even fall into the error of believing, as Josephus did, that it was referring to the completion of the building.[63]

---

[62] 5:52, 56, 59, 60 (Ezr 3:6, 10, 11, 12).

[63] Ant. XI, §80. Just as Josephus misinterpreted I Esd the Syriac translator misinterpreted the MT; for details see Talshir (1983).

IV. The Interpolation of the Story of the Youths

a. Duplication in the Sequence of Events

Where is the text leading in Ezr 4:24, or its equivalent in I Esd 2:25? In Ezr, it prepares the ground for the initiative taken at the start of Darius' reign to renew the building (Ezr 5:1 ff). In I Esd, it provides a springboard for the Story of the Three Youths, I Esd 3:1 ff, which takes place in Darius' reign. Both links seem quite plausible – but only at first sight. The problems come to light if one considers the entire span of the story. In Ezr, we are told that the building was interrupted till Darius' second year (Ezr 4:24); at that point, Haggai and Zechariah prophesied inspiring the rise of the leaders Zerubbabel and Jeshua, who renewed the construction; despite the intervention of the local authorities, the work was brought to a successful close (Ezr 5-6). Not so in I Esd. There, too, the work is suspended till Darius' second year (I Esd 2:25), but then the king holds a banquet (in his second year, 5:6) during which Zerubbabel's wisdom is revealed, as a consequence of which he receives the permits necessary to go to Judah and resume the building (Story of the Youths, 3:1–5:6). He indeed reaches Judah – a list of the immigrants is provided, 5:7-45 (Ezr 2) – the altar is built and first steps are made to build the Temple itself, but then the adversaries of Judah and Benjamin interfere and the work is halted through the entire reign of Cyrus until Darius' accession to the throne, 5:46-70 (Ezr 3:1–4:5). It is then renewed with the prophets' encouragement in Darius' second year, 6:1 ff (Ezr 5:1 ff).

The sequence of events in I Esd is basically impossible: the work is interrupted twice until the beginning of Darius' reign. It is resumed twice, each time in Darius' second year. The interruption of work is documented twice in parallel passages – 2:25, 5:70 – and continued twice, once in the Story of the Youths and a second time on the initiative of the prophets.[64]

---

[64] At first sight one might suggest a *Wiederaufnahme* in I Esd, but with the literary

In other words, the plot of I Esd goes forward from the same point in two different directions, the two accounts subsequently meeting again at a new common point; hence, each account excludes the other.[65]

b. Cyrus' Reign and Darius' Reign

The sequence of the material is faulty in yet another respect. The Story of the Youths brings us into Darius' reign, but it is followed by material parallel to events recounted in Ezr as taking place under Cyrus, as if unaware of Darius' appearance in the Story of the Youths: (1) the preparations for the building of the Temple are done with Cyrus' permission, no mention being made of the new license granted by Darius. (2) After the neighbors' interference, the work halts for the duration of Cyrus' reign, up to Darius' accession – although we have already reached Darius' reign. (3) When the work is resumed with the encouragement of the prophets, and Tattenai and his associates write to Darius, the king investigates and rediscovers Cyrus' decree – as if his own permit had never been issued.[66]

---

units reversed. While in Ezr the units are 2:1-4:5, 4:6-23, with 4:24 as a *Wiederaufnahme* to 4:5, in I Esd the order is: 2:15-25 (Ezr 4:6-24), 5:7-70 (Ezr 2:1-4:5), with 5:70 (Ezr 4:5) as a *Wiederaufnahme* to Ezr 4:24. But there is a cardinal difference: In Ezr the letter of complaint is parenthetical, not part of the main sequence of events in point of chronology or substance. In I Esd the (hypothetical) parentheses enclose a large complex which is by no means extraneous to the sequence of events, but continues the plot.

[65] The difficulty exists even without the Story of the Youths. I.e., if one argues that the Story of the Youths is indeed not an integral element, but I Esd preserves the original position of the letter of complaint to Artaxerxes, one obtains the following sequence: Edict of Cyrus; letter of complaint, after which the work ceases till Darius' second year; list of returnees, building of the Temple and interference of the neighboring nations, causing a halt in the building till Darius' second year. This layout is, of course, impossible, the work on the Temple being halted once because of the letter and once because of the neighboring nations' interference.

[66] For the first two points see, in particular, 5:53, 68, 70; for the last point see the whole situation in chapter 6.

c. Darius' Permit – the Return of the Vessels, the Building of the Temple and the Rebuilding of the City

In the Story of the Youths, the king, impressed by Zerubbabel's sagacity, encourages him to ask for more than had been promised, in a verse – 4:42 – that serves as a transition between the two parts of the narrative. Thereupon Zerubbabel reminds the king of his previous vow, otherwise unknown; the only possible explanation is that he is referring to the edict of Cyrus. In that vow, says Zerubbabel, the king made three promises: (1) the Temple vessels would be returned; (2) the Temple would be restored; (3) Jerusalem would be rebuilt. Darius writes letters permitting the city and the Temple to be rebuilt and consents to the return of the vessels, yet the vessels have already returned to Jerusalem – with Sheshbazzar! Thus, the references to the vessels in the Story of the Youths, 4:44, 57, are inconsistent with the descriptions of the vessels being brought to Jerusalem in Cyrus' time, 2:13-14; compare also 6:17-18. It would appear that in I Esd the vessels are redeemed twice!

The other two topics, the building of the city and the Temple, are intertwined both in the vow and in Darius' letters. The letters clear the way for Zerubbabel and his companions to rebuild Jerusalem, 4:47; they allow them to procure wood for the construction of the city, 4:49, and allot generous funds for the construction of the Temple, 4:51. The text goes on to promise the builders of the city their freedom, 4:53, and to ensure that the Levites receive their part until the work on the Temple is completed and Jerusalem rebuilt, 4:55. When the people learn of the events from Zerubbabel, they bless God who has enabled them to go up and build Jerusalem and the Temple, 4:63. The rebuilding of the city is thus highly prominent in Darius' letters – but the promise is never fulfilled. The next chapters, which are parallel to Ezr, are confined entirely to the building of the Temple. Only very late, in the time of Ezra, is there a hint of the rebuilding of Jerusalem: καὶ δοξάσαι τὸ ἱερὸν τοῦ κυρίου ἡμῶν καὶ ἐγεῖραι τὴν ἔρημον Σιων, 8:78 (Ezr 9:9). Perhaps it is not surprising that 'Zion' is mentioned only in I Esd, whereas the MT is concerned with the Temple only: לרומם את בית אלהינו ולהעמיד את חרבתיו "to set up the house of our God, to repair its ruins".[67]

Besides the above references, the building of the Temple and the reconstruction of the city have already been mentioned together in I Esd – in the letter of complaint. This is a combination unique to I Esd; it would therefore be quite plausible to ascribe all these changes to the same hand.

We have seen that the position of the letter of complaint in I Esd is problematic on several counts: it is chronologically anomalous; it clashes with the sequence of events; and it poses literary problems. Nevertheless, one might say that these very aspects gave it its position in I Esd. In the canonical Ezr, most of the text prior to the letter of complaint is already acquainted with Zerubbabel; this is the case with regard to the list of returnees (Ezr 2), the building of the altar, the foundation of the Temple, and the interference of the adversaries of Judah and Benjamin (3:1-4:5).[68] This entire section (Ezr 2:1-4:5) must be deferred, therefore, to some place after the Story of the Youths, which first brings Zerubbabel onto the stage in I Esd. On the other hand, the letter of complaint to Artaxerxes is, of course, unacquainted with Zerubbabel, so there is no need to hold it back till after the Story of the Youths. In addition, the letter, and particularly its last verse 2:25, explains why the construction of the Temple was

---

[67] Note that the continuation of the verse, ולתת לנו גדר ביהודה ובירושלם "and to give us a fence [RSV: continuation] in Judea and Jerusalem", might have also contributed to the development discerned in I Esd. Some scholars considered this 'fence' to be a hint of Nehemiah's wall, even going so far as to conclude that Nehemiah and his actions preceded Ezra. However, see Rudolph in his commentary, p. 88, to the effect that there is no such hint, for the text is speaking of a fence 'in Judea and Jerusalem'.

[68] I.e., all the text apart from Ezr 1. The implication is, incidentally, that the author of this redaction did not identify Sheshbazzar with Zerubbabel; and cf. below, pp. 60-61.

interrupted till the reign of Darius, thus becoming an excellent springboard for the Story of the Youths. Essentially, it is not the letter of complaint that has been displaced, but the whole block of narrative revolving around Zerubbabel, Ezr 2:1-4:5, which has been moved to a position after the Story of the Youths. The reason for the new arrangement is really quite simple: to permit the introduction of the Story of the Youths.[69] However, the author/redactor who created this new layout did only half the work: he carefully formed a new outer frame, but failed to notice that the story could not be properly integrated in the surrounding material, as it led the plot forward from the same point of departure and to the same termination as the plot of another literary unit, parallel with the MT, which was also absorbed into I Esd.[70]

Thus, the Story of the Youths was not properly woven into the fabric of the book; it did not become a natural link in the chain of events.[71] This may suggest that the story was not originally written for the present context. Nevertheless, since it clearly aims at rounding out the figure of Zerubbabel, it is not inconceivable that the author himself, and not some later interpolator, thrust the story into this account of the early days of the Restoration.

d. Zerubbabel's Role in I Esdras

The direct result of introducing the Story of the Youths into the account of the Restoration period was to magnify Zerubbabel's role in the history of his nation. To be sure, Zerubbabel occupies a central position in Ezr. He leads the returning exiles (Ezr 2); together with Jeshua, it is he who builds the altar and lays the foundations of the Temple (Ezr 3), and is

---

[69] See Pohlmann (1970), p. 35.

[70] Kaufmann, p. 543, defined I Esd derisively as a 'literary miscarriage' – he was not far wrong in relation to the incorporation of the Story of the Youths.

[71] A similar case is the citation of the duplicate tradition of the division of the kingdom in the LXX to Kings (3Kgdms 12:24a-z). There, too, one has a tradition providing an alternative course of events.

consequently addressed by the adversaries of Judah and Benjamin (Ezr 4:1-5). Finally, it is he, once again with the high priest at his side, who resumes the construction of the Temple at the beginning of Darius' reign (Ezr 5).[72] The biblical account, however, does not credit him personally with changing the course of history: Cyrus issues his edict, and the people depart with Zerubbabel, Jeshua and others leading them. Later, the call of the prophets inspires the resumption of work, and the complaint of the governor Beyond the River induces Darius to renew Cyrus' edict. Zerubbabel invariably takes second place in shaping the course of events. Subsequently, Ezra will be credited with far more initiative when he immigrates during Artaxerxes' reign as a leader with official government recognition (Ezr 7), and the same is true of Nehemiah (Neh 2), but not so of Zerubbabel.

The Story of the Youths remedies the situation. In the author's hands, Zerubbabel, too, becomes a leader of the same – if not higher – status as the other leaders. By virtue of his wisdom, he persuades the Persian king to treat his nation favorably. Moreover, an examination of the favors bestowed by Darius on Zerubbabel quickly reveals that he achieves more than Ezra and Nehemiah: he journeys to Judah, provided with permits far exceeding what the immigrants received from Cyrus and Darius and Ezra and Nehemiah from Artaxerxes. One receives the impression that the author borrowed whatever possible from the material at his disposal – and then added more.

1. In the Story of the Youths, Zerubbabel returns to Judah with the Temple vessels – armed with Darius' letters, 4:44, 57, as Sheshbazzar does with Cyrus' permission (Ezr 1:7-11). He has permission to build the Temple, 4:45, 51, just as Sheshbazzar, and later Zerubbabel himself, did

---

[72] Observe, too, Neh 12:47, which endeavors to sum up the whole period: וכל ישראל בימי זרבבל ובימי נחמיה נתנים מניות המשררים "And all Israel in the days of Zerubbabel and in the days of Nehemiah gave the daily portions for the singers". There is no need to belittle Zerubbabel's role in Ezr-Neh, as Eskenazi does (p. 45), solely in order to stress his central position in I Esd.

with Cyrus' and Darius' permission (Ezr 1 and 6), and to build the city like Nehemiah (Neh 2). He receives everything necessary to build the Temple, 4:51, just as Darius found recorded in Cyrus' edict in his archive (Ezr 6:4 "Let the cost be paid from the royal treasury") and reaffirmed himself (Ezr 6:8 "The cost is to be paid to these men in full and without delay from the royal revenue, the tribute of the province from Beyond the River"). He receives funds for all the needs of the Temple, 4:52, just as Darius had written, (Ezr 6:9 "And whatever is needed... for burnt offerings to the God of heaven... let that be given to them day by day without fail"; cf. Ezr 7:17, 20-22). The returning exiles and the priests receive generous tax exemptions, 4:49, and cf. 4: 50, 53, just as Ezra received for the Temple servants (Ezr 7:24 "We also notify you that it shall not be lawful to impose tribute, custom, or toll upon any one of the priests, the Levites, the singers, the doorkeepers, the temple servants, or other servants of this house of God").[73]

2. The similarity is even closer if one considers the permits awarded in the Story of the Youths as against those given to Nehemiah.[74] This comparison is particularly interesting in light of the make-up of I Esd, in which there is no trace of Nehemiah's activities.

Nehemiah requests: אגרות יתנו לי על פחוות עבר הנהר אשר יעבירוני עד יהודה אל אבוא אשר "...let letters be given me to the governors of the

---

[73] The freedom granted to the land and to the new arrivals (4:49, 50, 53) is more similar to the benefits offered by Demetrius to the Jews in 1 Macc 10:29, 31; or to Judah's request from the king, 11:28 ποιῆσαι τὴν ᾿Ιουδαίαν ἀφορολόγητον, as in our v. 50: καὶ πᾶσαν τὴν χώραν, ἣν κρατήσουσιν, ἀφορολόγητον αὐτοῖς ὑπάρχειν. The warning to officials not to approach the Jews' homes (v. 49) is not clearly paralleled in Ezr-Neh; perhaps it may be seen as an echo of Ezr 6:6 כען תתני פחת עבר נהרה.... רחיקין הוו מן תמה "Now therefore, Tattenai governor of the province Beyond the River... keep away".

[74] Kellermann (1967), p. 130-144, draws far-reaching conclusions, arguing that the account in I Esd is a polemic against Nehemiah and portraying each and every detail in Darius' letters as a controversy with Nehemiah.

province Beyond the River, that they may let me pass through until I
come to Judah" (Neh 2:7), and Darius writes for Zerubbabel (4:47):

Καὶ ἔγραψεν αὐτῷ τὰς ἐπιστολὰς πρὸς πάντας τοὺς οἰκονόμους καὶ
τοπάρχας καὶ στρατηγοὺς καὶ σατράπας, ἵνα προπέμψωσιν αὐτὸν
καὶ τοὺς μετ᾽ αὐτοῦ πάντας ἀναβαίνοντας οἰκοδομῆσαι τὴν Ἰερουσαλήμ.

Nehemiah further asks for אגרת אל אסף שמר הפרדס אשר למלך אשר יתן
לי עצים לקרות את שערי הבירה אשר לבית ולחומת העיר "a letter to Asaph, the
keeper of the king's forest, that he may give me timber to make beams for
the gates of the fortress of the temple, and for the wall of the city" (Neh
2:8); while in I Esd 4:48 we read:

Καὶ πᾶσιν τοῖς τοπάρχαις ἐν Κοίλῃ Συρίᾳ καὶ Φοινίκῃ καὶ τοῖς ἐν
τῷ Λιβάνῳ ἔγραψεν ἐπιστολὰς μεταφέρειν ξύλα κέδρινα ἀπὸ τοῦ
Λιβάνου εἰς Ἰερουσαλὴμ καὶ ὅπως οἰκοδομήσωσιν μετ᾽ αὐτοῦ τὴν
πόλιν (cf. also Ezr 3:7).

These are the two specific requests made by Nehemiah: a letter of
safe passage and a permit to procure timber. These are precisely the two
first things granted Zerubbabel in the letters Darius writes for him.

Both personages, upon coming to Judah, are accompanied by a
considerable retinue. Neh 2:9 וישלח עמי המלך שרי חיל ופרשים "Now the king
had sent with me officers of the army and horsemen". I Esd 5:2 καὶ
Δαρεῖος συναπέστειλεν μετ᾽ αὐτῶν ἱππεῖς χιλίους ἕως τοῦ
ἀποκαταστῆσαι αὐτοὺς εἰς Ἰερουσαλὴμ μετ᾽ εἰρήνης. There is no hint
here of Ezra's hesitation: כי בשתי לשאול מן המלך חיל ופרשים לעזרנו מאויב
בדרך כי אמרנו למלך לאמר יד אלהינו על כל מבקשיו לטובה "For I was ashamed
to ask the king for a band of soldiers and horsemen to protect us against
the enemy on our way; since we had told the king, The hand of our God is
for good upon all that seek him..." (Ezr 8:22).[75] Above all, Nehemiah's
mission is to build the city: אשר תשלחני אל עיר קברות אבתי ואבננה "that you
send me to Judah, to the city of my fathers' sepulchres, that I may rebuild

---

[75] There is a parallel in I Esd to this last verse (8:52, 53), so that the two approaches
are maintained simultaneously in I Esd as in the canonical Ezr-Neh.

it" etc. (Neh 2:5), and similarly, the declared objective in Darius' letters is primarily to rebuild the city, 4:47 etc.[76]

Two further details in Darius' letters may allude to Nehemiah, although not to Artaxerxes' letters. Darius' letters express concern for the needs of the priests and the Levites: ἔγραψεν δὲ καὶ τὴν χορηγίαν καὶ τὴν ἱερατικὴν στολήν, ἐν τίνι λατρεύουσιν ἐν αὐτῇ. καὶ τοῖς Λευίταις ἔγραψεν δοῦναι τὴν χορηγίαν, 4:54, 55, a concern which is not present in the permits but recalls Nehemiah's constant efforts to ensure מנאות התורה לכהנים וללוים "...the portions required by the law for the priests and for the Levites" (Neh 12:44); ואדעה כי מניות הלוים לא נתנה "I also found out that the portions of the Levites had not been given to them" (13:10); and also 12:47 וכל ישראל בימי זרבבל ובימי נחמיה נתנים מניות המשררים והשערים "And all Israel in the days of Zerubbabel and in the days of Nehemiah gave the daily portions for the singers and the gatekeepers". In the Story of the Youths, the concern for the priests and Levites extends to the town guards as well: καὶ πᾶσι τοῖς φρουροῦσι τὴν πόλιν, ἔγραψε δοῦναι αὐτοῖς κλήρους καὶ ὀψώνια, 4:56. The only mention of these persons in the canonical books occurs in Nehemiah's activities (Neh 4:16-17; 13:22; 11:19[77]).

One more point, though perhaps rather far-fetched, deserves mention. The first part of the story, describing the argument among the three youths as to the most powerful thing in the world, may have roots in Neh 2. Nehemiah, the king's cupbearer, though very much afraid, makes so bold as to approach the king with his request. The king responds favorably – perhaps somewhat softened because of the wine and because of his consort at his side (Neh 2:1-6). Now it so happens that these are precisely the three subjects discussed by the youths: wine, royalty and womankind. In

---

[76] Although the building of the city is also the central subject in the letter of complaint to Artaxerxes.

[77] Regarding those 'who kept watch at the gates', see Zadok (1982), p. 298.

fact, not only does the story touch upon womankind in general, but the narrator, as an example, cites the actions of a certain woman, the king's consort (παλλακή) seated at his right, whose antics are tolerated by the king (4:28-31).[78] Perhaps the similarity is only accidental, the author of the Story of the Youths having assembled motifs from similar stories current in his time.[79]

Another point of contact with Neh may be found in I Esd 5:4-6, a passage most likely from the pen of whomever inserted the story into its present context and placed the list of returning exiles after it. The passage features a figure known to us only from Neh: Joiakim, the son of Jeshua (Neh 12:10); as he was a high priest, the time of his office is named for him: ...ובימי יויקים היו כהנים ראשי האבות "And in the days of Joiakim were priests, heads of fathers' houses..." (12:12); אלה בימי יויקים בן ישוע בן יוצדק ובימי נחמיה הפחה ועזרא הכהן הסופר "These were in the days of Joiakim the son of Jeshua son of Jozadak, and in the days of Nehemiah the governor and of Ezra the priest the scribe" (12:26). Now in I Esd 5:5 we find Joiakim mentioned along with the two leading figures, Zerubbabel and Jeshua: οἱ ἱερεῖς υἱοὶ Φινεες υἱοῦ Ἀαρών: Ἰησοῦς ὁ τοῦ Ἰωσέδεκ τοῦ Σαραίου καὶ Ἰωακὶμ ὁ τοῦ Ζοροβαβὲλ τοῦ Σαλαθιήλ. The text of I Esd, as it stands, is incomprehensible. First, we know of no Joiakim son of Zerubbabel. Second, it is not clear why the author used the plural, 'the priests', if he meant to mention only one priest, Jeshua. Finally, Joiakim son of Jeshua is well known in the tradition of the period. The original

---

[78] Beyond the literary interest, one might say that the monarch most likely to fit such a picture would be Artaxerxes Mnemon (404-359 B.C.E.). See Schalit (1947), esp. pp. 126-127. Besides the women who figured in his life and dominated him, the description of the king busy eating, drinking and sleeping (4:10) fits him, rather than the warrior Darius. See further below, pp. 84ff. The question is a literary one and has no implications for the identification of the historical king; the Artaxerxes of Nehemiah's time is generally identified as Artaxerxes I (465-421 B.C.E.).

[79] Stories of this genre were common, but one does not find the combination of wine, king, woman in this or any other order. See pp. 60ff.

text must have been as follows: הכהנים בני פנחס בן אהרן ישוע בן יוצדק בן
שריה ויויקים בנו, וזרובבל בן שאלתיאל "The priests, sons of Phinehas son of
Aaron: Jeshua son of Jozadak son of Seraiah and Joiakim his son, and
Zerubbabel son of Shealtiel", i.e., the people mentioned are the priests
Jeshua and his son Joiakim, and the governor, Zerubbabel.

3. The text in I Esd 5:5 departs in one further respect from the
tradition of the canonical books about Zerubbabel. It explicitly refers to
Zerubbabel's ancestry, specifically his being a scion of the Davidic dynasty.
In the canonical books we learn this explicitly only from 1 Chr 3:19;
although there Zerubbabel is referred to as the son of Pedaiah, not Shealtiel.
This proclamation of Zerubbabel's lineage endows him with a special
status, as one finds in the prophets Haggai and Zechariah, see Hag 2:21-23
אמר אל זרבבל פחת יהודה... ביום ההוא... אקחך זרבבל בן שאלתיאל עבדי נאם ה'
ושמתיך כחותם כי בך בחרתי "Speak to Zerubbabel, governor of Judah... On
that day..., I will take you, O Zerubbabel my servant, the son of Shealtiel...
and make you like a signet ring; for I have chosen you..."; Zech 3:8 עבדי
צמח "my servant the Branch"; and cf. Zech 6:12-13. Zerubbabel is referred
to by his official title, 'governor of Judah', on the one hand, and as 'my
servant', on the other. These titles are not mentioned in Ezr; nor is
Zerubbabel's ancestry.[80] The situation in I Esd is otherwise.

(a) In Darius' letter to Tattenai we read: שבקו לעבידת בית אלהא דך פחת
יהודיא ולשבי יהודיא בית אלהא דך יבנון על אתרה "Let the work on this house
of God alone – the governor of the Jews – and [let] the elders of the Jews

---

[80] Concerning the deliberate silence of the author of Ezr-Neh with regard to Zerubbabel's
lineage and official title, see Japhet (1982), pp. 71 ff. Japhet notes that, as Jeshua's
lineage and title are not mentioned either, the omissions need not necessarily be due
to a desire to conceal the messianic expectations that were linked with Zerubbabel.
Japhet suggests that the author had a tendency to shift the center of gravity of events
from the leaders to the people, as done elsewhere in Chr. To my mind, however, this
is a rather weak pretext for omitting any trace of the distinguished lineage and
position of Jeshua and Zerubbabel.

rebuild this house of God on its site" (Ezr 6:7). The parallel text in I Esd 6:26 reads: ἐᾶσαι δὲ τὸν παῖδα τοῦ κυρίου Ζοροβαβέλ, ἔπαρχον δὲ τῆς Ἰουδαίας, καὶ τοὺς πρεσβυτέρους τῶν Ἰουδαίων τὸν οἶκον τοῦ κυρίου ἐκεῖνον οἰκοδομεῖν ἐπὶ τοῦ τόπου. This Greek may reflect a text such as שבקו לעבדא דאלהא זרבבל פחת יהודיא "Let the servant of God, Zerubbabel, governor of the Jews". The MT is difficult: the words 'the governor of the Jews' seem to be detached from the rest of the verse. Although, it seems unlikely that an official Persian document would use the phrase 'servant of God'. The name 'Zerubbabel' may be explained as a late insertion, due either to the title 'servant of God' or to the title 'governor'. At any rate, Zerubbabel receives both titles in I Esd.

(b) Zerubbabel is again referred to as governor later on in the same passage, and again only in I Esd. In Ezr 6:8-9, Darius promises that נפקתא תהוא מתיהבא לגבריא אלך די לא לבטלא. ומה חשחן ובני תורין ודכרין ואמרין לעלון לאלה שמיא "the cost is to be paid to these men in full and without delay from the royal revenue... And whatever is needed – young bulls, rams, or sheep for burnt offerings to the God of heaven". The parallel text in I Esd 6:28 reads: σύνταξιν δίδοσθαι τούτοις τοῖς ἀνθρώποις εἰς θυσίας τῷ κυρίῳ, Ζοροβαβὲλ ἐπάρχῳ, εἰς ταύρους καὶ κριοὺς καὶ ἄρνας. Our interest is primarily in the words די לא לבטלא. ומה חשחן "without delay. And whatever is needed", which are not represented in I Esd; instead, that part of the verse reads: Ζοροβαβὲλ ἐπάρχῳ. These words disturb the syntax of the sentence and have therefore been explained as a wrongly placed gloss which should have come before the words τούτοις τοῖς ἀνθρώποις, as in the previous verse cited above. There the letter instructed the recipients to leave Zerubbabel the governor and the elders of the Jews alone, while here it tells them to give the expenses to these same persons. However, the fact that Ζοροβαβελ ἐπάρχῳ replaces certain words in the MT implies that this was the original position of the Greek words. The relationship between the Greek and Aramaic words was brilliantly explained by Bewer: he argues that the words די לא לבטלא have no parallel in I Esd; the words ומה חשחן, however, were translated by ἐπαρκῶς, their literal equivalent, which was corrupted at some stage of transmission to ἐπάρχῳ. The new reading inspired the addition of the name Zerubbabel, naturally by a Greek redactor. It is rather difficult to imagine a corruption in the Aramaic text – or a different *Vorlage*, for that matter.

(c) Zerubbabel appears once more in I Esd without any parallel in the MT, and in the same episode. In Ezr 5:14, we read that Cyrus gave the Temple vessels לששבצר שמה די פחה שמה "to one whose name was Sheshbazzar, whom he had made governor". In the parallel passage in I Esd 6:17, the vessels are given to Ζοροβαβὲλ καὶ Σαναβασσάρῳ τῷ ἐπάρχῳ.[81] If this is a duplicate version, stemming from an attempt to identify Sheshbazzar with Zerubbabel, the attempt could not have been made by whomever interpolated the Story of the Youths. That redactor made a clear distinction between Sheshbazzar and Zerubbabel, for he leaves Sheshbazzar in place in the account of the edict of Cyrus, I Esd 2:11, 14 (Ezr 1:8, 11), while first introducing Zerubbabel in the Story of the Youths. It would appear, therefore, that the addition of Zerubbabel at this point is a late interpolation, whether as an alternative to the name of Sheshbazzar or as an adjunct to the title 'governor', as we have explained the previous cases.[82]

As the Story of the Youths brought out the figure of Zerubbabel, it must have encouraged references to him in the above three passages of I Esd, whether in the source, in the first translation, or in a reworked version of the latter.

In view of the many points of contact between the benefits granted Zerubbabel in the Story of the Youths and Nehemiah's activities, one

---

[81] Unlike the previous references, only part of the manuscripts of I Esd feature the extended reading of I Esd that includes Zerubbabel.

[82] Note that the Story of the Youths itself does not endow Zerubbabel with the title.

might suggest that the character of Zerubbabel was constructed in the Story of the Youths as a substitute for Nehemiah, and that Nehemiah's memoirs were deliberately eliminated from the book.[83] The relative weight assigned the central figures in the Restoration period in I Esd is surely not the same as in the Book of Ezr-Neh. Zerubbabel essentially takes Nehemiah's place.

There is no inherent reason for the substitution. Zerubbabel's character, as reshaped by the Story of the Youths, is no different from that of Nehemiah. Both hold high office in the royal court, both are permitted to come to Judah out of the kindness of the foreign king's heart. Is it a question of lineage? After all Zerubbabel is a scion of the Davidic dynasty, the target of prophetic expectations; while Nehemiah obtained his position solely from the Persian authorities.[84] It is worth noticing, however, that Zerubbabel's lineage is not mentioned in the Story of the Youths but only in the transitional passage between it and the surrounding context (5:5).

On the whole, I Esd clearly reveals here the common tendency of aggadic homilies to build up one character by borrowing traits from another.

4. The idea that one character has been ousted in favor of another makes good sense, given the strained relations among the central figures of the period – Sheshbazzar versus Zerubbabel, Ezra versus Nehemiah – as evidenced by major difficulties encountered in the Book of Ezr-Neh and by post-biblical literature:

(a) Ben Sira mentions Nehemiah, but not Ezra, in his 'Praise of the Fathers' (Sirach 49:1-3).

(b) The Second Book of Maccabees develops the figure of Nehemiah but entirely ignores Ezra. In the second letter of the Jews of Jerusalem to

---

[83] In contrast, Böhler (1997), pp. 307 ff, is convinced that Nehemiah's memoirs are a later addition not yet known to the author of the original edition of the book as preserved in I Esd.

[84] Eskenazi, pp. 44-51, places much emphasis on this point. She is apparently unacquainted with Talshir (1984).

their brethren in Egypt, Nehemiah overshadows the other heroes of the
Restoration period: ἵνα καὶ αὐτοὶ ἄγητε σκηνοπηγίας καὶ τοῦ πυρός,
ὅτε Νεεμίας ὁ οἰκοδομήσας τό τε ἱερὸν καὶ τὸ θυσιαστήριον
ἀνήνεγκεν θυσίας (2 Macc 1:18). The celebration of the Feast of Booths
and the erection of both altar and Temple, attributed here to Nehemiah,
are 'borrowed' from Zerubbabel's activities as described in Ezr 3. In the
sequel, Nehemiah earns further glory as the hero of the story of the search
for the hidden fire and the discovery of 'thick water' that burst into fire on
the altar. The author in fact refers to 'the writings and memoirs of Nehemiah'
and describes Nehemiah's establishment of a 'collection of books' which
the Sages of the Talmudic period would have ascribed to Ezra:

> Ἐξηγοῦντο δὲ καὶ ἐν ταῖς ἀναγραφαῖς καὶ ἐν τοῖς ὑπομνηματισμοῖς
> τοῖς κατὰ τὸν Νεεμιαν τὰ αὐτὰ καὶ ὡς καταβαλλόμενος βιβλιοθήκην
> ἐπισυνήγαγεν τὰ περὶ τῶν βασιλέων βιβλία καὶ προφητῶν καὶ τὰ
> τοῦ Δαυιδ καὶ ἐπιστολὰς βασιλέων περὶ ἀναθεμάτων (2 Macc 2:13).

It is not very likely that the authors of these works, in the 2nd
century B.C.E., were acquainted with only the memoirs of Nehemiah but
not with the historical chronicle that also included the story of Ezra. More
probably, Nehemiah was more highly regarded at that time; alternatively,
they may have had ideological reasons to suppress the memory of Ezra.[85]

(c) Josephus, too, expands at length on Nehemiah's activities going
beyond the biblical account. Nehemiah requests the king: "Do but graciously
permit me to go there and raise up the wall and complete the building that
remains to be done on the temple" (Ant. XI, §165, repeated in §169) – this
in itself is reminiscent of the treatment of Zerubbabel and in contrast to
the secretive nature of Nehemiah's early activities in the canonical book.
Underlying Josephus' version of the events, which credits Nehemiah with
having participated in the building of the Temple too, is the complex text
of Neh 2:8. In I Esd, it is Zerubbabel who builds both Temple and city.

---

[85] See Höffken (1975).

(d) Also important for our purposes is the Rabbinic midrash identifying Zerubbabel with Nehemiah on the basis of a popular etymology: ,זרבבל' שנזרע בבבל. ומה שמו? נחמיה בן חכליה שמו' "Zerubbabel – [so called] because he was conceived in Babylon. And what was his name? Nehemiah son of Hacaliah was his name". In other words, 'Zerubbabel' was a mere nickname of Nehemiah, so called because he was conceived in Babylon.

Perhaps some such homily provided the impetus for the composition of I Esd; alternatively, the author might have followed a homily of his own granting Zerubbabel some of the virtues of Nehemiah and pushing the latter out of the picture – an opposite thrust to that of Ben Sira and II Macc. The Rabbis are explicitly critical of Nehemiah,[86] and this may be true of the author of I Esd as well.

Notably, the figure of Ezra receives more emphasis in I Esd than in the canonical Ezr-Neh, although this emphasis may well be due to the translator: Ezra is described three times as the high priest, in 9:39, 40, 49 (Neh 8:1, 2, 9), while in the MT he is merely 'Ezra the priest'. Similarly, Ezra's clothing (בגדי ומעילי "my garments and my mantle") is referred to in I Esd as sacred vestments: τὰ ἱμάτια καὶ τὴν ἱερὰν ἐσθῆτα, 8:68, 70 (Ezr 9:3, 5).

In sum, it is probable that the author of I Esd omitted the story of Nehemiah from his narrative and instead built the history of the Restoration around the figures of Zerubbabel and Ezra.

---

[86] Babylonian Talmud, Sanhedrin 93b, מכדי, כל מילי דעזרא נחמיה בן חכליה אמרינהו ונחמיה בן חכליה מאי טעמא לא איקרי סיפרא על שמיה? ...מפני שהחזיק טובה לעצמו... מפני שסיפר בגנותן של ראשונים "Insofar as it was Nehemiah son of Hacaliah who uttered all the words of Ezra, why was his book not named for him?... Because he spoke vainly of himself... because he spoke disparagingly of his predecessors".

V. The Story of the Youths

The Story of the Youths is the high point of I Esd. It is the cause of at least some of the main discrepancies between I Esd and the canonical books. No doubt its inclusion was the reason for the structural changes in the unit Ezr 1-6. Possibly, it may also have influenced the omission of Nehemiah's life story from the book. For those who believe I Esd to be a fragment of a work that included all of Chr-Ezr-Neh, the Story of the Youths is simply a late interpolation that caused much confusion at one point in a large-scale history.[87] But if – as I am indeed arguing – I Esd as we have it today more or less preserves the original plan of the book, then the Story of the Youths was the catalyst for the formation of I Esd – its *raison d'être*. I Esd was created in order to interpolate the Story of the Youths into the story of the Restoration, and the whole book has no real existence without it.[88]

It is clear from the previous sections that the Story of the Youths, in its present context, essentially upsets the logical course of events.[89] Consequently, it was most probably not written with that context in mind, rather as an independent literary unit which was only later inserted into

---

[87] Torrey (1945), p. 396, offers the very attractive (though unacceptable) explanation that I Esd has preserved precisely that part of the large-scale work whose version of history deviated from what was commonly accepted. If this were true, I Esd would owe its very survival to the Story of the Youths.

[88] Gardner's (1986) article, entitled 'The purpose and date of I Esdras', makes almost no mention of the Story of the Youths. If the primary purpose of the book revolves around the doctrine of reward and punishment, the temple and the lessons of history, Gardner's article more aptly relates to Chr-Ezr-Neh, not I Esd. The promise held out by the ambitious title is not kept. The comparison with 2 Macc is superficial and unconvincing; it certainly does not justify the conclusion that I Esd was composed 'in the time of the Maccabean Crisis'.

[89] Howorth (1893*), p. 106, is the only authority to argue that I Esd preserves an original version, including the position of the Story of the Youths.

the plot of Ezr.[90] This conclusion is supported by the clearly demarcated limits of the story and the self-sufficiency of the content. That is not to say that the story is a homogeneous unit: it, too, reveals various 'seams' indicating different stages of formation. However, these difficulties do not attest to the history of the Book of I Esd as a whole, but rather to the evolution of the story itself.

a. Composition of the Story of the Youths

1. The Scope of the Story

The scope of the Story has been determined as 3:1-5:6, as this unit has no parallel in the canonical books. The story consists of two clear-cut parts: 3:1-4:41 and 4:42-63. The first part begins with a description of a feast held by Darius for the high-ranking officials of his kingdom. This feast gives the king's three bodyguards an opportunity to debate the question, 'What is the most powerful thing of all?' as a contest between the three. The style of the opening (3:1-16) recalls that of the Books of Esther and Daniel. Thereafter (3:17-4:41), the style changes, and the youths' speeches on the relative merits of wine, the king, womankind and truth are essentially discourses in a style reminiscent of wisdom literature. Zerubbabel, the youth found to be the wisest of the three, enjoys the fruit of his victory in the second part, 4:42-63, where he requests – and receives – from the king letters to facilitate his return to Jerusalem and permit him to rebuild the city. Here the dominant style is a historiographical one, reminiscent of the Book of Ezr-Neh. The last section, 5:1-6, is not part of the story proper, but a connecting link between the story and the context, written in the style of the subsequent passage, parallel to Ezr 2, yet by a palpably different hand. Parts of the story as we have it today are well rooted in biblical literature and derive from there. That is the case in the first verses (3:1-16)

---

[90] This is the conclusion of Goodman's third chapter (1972).

and the last part (4:42-5:6). Nevertheless, even these sections possess features in common with extrabiblical literature, such as the Books of Maccabees. The section describing the contest among the youths carries the story far beyond its present framework.

2. The Genre

The point of departure for the youths' contest is the ancient universal question, 'What is the most powerful thing of all?' (3:5 ἕνα λόγον, ὅς ὑπερισχύσει). The background to the question is surely contemplation of the powerful elements of nature, as expressed at the beginning of the fourth discourse (on truth), toward the end of the whole cycle:

Μεγάλη ἡ γῆ, καὶ ὑψηλὸς ὁ οὐρανός, καὶ ταχὺς τῷ δρόμῳ ὁ ἥλιος,
ὅτι στρέφεται ἐν τῷ κύκλῳ τοῦ οὐρανοῦ καὶ πάλιν ἀποτρέχει εἰς
τὸν ἑαυτοῦ τόπον ἐν μιᾷ ἡμέρᾳ.
The earth is great and the heavens are high and the sun rapidly runs its course around the heavens, returning to its place in a single day (4:34).[91]

The various answers to this intriguing conundrum may include, besides the elemental forces of nature, a broad spectrum of components in innumerable combinations. To illustrate, let us consider a few sample answers from the literature of the East and from Rabbinical sources.

---

[91] D. Flusser (oral communication, 1980) defined this passage as the earliest response known to him to the universal question, 'What is the most powerful thing in the world?' For the content of the passage, cf. Eccl 1:4-7, from a different standpoint: והארץ לעולם עומדת. וזרח השמש ובא השמש ואל מקומו שואף זורח הוא שם. הולך אל דרום וסובב אל צפון סובב סבב הולך הרוח על סביבתיו שב הרוח. כל הנחלים הלכים אל הים והים איננו מלא אל מקום שהנחלים הלכים שם הם שבים ללכת "But the earth remains for ever. The sun rises and the sun goes down, and hastens to the place where it rises. The wind blows to the south, and goes round to the north; round and round goes the wind, and on its circuits the wind returns. All streams run to the sea, but the sea is not full; to the place where the streams flow, there they flow again".

An Indian folktale tells the story of a holy man who turns a mouse into a girl and raises her as his daughter. When she reaches the age of twelve, he tries to marry her off. He proposes that she marry the sun, but the girl does not consider it a worthy partner. Thereupon the man asks the sun, "who is superior to you?" to which the sun answers, "the cloud". So on the story goes: the cloud declares that the wind is superior, the wind suggests the mountain, and the mountain finally suggests the mouse.[92]

A typical Ethiopian chain-proverb strings several components together as follows: iron is strong, but fire is stronger; fire is strong, but the clouds are stronger; clouds are strong, but the earth is stronger; the earth is strong, but man is stronger; man is strong, but sorrow is stronger; sorrow is strong, but wine is stronger; wine is strong, but sleep is stronger. And woman is stronger than them all.[93]

A Pehlevi text preserves an authentic Sassanid version of a literary type in which the framework story has three or four members of different nations expressing their views, the last word being that of the Persian: One day wise men from Byzantium and India, together with Adorbad son of Mahrasfend, were seated before the King of Kings. The king asked them, 'Who is the happiest person in the world?' The Byzantine replied, 'An unopposed ruler'. The Indian answered, 'One who is young and wealthy'. But Adorbad said, 'One who has fear neither in this world nor in the next'. The king then asked, 'Who is the unhappiest person in the world?' (The Byzantine replied, ...). The Indian said, 'One who is childless and destitute'. But Adorbad answered, 'Death is worst of all, after evil'.[94]

---

[92] See *The Panchatantra* (1949), pp. 304-309. I am indebted to Professor D. Flusser for this reference.

[93] Cited in Latin translation by Laqueur (1911), p. 172 note (a lengthy comment on our story, though the article is devoted to a different subject).

[94] Shaked (1984) cites other examples of such tales in Arabic literature and argues for their Persian ancestry.

A talmudic anecdote recounted in Bava Batra 10a is very similar to the chain-proverb cited above, except for its punch-line:

תניא. ר"י אומר: גדולה צדקה שמקרבת את הגאולה... הוא היה אומר: עשרה דברים קשים נבראו בעולם. הר קשה, ברזל מחתכו. ברזל קשה, אור מפעפעו. אור קשה, מים מכבין אותו. מים קשים, עבים סובלים אותן. עבים קשים, רוח מפזרתן. רוח קשה, גוף סובלו. גוף קשה, פחד שוברו. פחד קשה, יין מפיגו. יין קשה, שינה מפכחתו. ומיתה קשה מכולם. וכתיב: וצדקה תציל ממות.

We have learned the following. R. Yose said: Great is charity, for it hastens the approach of redemption... He used to say, Ten hard things were created in the world. A mountain is hard, iron cuts it. Iron is hard, fire melts it. Fire is hard, water quenches it. Water is hard, clouds carry it. Clouds are hard, wind scatters them. Wind is hard, the body endures it. The body is hard, fear breaks it. Fear is hard, wine dispels it. Wine is hard, sleep sobers from it. And death is the hardest of all – but it is written, Charity delivers from death.

The same literary genre was used to answer the question, 'Who is worthy of being worshipped?' Probably the earliest source of such tales is a passage in Bereshit Rabba, Pisqa 38 (ed. Theodor-Albeck, p. 363):

אמר ליה: ולא ישמעו אזניך מפיך, נסתיה ומסרתיה לנמרוד. אמר ליה: נסגוד לנורא. אמר ליה: נסגוד למייא דמטפין לנורא. אמר ליה: ונסגוד למיא. אמר ליה: נסגוד לעננו דטעני מיא. אמר ליה: ונסגוד לעננא. אמר ליה: נסגוד לרוחא דמובלי עננא. אמר ליה: ונסגוד לרוחא. אמר ליה: נסגוד לבר נשא דסביל רוחא. אמר ליה: מלין את משתעי לא נסגוד אלא לאור הריני משליכך בו.

Said [Abram to Terah]: Cannot your ears hear what your mouth is saying?! He [Terah] took him and delivered him to Nimrod. Said [Nimrod to Abram], Let us worship fire. He said to him, Let us worship water, which quenches fire. He said to him, Well then, let us worship water. He said to him, Let us worship the clouds, which bear water. He said to him, Well then, let us worship the cloud. He said to him, Let us worship the wind, which moves the cloud. He said to him, Well then, let us worship the wind. He said to him, Let us worship man, who endures the wind. He said to him, You are talking nonsense! We shall worship only fire, behold, I am throwing you into it.

The same theme is featured in a late midrash, Ma'aseh Avraham, which provides a good typological example of the birth of such questions about 'the most powerful things':

כשהיה בן שלש שנים יצא מן המערה. הרהר בלבו: מי ברא שמים וארץ ואותי. התפלל
כל היום כולו לשמש, ולערב שקע השמש במערב וזרחה הלבנה במזרח. כשראה הירח
והכוכבים סביב הירח. אמר: זהו שברא השמים והארץ ואותי והכוכבים הללו שריו
ועבדיו... לבקר שקע הירח במערב וזרח השמש במזרח. אמר: אין ביד אלו כח. אדון יש
עליהם.

When he was three years old he came out of the cave. He thought to
himself, Who created the heavens and the earth and myself? All day long
he prayed to the sun, but in the evening the sun sank in the west and the
moon rose in the east. When he saw the moon and the stars around the
moon he said, it must be the moon who created the heavens and the Earth
and myself and those stars are his princes and servants... In the morning
the moon sank in the west and the sun rose in the east. He said, These are
powerless! Surely they have a Master![95]

In the much older Book of Jubilees the situation is presented without
any hint of the puzzle motif, and the solution is known in advance: "And
there came a thought into his mind, and he said, All the signs of the stars
and all the signs of the Heavens and the moon – all are in the hands of the
Lord – so why should I inquire further?!" (Jub 12:17).

Finally, mention should be made of the dypno-sophist scene in the
Letter of Aristeas (§§181-194). In the course of a seven-day feast, the
king asks ten different questions each day mainly pertaining to wise
government. He addresses his questions to various guests at the feast and
is satisfied with all the answers.

None of these tales resemble the Story of the Youths, although grown
from a similar seed; most of all, they fall short of that story in their
development of the themes. They also differ from one another, both in
framework and in presentation. The Persian texts and the Letter of Aristeas
are concerned primarily to arrive at an outstanding answer, but they do not
reject the other answers or explicitly present the last one as more powerful;
its power is self-evident. This may be due to the topics treated, which are
more philosophical in nature. Yet, even in the chain-proverb, whose salient
feature is the ascending order of the statements, the closing statement –

---

[95] Jellinek (1938), II, p. 118.

the greater power of womanhood – is not related to or inherently implied by any of the other links in the chain. On the contrary, the proverb owes its attraction to this element of unexpectedness and surprise. The sudden appearance of a theme that does not follow naturally from the argument and sometimes seems like an artificial leap to another plane is worthy of attention; that is the case with regard to death and evil in the Pehlevi text, or death and charity at the end of the talmudic text.

3. Wine – King – Women

One of the major difficulties in the Story of the Youths is the relationship among the different themes. We may start with the question of the relationship among the three first themes – wine, king and woman. In this literary genre, one expects the first theme to be one whose power is self-evident,[96] while the others surprise the listener. In the present case, there could have been no better opening than the king, since the framework places the entire event at the royal court. Surprisingly, however, the story begins with wine.

The linkage between the themes is also puzzling. The first theme is wine, which is said to be 'powerful' because it muddles people's minds. The second is the king, whose power consists in his absolute rule over his subjects; there is no reference to the previous theme, wine. It is questionable whether the two themes can be compared at all – in what sense is the king more powerful than wine? The third theme is woman, or womanhood. While wine and royalty remain disconnected, women are compared with both king and wine: women are superior to both, as they give birth both to the king and to the vintners who manufacture the wine. The connection with wine, however, is artificial.[97] Women's sway over people and over the king in particular is fully explained in the rest of the discourse.

---

[96] See Laqueur (1911), p. 172 note. The chain-proverb that he quotes indeed begins with iron, whose power is obvious.

[97] In the same way one might say that the king rules the vintners; there is no inherent connection.

Many scholars have questioned the logic underlying the order 'wine – king', suggesting that the text has inverted the original order. The source, they argue, presented the themes in the order: the king; wine, which prevails over the king; and women, who triumph over both. Apart from the logical argument, there are two details in the story that appear to favor the order 'wine – king'. First, the discussion of wine already refers to the king: "It reduces to the same level the mind of the king and the orphan, the mind of the slave and the mind of the freeman, the mind of the poor man and the mind of the rich man" (3:18). However, this reference to the king does not necessarily mean that the king preceded wine in some previous, differently structured version of the story. It is merely part of the description of wine's ability to rule out the differences in the minds of three opposing pairs: 'king – orphan', 'slave – freeman', 'poor man – rich man'. The king enjoys no advantage over the others. Even less indicative of a different order is the second mention of the king in the 'wine' speech: one effect of wine is to erase all memory of king and governor (3:20). Here, too, the king is merely part of the presentation of wine and there is no hint that he is inferior to wine. Nevertheless, the reference to the king in the discourse on wine, while royalty is the next theme to be discussed, indeed detracts from the literary merit of the story.

Another possible indication that the story might have been differently constituted is a passage at the beginning of the discussion of womanhood. The speaker refers to the two previous themes, but in an order different from that in our present text, mentioning first the king and then wine:

> Is not the king great, are not men mighty, and is not wine powerful? But who now is their master?... Women have given birth to the king and all the people who rule over sea and land. They were born of them and they reared those who planted the vineyards from which comes wine (4:14-15).

This proof is convincing, especially when combined with the following argument: unlike the author of the passage on women, who knew the story in its previous version, whoever added the discussion of truth was already familiar with the present order, and wrote, "Wine is deceptive, the king is deceptive, women are deceptive" (4:37) – first wine and only then the king.[98] However, this, too, is not conclusive proof, for the author might have referred to the two themes preceding womanhood in inverted order; the order is irrelevant in the discussion of women since there is no implication that wine is more powerful than the king and since women prevail over both. Moreover, there is an additional element here – 'people', and this may affect the order of the themes.

Further support for the thesis that the original order was king-wine-women is allegedly found in Josippon.[99] Josippon tells the whole Story of the Youths, first referring to the king's power and only then going on to wine. He begins as follows:

ויביאו את קסת הסופר והמגילה, ויפילו הגורל לאחד, ויכתב על המגילה לאמר: אין כמלך חזק בארץ, והשני כתב: אין כיין חזק בארץ, והשלישי, הוא זרובבל, כתב: אין כאשה חזק בארץ.

And they brought the scribe's inkstand and parchment and cast lots. One wrote on the parchment as follows: There is nothing so powerful on earth as the king; and the second wrote, There is nothing so powerful on earth as wine; and the third, that is, Zerubbabel, wrote, There is nothing so powerful on earth as woman (Josippon 6:47).

It does not seem likely that Josippon was drawing on some earlier source, such as a cycle of Zerubbabel stories, which had also been at the disposal of the author of I Esd. One doubts whether he had any sources at all other than those currently available, in particular for the episode of the youths. Far more probably, he reshaped the story on his own initiative.[100] In fact, he anticipated the order king-wine at the very beginning, when he wrote, describing the drunken king (here, too, there is no parallel in

---

[98] Laqueur, *ibid.*

[99] See Neuman (1952).

[100] Flusser, I (1978), p. 37, writes: "However, Josippon rightly observed that wine also vanquishes the king and therefore inverted the order.... There is therefore no substance to the arguments of some scholars... that Josippon preserved the original order, which had reached him from a source earlier than III Esdras – that argument in itself is questionable, since Josippon did not use primary, early sources".

ויעמדו סביבות המלך עד עת תעורתו והמלך כבד בשנתו כי נשתכר ביין :(I Esd)
"They stood around the king until he awoke; and the king slept heavily,
for he had been intoxicated by wine" (Josippon 6:37). Besides changing
the order, he added an opening passage to the discussion of wine, linking
it to the previous theme: ואף היין חזק מן המלך כי כל גבורת המלך אמת הוא,
וכאשר ישתה, היין ימשול בו ויך לבו "And wine, too, is more powerful than the
king, for all the king's valor is true, but when he drinks, wine rules him
and diverts his heart" (Josippon 6:73-74). Moreover, the 'wine' speech is
oriented around the king: Josippon explicitly speaks of the power of wine
over the king, while I Esd is concerned with the power of wine over
people in general. The king is indeed mentioned in the 'wine' speech of
I Esd (3:18, see above), but the reference is incidental. Josippon is very
consistent in this order. He even inverts the order in the discussion of
truth, where our text of I Esd (4:37) lists the previous themes in the order
wine-king: ...והבל היין ... הבל המלך... "Vanity is the king... and vanity is wine..."
(Jossipon 6:130).[101] There are further interventions of Josippon elsewhere
in the story. Thus, in his version, truth is not mentioned at the beginning
of the third youth's address (see Jossipon 6:47, 59-60, *contra* I Esd 3:12,
4:13), but only at the end so as not to spoil the reader's surprise. Beyond
this particular episode, indeed, Josippon not infrequently reworks his sources
and rebuilds them. For example, he makes Zerubbabel Daniel's successor
as adviser to the Persian king in order to create a 'historical' continuum.
The literary superiority of the story in Josippon's version does not, therefore,
testify to its authenticity.

The order in the present text of I Esd, wine-king-women, is indeed
rather perplexing, while the ascending order king-wine-women seems

---

[101] Contrary to the aforementioned suggestion, that the author of the discourse on truth
was familiar with the present order of I Esd, this cannot be said of Josippon; though
he seems to recognize the original order of king-wine, he is also acquainted with the
expanded story, including truth, and in fact takes care to write king-wine, adhering
to his own order, there as well.

preferable. Nevertheless, there is no real proof that the story ever existed in that order. More plausibly, the author of the Story of the Youths drew on different sources, which featured the themes wine/king/women solely or in different combinations in relation to one another or to yet other themes. In any case, these particular themes do not constitute a convincing threesome. 'King-wine' is a likely combination, as is 'king-women'. The three together, however, whatever the order, form an artificial combination. Moreover, if we assume that the author of the story in I Esd tampered with the original order, we must explain why he did so, and there is no obvious reason for him to place wine before the king.[102]

Finally, it is noteworthy that the author develops the themes gradually, beginning with a brief discourse on wine, expanding somewhat with regard to the king and discussing women at greater length. This gradation provides yet another indication that he was constructing the story in the existing order.

Aside from the wine theme, the discourses on the king and on womanhood seem convincingly related. The account of the king begins with a declaration of the greatness of men in general, as something self-evident: "Are not men incomparably strong, since they exercise control over land and sea and all things in them?" (4:2).[103] Although people in general occupy a prominent place in the subsequent arguments as well, that does not necessarily imply that they were ever treated in a separate speech. The reference to their power at the beginning of the 'king' speech is characteristic of the author's style, introducing the central topic gradually (cf. the beginning of the discourse on truth, 4:34-35, and also 4:28). The king's power, then, is based on his rule over people: "He rules over them and has dominion over them and to everything he decrees they submit"

---

[102] He surely had no scruples about degrading the king in comparison with wine – for, as it is, he forthrightly criticizes the king and treats him with considerable contempt (esp. 4:10, 28-31).

[103] For man's control of the universe cf. Gen 1:26, 28; Ps 8:6-9.

(4:3). Similarly, the discourse on womanhood begins with a proclamation of the greatness of the king and men in general, and the power of wine, too, is mentioned. Then comes the key question: Who has power over them, if not women? (4:14). Women gave birth to the king and to people (4:15), and – as an addendum – to the planters of vines (4:16). Thus far the opening section; however, the vintners are not mentioned at all in the main body of the speech. There the youth speaks of woman's power over men (4:17-27), citing as the ultimate proof her power over the king (4:28-31). One cannot deny wine its place in the discourse on womanhood, but it plays a very ancillary and rather artificial role. Most of the stage is occupied by the king, men and women. In the discourse on truth, too, wine is denied a logical place alongside the king, women, people in general and all their actions (4:37). Wine, therefore, seems to be an extraneous theme, however it is woven into the story.[104]

4. The Discourse on Women

The texture of the discourse on women is also rather nonuniform. It reveals two different faces of womanhood. One is the beautiful woman, to whom men are attracted and for whom men are ready to give up practically everything. This is the face of woman that makes men toil, even steal and cheat for her sake, sometimes even bringing them to rack and ruin. The other face is the faithful wife, for whom man leaves his father and mother, to whom he cleaves for love. This last aspect of womanhood is uppermost in 4:20-21, 25 – passages thought to be an expansion of the original speech. It has been argued that the original narrative was devoted to the woman who dominates man, exploiting and taunting him (like wine).

---

[104] The extraneous nature of wine in this context is also brought out by the rather incongruous Greek adjective describing it: ἄδικος ὁ οἶνος. If the source underlying ἄδικος was הבל 'vanity', the word chosen by Josippon here, the predicate would not be so foreign to the subject in the source as it is in the translation. See below, n. 146.

Whoever placed this discourse on women in Zerubbabel's mouth tacked
on evaluations of a different kind, in the spirit of Gen 2:24 על כן יעזב איש
את אביו ואת אמו ודבק באשתו והיו לבשר אחד "Therefore a man leaves his
father and his mother and cleaves to his wife, and they become one flesh".
The text thus presents a mixture of ideas from different areas.[105] However,
the distinction is not so clear-cut as to define the aforementioned verses as
an accretion to an existing text. For indeed, the opening section of the
discourse describes woman as prevailing over the king and over people in
general, but she is also said to give birth to the king and to the people,
cloth them, and care for their needs; they cannot live without her. The
aspect of womanhood exalted in these verses is rather that of the wife-mother.
Moreover, these verses belong to the framework, the skeleton of the story,
that links the different themes together, and so, cannot be an accretion. In
other words, whoever constructed the story had already merged the two
faces of womanhood.

The evolution of the story that emerges from the composition of the
discourse on women accords with that implied by the previous discussion:
our text was produced not by expanding and modifying an existing narrative,
but by using existing raw materials with different subjects, pouring them
into a new mold which did not always suit the constituents, whether
because it altered the original intent (woman), or because it forced them
into an incongruous relationship (wine-king-woman).

5. The Fourth Theme – Truth

The skeleton of the story seems to be completely violated by the
fourth theme – truth. There are only three youths (3:4), each of whom

---

[105] Zimmermann (1963/64), pp. 183f., points out the different orientation of vv. 20, 25.
He suggests that this was due to a translator's error: the original text read אנתתה
(woman), but the translator understood this as a noun with a pronominal suffix,
meaning 'his wife'; however, the conceptual difference is not explained by this one
slip.

undertakes to suggest one theme: Εἴπωμεν ἕκαστος ἡμῶν ἕνα λόγον (3:5). Subsequently, each youth pens his contribution (3:8), and their efforts are placed at the head of the king's bed for him to read and judge (3:9). Surprisingly, one has written about wine and the second about the king, but the third has taken up two themes – women and truth (3:12). Moreover, his discourse is explicitly introduced as being devoted to women and truth (4:13), and he indeed proceeds to present two separate speeches, one about women (4:14-32) and another about truth (4:34-40). In addition to the incongruity of three speakers versus four themes, there is a fundamental difference between the first three themes and truth, which is an abstract philosophical element. Scholars have concluded that truth is an addition, superimposed on an existing story – either when the story was assimilated into Persian culture, which reveres truth as a central notion,[106] or when its wanderings brought it into Jewish circles, which were eager to grant Zerubbabel a worthy subject.[107] However, this generally accepted thesis raises several objections:

(1) The argument that the narrative involves an inner contradiction – three youths, one theme each, but the third youth presents two themes – is based on interpreting ἕνα λόγον (3:5) as a noun-number combination; yet here, εἷς, or its hypothetical source ‏תן(א)‏, may serve as the indefinite article.[108]

(2) The argument that the connection between truth and the rest of the story is artificial, thus proving that it was added at a late stage, is unsound. Whoever wove truth into the narrative took considerable pains

---

[106] See Widengren (1956), p. 218; Grintz (1963), pp. 141-143; Goodman (1972), pp. 204-209, cites parallels from Persian literature but does not conclude that our story has a Persian origin.

[107] Schalit (1947); Pohlmann (1980), pp. 42-45, cites parallels from biblical and apocryphal literature.

[108] This is the case in 4:18 καὶ ἴδωσιν γυναῖκα μίαν, "and they saw a woman"; see Torrey, p. 24.

to do so. It appears from the start as the third youth's second theme (3:12); and, the third youth himself does not 'forget' to mention it at the beginning of his discourse (4:13). When the discourse on women comes to an end there is an obvious pause, stressing the change of theme: "Then as the king and the magnates looked at one another, he proceeded to speak about the truth" (4:33). Moreover, the youth's words relate quite clearly to the previous themes. First he creates a tie to womanhood: "Men, are not women strong?" (4:34), as if to say: You see, I have been able to demonstrate that women prevail over everything suggested by the others, on the level of the discussion up to this point; however, all these things are trifling compared with the really great ones. Their triviality is clearly defined in 4:37, and truth is described in subsequent verses as the antithesis of all the previous themes. In other words, whoever wrote the discourse about truth was intensely aware of the preceding discourses. The 'fourth' discourse was not simply inserted into a given narrative, but carefully composed with consideration for the development of the story up to that point. In any case, the very genre being used here would not easily allow a more explicit reference to truth in the discourses on the other themes.

(3) As to the difference in the nature of the themes, one might argue, on the contrary, that that is precisely what qualifies truth for its special literary and ideational position in the story. As we have seen, the uniformity of the narrative is violated even in other, more 'primitive' literary genres devoted to the idea of the 'most powerful thing in the world'. Thus, the chain-proverb listing several things, each stronger than its predecessor, ends with 'and woman is stronger than them all'; although, the theme of 'woman' has absolutely nothing to do with any of the previous themes (iron, fire, etc.). Death, too, and of course evil, are quite unexpected in the Pehlevi text about people who have met happy or unhappy fates. Similarly, death and charity do not follow naturally on 'Ten hard things... created in the world' (mountain, iron, etc.) in our talmudic text. In all these cases,

the shift to a new plane is quite intentional. Perhaps the writer of the discourse about truth was out of touch with modern literary taste, but he was not violating ancient conventions.

(4) The structure of three and four is by no means less expected, and in such narratives in particular, than a structure of three.[109]

(5) Furthermore, a certain structural feature of the discourse on truth is closely reminiscent of the presentation of the other themes. It begins by praising something entirely different: "Great is the earth, high is heaven, and swift is the sun in its course", and only then is the superiority of truth mentioned (4:34-35). The same occurs in the speech about the king; the youth first speaks of the greatness of men in general, only then observing that the king rules them all (4:2-3).[110]

These points explain the intentions of the author in structuring his story as it is today. One is nevertheless left with the impression that the three first constituents of the story enjoyed some previous, independent life, before being joined by truth.

6. God of Truth

The discourse on truth raises yet another difficulty. The acclamation of truth, so it is argued, has pagan overtones and the Jewish author had reservations about using it unmodified; he therefore twisted the text around so as to ensure that God be assigned His proper place as the real supreme power.[111] The youth describes truth as an eternal force, the source of all

---

[109] Cf. the examples cited by Shaked, which describe disputes between members of nations from the four corners of the earth. See also Zakovich (1978), pp. 249-254.

[110] For a similar style of discourse compare the opening verse of the speech about women (4:16) and the verse effecting the transition to the section stressing woman's hold over the king (v. 28). In those cases, however, the theme has already been mentioned and it is naturally referred to again in order to show that the new theme is superior.

[111] Rudolph, in the introduction to his commentary, p. VI; Grintz (1963), p. 143.

order in the universe and the embodiment of justice. The audience supports
him at the end of the speech, crying, "Great is truth and incomparably
strong" (4:41). There is no reason to involve any other power. Nevertheless,
God is involved three times: in the opening verses, after the greatness of
heaven, earth and the sun is mentioned, we read: οὐχὶ μέγας ὃς ταῦτα
ποιεῖ "Is not he who does these things great?" (4:35).[112] The next verse
goes on to speak of truth as prevailing over all, but it ends with the words:
καὶ οὐκ ἔστιν μετ᾽ αὐτοῦ ἄδικον οὐθέν "and not a single injustice is
with him" (4:36), i.e., the pronoun refers to God and not to truth.[113] Finally,
at the end of the discourse, the text states: εὐλογητὸς ὁ θεὸς τῆς ἀληθείας
"Blessed is the God of truth" (4:40).

It is doubtful whether these 'divine intrusions' in the text are all
attributable to similar causes. One reason might be a misunderstanding on
the translator's part (see below). There is also room for some variety at
the level of transmission of the original text. For example, the pronoun
referring to God in 4:36 could hardly be the result of a deliberate change
meant to belittle the power of truth. The idea that "not a single injustice is
with it [= truth]" is not inappropriate and there would be no reason for an
editor / translator to take the trouble to make the sentence refer to God.
There are several passages where such a change would be more necessary;
cf., e.g., v. 40, where truth is credited with valor, kingship, government
and greatness for all time – and there, too, a mere change of the pronominal
suffix would have sufficed to enforce a reference to God. It is not
inconceivable, therefore, that our text of v. 36 is accidental and that the
original reading indeed referred to truth.

The references to God at the beginning and, in particular, end of the
discourse are a different matter. These references do indeed disturb the

---

[112] This is of course not the case if the words in question refer not to God but to the
sun; Rudolph, loc. cit.

[113] One group of manuscripts reads here μετ᾽ αὐτῆς, referring to truth.

dynamics of the discourse on truth. Nevertheless, they do not seem to be late additions intended to reorient the text away from truth and toward the divine power; it is not inconceivable that, for this author, it was quite natural to consider God and truth in the same breath. Perhaps what appears to modern minds as two themes – God and truth – was a single theme for the author, who intended to praise truth not as an independent, self-sufficient entity but as an attribute of divine government.

Truth is described in the terms of the same ideas and language used in the Bible to describe God. Even the opening verse, with its praise of the greatness of truth, which prevails over everything, sounds like an echo of the 'great and mighty God' (Jer 32:18). Further on, all the earth calls to truth; the heavens bless it and all the 'works'[114] tremble before it; this recalls, say, Ps 19:2 (1) השמים מספרים כבוד אל ומעשה ידיו מגיד הרקיע "The heavens are telling the glory of God; and the firmament declares his handiwork"; 103:22 ברכו ה׳ כל מעשיו "Bless the Lord, all his works" (also 145:10; 148:2, 7); 104:31-32 יהי כבוד ה׳ לעולם ישמח ה׳ במעשיו המביט לארץ ותרעד יגע בהרים ויעשנו "May the glory of the Lord endure for ever, may the Lord rejoice in his works, who looks on the earth and it trembles, who touches the mountains and they smoke". Truth is never guilty of partiality or bribery (I Esd 4:39) and its verdict is never unjust (v. 40; cf. v. 36); compare 2 Chr 19:7 כי אין עם ה׳ אלהינו עולה ומשא פנים ומקח שחד "For there is no perversion of justice with the Lord our God, or partiality, or taking bribes". Truth exists and always prevails, living and governing forever (I Esd 4:38) – compare Dan 6:27 אלהא חיא וקים לעלמין "He is the living God, enduring for ever". And, finally, truth possesses might and kingship and greatness for ever and ever; cf. 1 Chr 29:10-12 ברוך אתה ה׳ אלהי ישראל... לך ה׳ הגדלה והגבורה והתפארת והנצח וההוד... לך ה׳ הממלכה... "Blessed art thou, O Lord, the God of Israel... Thine, O Lord, is the greatness, and the power, and the glory, and the victory, and the majesty...; thine is the

---

[114] The 'works' of creation is a much more natural term if the subject is the deity.

kingdom...". Similar praise of the Lord's greatness and power is heard in Ps 145:13 מלכותך מלכות כל עלמים וממשלתך בכל דור ודור "Thy kingdom is an everlasting kingdom, and thy dominion endures throughout all generations". As in our narrative, the Bible, too, speaks of God as אל אמת the 'true God/God of truth' etc.; see Jer 10:10; Ps 19:10 (9); 31:6 (5); 2 Chr 15:3. Also, truth is associated in the Bible with God's justice and eternity: ואתה צדיק על כל הבא עלינו כי אמת עשית ואנחנו הרשענו "Yet thou hast been just in all that has come upon us, for thou hast dealt faithfully [= truthfully] and we have acted wickedly" (Neh 9:33); וה' אלהים אמת הוא אלהים חיים ומלך עולם "But the Lord is the true God; he is the living God and the everlasting King" (Jer 10:10).[115]

It is also relevant here to mention the talmudic homily identifying God with truth:

מהו חותמו של הקדוש ברוך הוא, רבי בבי בשם רבי ראובן: אמת. א"ר בון: שהוא אלהים חיים ומלך עולם. אמר ריש לקיש: אל"ף רישיה דאלפא ביתא. מ"ם באמצעותה. ת"ו בסופה. לומר אני ה' ראשון... ואת אחרונים אני הוא.

What is the seal of the Holy One, blessed be He? Rabbi Bebai [said] in the name of Rabbi Reuben: Truth. What is truth? Said R. Bun: That He is the living God and King of the universe. Said Resh Lakish: *Aleph* is the first letter of the alphabet, *mem* is in the middle and *tav* at the end [= the three letters of אמת 'truth']. That is to say, I, the Lord, am the first..., and with the last, I am He (Palestinian Talmud, Sanhedrin 18a).[116]

The close resemblance to biblical phraseology indicates that, even if the discourse on truth was originally part of a pagan or Persian narrative, the present version has been shaped by Jewish hands.

---

[115] The ambivalent description of truth as an independent force, but nevertheless subordinate to God, is reminiscent of the account of wisdom in Prov 8-9 and Job 28. See Pfeifer (1967), p. 36.

[116] See Wasserstein (1983), pp. 496-498.

7. The Historical Setting

The discourses on the various themes are inherently universal. In the Story of the Youths, however, they are delivered in a well-defined historical setting, even if considered in isolation from their present literary context. That this is the case is obvious on three counts, namely, 1) the identity of the king, 2) the identity of the third youth, and 3) the identity of the king's concubine.

(a) The king is Darius, as stated in 3:1, 3, 7 (twice), 8. Thus, the identity of the king is firmly established in the opening verses. It is not probable that the failure to mention the king by name in the dispute itself testifies to the secondary nature of the name in the opening verses. It would be out of place to repeat the identification in the discourses themselves. Indeed, were the identification secondary, it would hardly have been repeated five times. At any rate, the presentation of the scene on a definite historical background is not exceptional – cf., e.g., the story in the Letter of Aristeas.

(b) The identification of the third youth seems to be entirely disjointed from its context: οὗτός ἐστιν Ζοροβαβέλ "he was Zerubbabel" (4:13) – that is all.[117] Nevertheless, this does not necessarily imply that the story ever subsisted in its present 'historical' context – Darius' court – without Zerubbabel. Furthermore, it is not surprising that only the main character, i.e., the victor in the contest, should be named, as in the Persian text quoted above (pp. 67-68).

(c) Our story also identifies the king's concubine as 'Apamē the daughter of Bartacēs' (4:29). However, this particular lady cannot be

---

[117] The identification is quite unexpected in the context of I Esd, as Zerubbabel has not yet been mentioned. The Syriac and Old Latin texts expand somewhat: "Zerubbabel the son of Salathiel from the tribe of Judah", clearly out of sensitivity to the problem raised by the laconic identification in I Esd. Josephus (Ant. XI, §§31-32) and Josippon (6:29 ff.), each in his own way, took care to acquaint their readers with Zerubbabel in advance.

identified with any concrete historical personality at the court of Darius or, indeed, of any other king.[118] The presumption that the king in question is in fact Artaxerxes Mnemon is highly plausible (irrespective of the name of the concubine or of her father). The many stories about that king provide an excellent backdrop for the description in our text.[119] Nevertheless, one cannot assert that the Story of the Youths preserves this particular historical memory – or any historical memory at all.[120]

Admittedly, the reference to Apamē is very convincing from a literary point of view, occurring as it does at the climax of the discourse on women who rule even the king. The lively wording of the passage could well be an eye-witness report of the concubine's control of the king. If the narrative originally concerned a different king, the adaptation to Darius' reign were clearly done by someone who wished to construct the story around Zerubbabel. At any rate, whoever involved Zerubbabel in this wisdom-type debate also wrote the second part of the story, 4:42-5:6. That

---

[118] Schalit (1947), based on a broad spectrum of historical data and assumptions piled up on one another (including some radical corruptions of names), reconstructs the characters on their historical background, as well as the history of the tradition. He suggests that the original story was Indian; it reached Persia as a folktale about the power of wine, king and women. The story of Artaxerxes Mnemon's concubine Artakame – that was her original name, not Apame (known in the 3rd century B.C.E. as the name of several wives of Hellenistic rulers) – was added, as an example of woman's power, during the reign of that monarch. This Artakame was a member of a local ruling family in Phrygia whose name was Artakama (and that is the name underlying the corrupted name of Apame's father). The latter also carries the title θαυμαστοῦ, which actually derives from the name of a place, Θεμισώνιον, named for its founder – the independent ruler of a region of southern Phrygia in the late 3rd century B.C.E. When the story fell into Jewish hands the youth was identified as Zerubbabel and the discourse on truth was added.

[119] See above, n. 78.

[120] Identification of anonymous figures is a typical feature of Midrash; see Heinemann (1950), p. 21. Compare the identification of Jeroboam's wife in the tradition of the LXX, 3Kgdms 12:24, §§g, k, l; Talshir (1993), p. 209; the identification of Jaddua's wife in I Esd 5:38 (Ezr 2:61) may be a result of textual development rather than of tradition.

part of the story is well rooted in a pseudo-historical situation and has no independent subsistence otherwise. The youth is Zerubbabel and the king is Darius; together, they, as it were, determine certain historical developments associated exclusively with themselves.

8. Second Part of the Story

The wisdom-type story, in its historical guise involving King Darius and the young Zerubbabel, leads into the second part of the narrative (4:42-5:6). This section is fully 'historical' and shows considerable similarity with the Book of Ezr-Neh (see pp. 65-66). Verse 42 is a transition to the sequel in which the victorious youth is told to ask for more than he had originally written: Αἴτησαι ὃ θέλεις πλείω τῶν γεγραμμένων, καὶ δώσομέν σοι, ὃν τρόπον εὑρέθης σοφώτερος.

Torrey's theory that a large section of this unit is an original text omitted from the MT, which had filled the gap between Ezr 1 and Ezr 2,[121] is untenable. This is clearly indicated by the juxtaposition of city and temple, which is foreign to Ezr (see above, p. 40). The section is the peak of this Hellenistic-Jewish account of how a Jewish youth, the king's bodyguard, successfully secured an advantage for his people, thus joining the ranks of various figures in the Books of Nehemiah, Esther, Daniel, Judith, 2 Macc, etc.[122] As in some of these books, the framework in I Esd is also one of legend.[123]

---

[121] Torrey (1910), pp. 57ff. For a comprehensive and instructive response to Torrey see Bewer (1919), pp. 18-26. Torrey reiterated his theory in 1945, p. 396.

[122] See Fischer (1904), for the far-reaching view that a single author was responsible for the final version of all these books, the goal of his work being to buttress national consciousness.

[123] A historical echo – at least, in its reflection of the author's period – may be found in the king's decree ordering the Edomites to evacuate Jewish homes. However, one can hardly draw definite conclusions from this point. See Cook (1913), pp. 13-14. I disagree with attempts to associate the decree with the situation described at the beginning of Neh, as claimed by Smith (1971), p. 127.

In sum: there are a good many fissures or, better, seams in the Story of the Youths, usually understood as indicating different layers of development. There are internal problems in the discourses on womanhood (the two faces of woman) and on truth (the 'intrusion' of God). The difficulties due to the integration of the different themes are readily visible, as in the questionable link between wine and the other themes and the treatment of two themes by a single disputant. The historical frame of the wisdom-type speeches also heightens uncertainties concerning the evolution of the narrative. Was the story written by a single author, despite the difficulties or did shifts occur in its form and content, as it was reworked and adapted to the version currently before us? Certain parts of the story presumably had previous 'lives' in other contexts. The themes treated are hardly new in the world of wisdom literature, neither is the narrative genre that the story represents. Nevertheless, I suspect that the 'evolutionary stages' seemingly implied by the various difficulties in the text are simply the outcome of conventional patterns in scholarly treatments of the history of traditions. We do not have sufficient proofs for the thesis that there once existed a more polished narrative devoted to king, wine and women, which fell victim to the efforts of some later editor who rearranged the material, tacked on the discussion of truth and placed it in a historical framework. Today, the history of the story is concealed behind a fairly homogeneous veil: the story of the contest reads as if it were written precisely for this historical frame, for Zerubbabel.

The Story of the Youths, then, was written for the sake of Zerubbabel, probably borrowing from extant wisdom-type material and from the Book of Ezr-Neh, in particular from Nehemiah's activities. It was not well integrated into the biblical material despite the redactor's efforts to adapt the context so as to suit the Story of the Youths.

b. The Original Language of the Story of the Youths
(In collaboration with David Talshir)

The aim of this section is to take another look at the question of the original language of the Story of the Three Youths which has come down to us in Greek alone. Scholarly opinion rarely goes beyond a general impression of the subject, and all of it takes its cue from Torrey,[124] who contended that the story was translated from a Semitic-language original. His most commonly noted evidence is the frequent use, alien to the Greek language, of the word τότε 'then' which he identified as a reflection of the common Aramaic word אדין. He further adduced several other phrases that pointed in the same direction, and therefore he concluded that the original language of the story was Aramaic and not Hebrew.[125] Since that time, only Zimmermann has sought to continue in Torrey's path and to uncover other Aramaic constructions hiding behind the veil of Greek.[126]

The question on the agenda is, thus, twofold: was the story originally written in Greek, and, if not – was it written in Aramaic or in Hebrew? At the basis of the problem is the difficulty in making the material yield

---

[124] Naturally, those who argue that the story originated in Greek made do with a general impression, as though the burden of proof is not on them. So, for example: Fritzsche (1851), p. 1; Guthe (1900), p. 1. Jahn (1909), pp. 177-188, on the other hand, offered a methodologically curious reconstruction of the entire book into Hebrew, including those parts which already have an Aramaic (!) parallel in the MT. The evidence adduced by Torrey (1910) is noted on pp. 23-25, 50-56, 125-131. Those who followed in his footsteps quoted the major part of his words. See for example Bayer (1911), pp. 123ff.; Walde (1913), pp. 119-120, and many others.

[125] And more precisely, that most of the story was indeed Aramaic, with the exception of its last part (4:47 *et seq.*), which was largely Hebrew; a lost part of the Proto-MT which originally came between Ezr 1 and 2. But what could have been the logic in quoting the letters of the later kings in Aramaic and the letters of Cyrus in Hebrew (as Torrey would have it, when I Esd is speaking of Darius)? Nor would the content seem to justify the opinion that this part ever formed a bridge between Ezr 1 and 2.

[126] Most of Zimmermann's suggestions (1963/4), although interesting, are rather extreme.

negative evidence, such is to say, evidence that specific expressions could not possibly have been written in a given language. On the surface, there would seem to be little difficulty in determining between the Greek language and a Semitic one; only, most claims of 'barbarisms' could be countered by dredging out evidence of nuance or syntax that prove the ostensible 'barbarism' to be legitimate usage of the Greek language. Even if a parallel is not to be found in other Greek texts, one can always explain away the oddities as a personal idiosyncrasy on the part of the author, or attribute it to his cultural environment.[127] Indeed, the problem is not a minor one seeing that the Greek we are dealing with is κοινή, probably influenced by the native languages, and that the milieu in which the story was created may have been a bilingual or trilingual society.[128]

On the other hand, there is little point in hunting down constructions that could not possibly have been written in a Semitic language since these can always be attributed to the individuality of the translator. To cite one example, let us take the concept of φιλανθρωπία, which is a Greek concept *par excellence* and hard to imagine as having an Aramaic or Hebrew source. Yet if its appearance in Addition E to Esther is adduced as evidence that this pericope was originally written in Greek, what happens when we find the term turning up in I Esd, and not in the Story of the Three Youths, but in the translated parts, 8:10 (Ezr 7:12)? The fact that it has no clear equivalent here makes little difference at all. What is important is that it appears in the translated material, and thus totally undermines the basis of the conclusion in relation to Esther.

The same can be said for the attempt to determine between Hebrew and Aramaic; these two languages went side by side over a long period of time, and there can be no telling when and where the forms and constructions common to one language might have strayed into the other.

---

[127] Rudolph (1949), pp. viii-ix. These are precisely the two sides of the approach adopted by Rudolph: first of all, this is Judeo-Greek. Secondly, every problem in the Greek text is necessarily rooted anywhere but in its *Vorlage*.

[128] Barr (1989).

Together with this, it would seem that a more precise evaluation of the kind of Greek used in The Story of the Three Youths shows that it is translation-Greek, and observation of the kind of language which it reflects indeed sways the pendulum over to Aramaic.

1. The Kind of Greek Used in the Story

The language of The Story of the Three Youths has been described more than once as natural and free-flowing. In order to study the kind of Greek in which the story is written, it is best to use criteria as precise as possible in examining what stands behind the outer facade. Is the story's language closer to original Greek or to translation-Greek? As a rule, if the language of the story is compared with patterns of non-translation Greek and the Greek of the LXX, we find that it does not easily disengage itself from the latter. In order to set these assessments on a sound basis, we will employ the criteria established by the researchers of the New Testament language in their search after its *Vorlage*.

Let us first recall a few phrases encumbering the fluency of the Greek in the story. Even if these examples are not enough to give the work the indelible stamp of translation, their presence does call for explanation.[129]

(a) The Semitic patterns of *verba dicendi*, such as: εὐλόγησεν... λέγων (4:58); ἐφώνησεν καὶ... εἶπον (4:41). Or, the use of πρός after verbs of saying, even if it is not a rarity in κοινή:[130] εἶπαν ἕτερος πρὸς τὸν ἕτερον (3:4).

(b) The same is true for the place of the pronoun in 4:16 ἐξέθρεψαν αὐτοὺς τοὺς φυτεύοντας.[131]

---

[129] See Mowinckel's criticism (1964) of Rudolph: "Es wäre jedoch merkwürdig, wenn es dem behaupteten griechischen Verfasser gelungen wäre, fast sämmtliche Anomalien des gesprochenen Judengriechisch in seine Erzählung zu unterbringen" (p. 11).

[130] Turner (1976), p. 54.

[131] Black (1967), pp. 96ff.

(c) Ἄρχειν, as an auxiliary verb meaning 'to begin', is not common in Greek,[132] yet in the story before us now, it reoccurs in the opening words of the youths: Καὶ ἤρξατο ὁ πρῶτος... καὶ ἔφη (3:17, and also in 4:1, 13, 33).

(d) The particle ἵνα, which may possibly reflect the Aramaic די,[133] also reappears, and the fact that it recurs in adjacent verses may be evidence of over-adhesion to a non-Greek *Vorlage*:

4:46 δέομαι οὖν ἵνα ποιήσῃς.

4:47 καὶ ἔγραψεν... ἵνα προπέμψωσιν.

4:50 καὶ ἵνα οἱ Ἰδουμαῖοι ἀφιῶσι.

(e) Let us also mention here the use of ποιεῖν, which may possibly reflect a causative verb in Hebrew or Aramaic: ποιεῖ πλουσίας... ποιεῖ λαλεῖν (3:20); καὶ ἐποίησεν αὐτοὺς συναναβῆναι (5:3).[134]

The following data also testify to a Semitic construction, but in a more controlled way.

(f) Substantial evidence for the existence of a Semitic *Vorlage* emerges from the position of the particle πᾶς, a secondary detail in itself, but one which assumes importance precisely for this reason. Of the four patterns in which the word can be used, the Story of the Youths shows a clear preference for the biblical patterns. The forms common to independently-written Greek, ὁ x πᾶς or ὁ πᾶς x, both in the singular and plural, are represented in the story only three times, as opposed to the forms of πᾶς x and especially of πᾶς ὁ x, generally in the plural, which appear some thirty times. There is a similar trend in certain parts of the New Testament,[135] unlike the trend increasingly evidenced by papyri beginning with the third century B.C.E., in which a striking preference for the constructions of Classical Greek becomes apparent.[136] It is not that the preferred constructions in the

---

[132] Turner (1976), pp. 20, 46.

[133] Burney (1922), pp. 69ff.

[134] See Tov (1982), pp. 417-24.

[135] Turner (1976), p. 95.

[136] According to: Mayser (1934), II, 2, p. 102.

Story of the Youths are utterly impossible in Greek, for they do appear dozens of times in the papyri. Yet, had the story been written in Greek to begin with, we would have expected a different ratio between the various kinds of constructions.

(g) The same trend emerges in the following table, which presents the ratio between main and subordinate verbs:[137]

New Testament	- for every main verb: 0.4 subordinate verbs
Selected Papyri[138]	- for every main verb: 0.7 subordinate verbs
Classical Greek	- for every main verb: 1.4 subordinate verbs
The Story of the Youths	- for every main verb: 0.5 subordinate verbs

The table shows that the story has more main verbs than subordinate verbs, indeed almost twice as many, which stands in contrast to the trend of Classical Greek. Is this not indicative of a *Vorlage* which prefers paratactic sentences?

The above-noted relationships assume even more importance in view of the following considerations. First of all, while there is little discrepancy between the Greek of the story and independently-written Greek when compared with the papyri from the same time span, one cannot define the story's language simply as κοινή, for the distance between them is still a long one and paved with Semitic stumbling blocks. We must also lay stress on an additional point arising from another aspect in the study of I Esd, namely, the study of the technique used by the translator in those parts where the *Vorlage* has come down to us. An examination of his method reveals that he does not transmit the content together with the form, so to speak, but often exchanges a form of expression preferred in Hebrew and Aramaic for one more at home in the Greek language. If this is the kind of translator responsible also for the Greek in the Story of the Youths, we would hardly expect to find a profound difference between the language of his translation and that of the Greek of his own day. For this

---

[137] Turner (1976), p. 51.

[138] The findings from the papyri in this case are less conclusive due to their literary nature, which leaves little room for using complex constructions of main and subordinate sentences.

reason, these Semitic traces in the story are all the more significant and
provide cogent support for our hypothesis that the story is indeed a
translation.

This assessment is well illustrated by the relation between the verbs
in the main and subordinate sentences. In the translated parts, paratactic
constructions are exchanged for hypotactic constructions thirty-five times,
and we could further mention no fewer number of places in which a
subordinate clause rejects other syntactical constructions. In view of this,
the two-to-one ratio between main and subordinate verbs in the story
becomes highly important as proof that we are dealing with translation-
Greek.

(h) In Sollamo's tables of semi-prepositions, as she terms them,
I Esd ranks high as a book in which it is difficult to find mistaken,
un-Greek like use of prepositions. This is true for the book as a whole,
both the story and the translated parts. Indeed, out of all the Apocrypha,
I Esd takes its place at the bottom rungs of the ladder among those works
which make the least use of prepositions derived from parts of the body.[139]
This is still not enough to draw it closer to the non-translated books,[140] but
it does give it a unique status among the other translations, and it shows
its author as one who managed to free himself from the language of his
Vorlage and to preserve the vitality of the target language.[141]

The relatively authentic Greek appearance of the Story of the Youths
does not, then, constitute an anomaly within the larger framework of

---

[139] Sollamo (1979), pp. 290 ff.

[140] In I Esd there is one such preposition for every 16 verses, whereas in 2-4 Macc the
ratio is 1:90, 1:277, 0:284, respectively.

[141] Even so, every now and then the choice of prepositions is surprising, as in the use
of ὑπέρ for νικᾶν in 3:12 ὑπὲρ δὲ πάντα νικᾷ ἡ ἀλήθεια; or εἰς for πλεῖν in 4:23
εἰς τὴν θάλασσαν πλεῖν; in Greek, one sails to a given place, but sails in the sea,
or better yet: πλεῖν τὴν θάλασσαν, without any preposition at all. However, it is
difficult to point with certainty to the nature of the original: Zimmermann (1963/4),
p. 200, suggested that the translator found פרש לימא before him, but no Aramaic
usage such as this is documented; in Hebrew see the Palestinian Talmud Mo'ed
Qatan, the beginning of chapter 3 (81:3) אסור לפרש לים הגדול "it is forbidden to sail
at the big sea".

I Esd. Similar to the translated parts, the story may also owe its elegant Greek to the translator.

In light of all the above, it is worth noting the internal relationships between the story and the translated parts of the book in connection with certain phenomena. Let us call into use here two of the criteria suggested by Martin.[142]

(i) Martin examined the frequency of the preposition ἐν in relation to that of other prepositions, and reached the conclusion that in the original Greek material the latter appear far more frequently; whereas, in the translations, the opposite is true. Examination of this relationship in I Esd, in the Story of the Youths on the one hand, and in the translated parts on the other, reveals that the entire book stands firmly in the no-man's land between translated and original Greek.[143]

(j) Another relation examined by Martin is the usage of καί versus that of δέ. He found that translated Greek has at least two καί for every δέ; whereas, original Greek has significantly fewer καί than δέ. In real samples, the curve in the LXX moves from six καί for every δέ (chapters from the LXX to Genesis and the Aramaic parts of Daniel), up to 343 καί for every δέ (Theodotion for the Hebrew parts of Daniel). In contrast with this, in original Greek, there are 0.06 καί for every δέ (Polybius) and up to 0.39 καί for every δέ (the papyri). A quick glance at I Esd immediately

---

[142] Martin (1974), pp. 5ff.

[143] Table of frequency of the different prepositions versus ἐν:

	Original Greek	LXX	I Esd	
			Translation	Story
διά	0.01-0.18	0.1	0.3	0.19-3.0
εἰς	0.01-0.49	0.51	0.1	0.79-11.0
κατά	0.01-0.19	0.3	0.23	0.26-2.1
περί	0.01-0.27	0.05	0.41	0.28-1.2
πρός	0.01-0.024	0.15	0.47	0.19-0.26
ὑπό	0.01-0.07	0.06	0.11	0.13-0.51

In the translated parts of I Esd: διά, περί, ὑπό, borders on the LXX, εἰς, πρός is in the middle ground, κατά borders on the original language. In the story: διά, περί borders on the original language, κατά, πρός, ὑπό is in the middle ground, εἰς borders on the LXX.

reveals that the entire book, both the story and the parts parallel to the
MT, aligns itself firmly on the side of the LXX making more intensive use
of καί than δέ. In the translated parts the ratio is 7:1, while in the story
this ratio climbs even higher – 8.5:1. This criterion, similar to that which
we have examined up till now, shows that the Story of the Youths, like
I Esd in its entirety, is closer to independent Greek than most books of the
LXX, yet together with this, it still shows clear signs of belonging to the
circle of translated books.

2. Traces of the Process of Translation

We have sought to show that the language of the *Vorlage* left its
imprint on the language of the story, and that this language is translation-
Greek. Let us now seek out the traces which the process of translation left
in the story, both in the way the material was handled and in its language
and content.

(a) Issues of Form

(1) We first mention a verse whose form would seem to actually
prove that the story is indeed a translation: οἱ σωματοφύλακες οἱ
φυλάσσοντες τὸ σῶμα τοῦ βασιλέως (3:4). Regardless of the language
of the *Vorlage*, this text is best explained as a double translation.[144] What
was the point of explaining the term οἱ σωματοφύλακες by its literal
components οἱ φυλάσσοντες τὸ σῶμα, if not because of an original
which was itself formed of separate parts?[145]

---

[144] The same can be said for ἐπεστάτουν τῶν ἱερῶν ἔργων... ἱεροστάταις, 7:2. Even
though its parallel in Ezr 6:13 has no clear equivalent, this is probably nothing more
than a double translation. Similar are double translations which repeat only one of
the elements, e.g., Gen 39:21-23 שר בית הסהר ≈ ἀρχιδεσμοφύλαξ τοῦ δεσμωτηρίου.
[145] We could not find an attested term in either Hebrew or Aramaic to answer to the

(2) The appearance of different wording in a place where one might expect repetition can also testify to the transition between languages. In listing the high privileges due to be heaped upon the lad who was found to be wise, the youths reel out: καὶ δεύτερος καθιεῖται Δαρείου (3:7). When the time comes for the King to pay off this debt, he says: καὶ ἐχόμενός μου καθήσῃ (4:42). That 4:42 fulfills the promise made in 3:7 we can easily learn from the other components common to these texts. The *Vorlage* must have used the same idiom in both places, whereas the translator conveyed the former in one way, and the latter in yet another.

(3) Finally, there is a stylistic detail which suggests that the text originated in another language. 4:7-9 contains seven pairs of verbs. In six of them, the pair is comprised of two forms of the same verb, while a seventh makes use of two different verbs: ἐὰν εἴπῃ ἀποκτεῖναι ἀποκτέννουσιν... ἀφεῖναι ἀφίουσιν... <u>πατάξαι</u> <u>τύπτουσιν</u>... ἐρημῶσαι ἐρημοῦσιν... οἰκοδομῆσαι οἰκοδομοῦσιν... ἐκκόψαι ἐκκόπτουσιν... φυτεῦσαι φυτεύουσιν. The exception would seem to be the result of translation, rather than an original formulation.[146]

Greek *terminus technicus* σωματοφύλαξ. In 1 Sam 28:2 שמר לראשי is ingeniously rendered by ἀρχισωματοφύλαξ. The latter stands also for שמרי הסף in Esth 2:21. In Josippon's version of our story he retranslates the Greek into שומרי ראש המלך (Josippon 6:30, 35); however, there is no evidence for the use of שומר-ראש in the technical meaning of 'bodyguard' before Josippon.

[146] See another list of verbs which is repeated with some variation in Greek in 4:23-24. There are a few other things which are tempting to believe but difficult to prove, such as the possibility of the intentional alliteration of עול-הבל in the discourse about truth (4:36-37). Or, the possible reflection of the phrase בגדי כבוד (Sirach 6:29 – in Greek, Hebrew: בגדי כתם; 6:31; 50:11, and see LXX-Isa 52:1), or in Aramaic לבושין דיקר (cf. Onkelos for כתנות עור in Gen 4:21), divided between two hemistichoi in 4:17 καὶ αὗται ποιοῦσιν τὰς <u>στολὰς</u> τῶν ἀνθρώπων, καὶ αὗται ποιοῦσιν <u>δόξαν</u> τοῖς ἀνθρώποις. This may be true, even though the second hemistich should probably be understood literally (cf. Esth 1:20 וכל הנשים יתנו יקר לבעליהן "all women will give honor to their husbands").

(b) Linguistic Patterns

The use of biblical phraseology is not necessarily the identifying mark of a translation, and yet, it is worth stressing that the language of the story does bear the biblical influence, as we see, for example, in:

(1) 4:54 τὴν ἱερατικὴν στολήν ἐν τίνι λατρεύουσιν ἐν αὐτῇ, cf. Ezek 42:14 בגדיהם אשר ישרתו בהן "their vestments in which they minister" (note the parroting of the Semitic relative clauses; also below).

(2) 4:60 εὐλογητὸς εἶ ὃς ἔδωκάς μοι σοφίαν καὶ σοὶ ὁμολογῶ δέσποτα τῶν πατέρων, has a close parallel in Dan 2:23 לך אלה אבהתי מהודא ומשבח אנה די חכמתא וגבורתא יהבת לי "I acknowledge and praise you, O God of my fathers, you who have given me wisdom and power",[147] and also in 1 Chr 29:10-12.

(3) 4:63 τὸ ἱερόν οὗ ὠνομάσθη τὸ ὄνομα αὐτοῦ ἐπ᾽ αὐτῷ, cf. Jer 7:10 בבית הזה אשר נקרא שמי עליו "in this house, which is called by my name", and elsewhere.

(4) It is particularly worth noticing passages such as 3:6 καὶ πορφύραν περιβαλέσθαι καὶ ἐν χρυσώμασιν πίνειν καὶ ἐπὶ χρυσῷ καθεύδειν καὶ ἅρμα χρυσοχάλινον καὶ κίδαριν βυσσίνην καὶ μανιάκην περὶ τὸν τράχηλον, a verse which has an echo, in content and terminology, in Dan 5:7 ארגונא ילבש והמניכא די דהבא על צוארה "shall be clothed in purple and wear a golden chain on his neck", and similar to this in Dan 5:16, 29),[148] and cf. also Esth 1:6-7; 8:15.

(5) Or, the list in 3:14 καὶ σατράπας καὶ στρατηγοὺς καὶ τοπάρχας καὶ ὑπάτους, which is identical with the LXX to Dan 3:2 לאחשדרפניא סגניא ופחותא אדרגזריא. While such examples demonstrate the proximity between the story and certain biblical passages, they also show that court phraseology which imbues the Greek with a dimension of authenticity, may nevertheless be the result of translation.

---

[147] And cf. also 4:40 with Dan 2:37; 7:14, 27.

[148] Admittedly, the word cognates המניכא (originally Persian) – μανιακής (which, like βύσσινος, is borrowed by the Greek from Aramaic), may mislead us into exaggerating the similarity between the texts.

Beyond the general similarity in linguistic pattern, a number of phrases foreign to Greek also stand out: these are best defined as loan-translations.

(1) The first of these is καὶ οὐκ ἔστιν παρ' αὐτῇ λαμβάνειν πρόσωπα οὐδὲ διάφορα (4:39). One cannot imagine a phrase such as λαμβάνειν πρόσωπα in Greek. It must have originated in the Hebrew נשא פנים / משא פנים or the Aramaic נסב / מסב אפין; cf. Deut 10:17 לא ישא פנים ולא יקח שחד "who shows no favor and takes no bribe".[149] The vitality of the Aramaic expression emerges from its independent use in the Aramaic translations.[150] Moreover, the first part of the sentence καὶ οὐκ ἔστιν παρ' αὐτῇ, and its parallel in v. 36 καὶ οὐκ ἔστιν μετ' αὐτῆ also bear a Semitic stamp. The entire verse finds a close parallel in 2 Chr 19:7 כי אין עם ה' אלהינו עולה ומשא פנים ומקח שחד "for there is no injustice or favoritism or bribe-taking with the Lord our God".

(2) 4:38, 40 εἰς τὸν αἰῶνα... εἰς τὸν αἰῶνα τοῦ αἰῶνος... τῶν πάντων αἰώνων apparently reflect the common expressions of לעולם, כל עולמים[151] and לעולם ועד.[152]

---

[149] Rudolph's comment (1949), p. ix, that the Semitic expression also needs a verb before διάφορα, that is שחד, does not invalidate the former conclusion, even though there is a certain justice to his words. One might, after all, say that the lack of a second verb or *nomen actionis* before 'bribery' proves that we are dealing with a Greek who used Hebrew expressions with a free hand. Only, this shortened form is also proper usage in Hebrew and Aramaic, though not in Greek; the fact remains that λαμβάνειν πρόσωπα has no life in Greek. It should also be noted that a similar phenomenon is found in the translated parts, 1:46 (2 Chr 36:13) ויקש את ערפו ויאמץ את לבבו ≈ σκληρύνας αὐτοῦ τὸν τράχηλον καὶ τὴν καρδίαν αὐτοῦ; again two verbs are condensed into one. It is interesting that καλὴν τῷ εἴδει καὶ τῷ κάλλει is also a kind of abbreviated translation for an expression made up of a recurring element; see below.

[150] Onkelos changed the structure in Deut, *ibid.*, to דלית קדמוהי מסב אפין; Neophyti also translated Deut 1:17 לא תכירו פנים במשפט with נסב אפין; and in the Peshitta נסב באפא is common.

[151] Εἰς τὸν αἰῶνα τοῦ αἰῶνος is used for לעולם ועד in the literal translation of Psalms, but also in LXX-Dan 12:3 (see also Susanna 64).

[152] כל עלמים is found in Ps 145:13, and, as for the Aramaic literature, in the Genesis

(3) 4:18 καλὴν τῷ εἴδει καὶ τῷ κάλλει is an expression foreign to Greek;[153] one may reasonably assume that this is a translator's solution to an expression such as יפת תואר ויפת מראה,[154] or its Aramaic counterpart יאיה בריוה ושפירה בחזוה.[155] Though the Aramaic formulation exactly corresponds to that of the Greek, a Hebrew *Vorlage* is as plausible, since other translators similarly replaced the constructs יפת תואר/יפת מראה with the dative case.[156]

(4) Since there is no such phrase as 3:1 ἐποίησεν δοχήν, one doubts whether a Greek writer would have used it of his own accord. The one who used it belonged to the milieu of translators accustomed to rendering עשה משתה (in Esther), or עבד לחם (in Daniel) as ποιεῖν δοχήν.

(c) Issues of Content

And finally, infelicities of content may well be the result of a mistake in translation; a phenomenon which is second to none in disclosing the fact that a work indeed originated in another language.

(1) A mistake is most probably lurking behind 4:4 ἐὰν δὲ ἐξαποστείλῃ αὐτοὺς πρὸς τοὺς πολεμίους, βαδίζουσιν καὶ κατεργάζονται τὰ ὄρη καὶ τὰ τείχη καὶ τοὺς πύργους. Why, after setting out against the royal enemies by command of the King, was it precisely the mountains which they conquered, together with the walls and the towers? One possibility is that in the *Vorlage*, the walls and towers were linked to cities, and not to mountains. The mistake could have occurred in a text that was either

---

Apocryphon 2:7 מלך כל עלמים (also common in Tobit). In independently written Greek, πᾶς would have been added to the singular.

[153] Torrey (1910) p. 53, note e, defined it as a barbarism.

[154] The repeated יְפַת is represented only once; see above, note 149.

[155] This is the formulation e.g., in the Fragments of the Palestinian Targum to Gen 29:17 (ᴍѕ E), see M.L. Klein (1986), p. 41; similarly in the rest of the Targumim.

[156] Cf. Gen 29:17; 1 Sam 25:3; Esth 2:7. I thank Prof. T. Muraoka for these references and considerations.

Hebrew הרים-ערים[157] or Aramaic טיריא[158] or קוריא-טוריא, but not in a Greek one.[159]

(2) There is a striking contradiction in the course of the story between 3:3 καὶ ἐκοιμήθη καὶ ἔξυπνος ἐγένετο and 3:13 καὶ ὅτε ἐξηγέρθη. First, we are told that the king was <u>awake</u> and then, that he <u>awoke</u> from his sleep. How did this come about? While it is possible that we have a combination of traditions here, a quite extreme solution in itself, it is also possible that the translator failed to understand his *Vorlage* in one of the texts: (a) A straightforward explanation would be that the *Vorlage* of 3:13 used the verb קום, implying that the king <u>rose</u>, and the translator understood it to mean that he <u>woke</u> from his sleep. In support of this cf. Dan 6:19-20 ושנתה נדת עלוהי באדין מלכא בשפרפרא יקום בנגהא, "and his sleep fled from him. Then at the first light of dawn, he <u>arose</u>". (b) Or, 3:3 could have originally meant that the king fell asleep and the translator understood just the opposite. We may conjecture that he found something like שנת המלך נהיתה עליו before him – meaning, that sleep fell upon the king,[160] which he took to mean that he was unable to sleep at all; cf. Dan 2:1 ותתפעם רוחו ושנתו נהיתה עליו "his spirit was agitated, yet he was overcome by sleep" (others, however: "and he could not sleep"). Although this explanation is not solidly grounded in linguistic usage, it is more in harmony with the

---

[157] As suggested by Kahana. And cf. 2 Chr 14:6 ויאמר ליהודה נבנה את הערים האלה ונסב חומה ומגדלים דלתים ובריחים "He said to Judah let us build up these cities and surround them with walls and towers, gates and bars".

[158] As suggested by Zimmermann (1963/4), p. 192.

[159] Interestingly enough, Josippon introduces a doublet: ואם יצוום להפוך ערים יהפכו ואם לחצוב הרים יחצבו ואם להרוס חומות יהרוסו "And if they command to overthrow the cities they will overthrow, and if to cut through mountains they will cut through, and if to destroy walls they will destroy" (Josippon 6:65-66).

[160] Cf. 1 Sam 1:18 פניה לא היו לה עוד, such is to say, and her face did not fall. In the language of the Tannaʾim, we find the expression יש שינה לפני, in the sense of 'to fall asleep', e.g., Mechilta de-Rabbi Ishmael, Shira, 5 (Horowitz-Rabin, p. 134).

spirit of the story, seeing that the story is not based on the motif of insomnia, and indeed just the opposite: the contest is planned while the king is sound asleep.[161] In addition, it is difficult to explain ἔξυπνος ἐγένετο as anything but an exact reflection of a Semitic expression.[162]

It becomes clear therefore – even without committing ourselves as to the exact nature of the *Vorlage* – that certain elements in the content of the Story of the Three Youths, as well as in its language and external design, prove that the work is indeed a translation.

3. Hebrew or Aramaic?

Let us turn now to a closer examination of the *Vorlage* in the attempt to discover whether its language was Hebrew or Aramaic. In the discussion below we shall have numerous occasions to refer to the important evidence brought by Torrey, but we shall attempt to refine and substantiate the evidence, and to round it out with material of our own.[163]

What, then, was the language of the *Vorlage* from which the translator worked, Aramaic or Hebrew? Does the Greek text reflect linguistic patterns found in only one of these languages? Does the meaning of the text offer a clue to the original language? This is no easy task, if only because it is difficult to make a Greek translation our yardstick for distinguishing between Hebrew and Aramaic. In addition to this, our knowledge of these languages is based on limited sources and lack of documentation for either of these languages may well be a matter of chance. Finally, the closeness between

---

[161] Josippon is very articulate on this point: והמלך כבד בשנתו כי נשתכר ביין "and the king was heavily asleep since he got drunk" (Josippon 6:35).

[162] This pattern of translation is even more striking in the above mentioned Dan 2:1 καὶ ὕπνος αὐτοῦ ἐγένετο ἀπ᾽ αὐτοῦ.

[163] Note that Torrey (1910) did not even attempt to show that Hebrew responds less to the text than Aramaic. So, for example, he suggested (p. 25) עם דנה as the original to πρὸς τούτοις (4:10, 41), on the basis of עם זה (Neh 5:13).

Hebrew and Aramaic makes it harder to choose decisively between them, given the fact that we are dealing with a bilingual society, and linguistic patterns common to one could easily become part and parcel of the other. Nonetheless, there are a few cases where it seems that the Greek text before us can be well explained on the basis of an Aramaic *Vorlage*, while a Hebrew text would not fit the bill. On the other hand, it is hard to find evidence pointing exclusively to a Hebrew *Vorlage* alone, such is to say, features of language or content that could not also be explained on the basis of Aramaic.

(a) Linguistic Patterns

A few linguistic patterns reflect the Official and Middle Aramaic, but have no counterpart in Hebrew.

(1) Let us first mention the conjunction noted by Torrey (pp. 23-24), and which is frequently repeated in the literature: the high frequency of the word τότε in the Story of the Youths – 3:4, 8; 4:33, 41 (twice), 42, 43, 47, as in the rest of I Esd (7 times). This is not characteristic of Greek, and its presence can only be explained through reference to the common Aramaic conjunction in Official Aramaic: באדין(ב).[164]

(2) 4:36 σείεται καὶ τρέμει. This is practically a carbon copy of one of the Aramaic expressions: זאעין ודחלין; see Dan 5:19; 6:27,[165] or רעדין ודחלין in the Aramaic Book of Enoch, 4QEn^d2 II, 30.[166] In Aramaic, therefore, this is a common expression, whereas Hebrew has nothing like it.[167]

---

[164] The Hebrew parallel אז is not frequently used as a conjunction, and the same is true for the later בכן.

[165] And in reverse order: דאלין וזאעין, Genesis Apocryphon 3, Beyer, p. 166.

[166] Milik, p. 223, and cf. also 4QEn^c 4, 1, Milik, p. 204.

[167] The closest expression which we found for this is: פחדו ורגזו (Jer 33:9).

(3) 4:39 τὰ δίκαια ποιεῖ ἀπὸ πάντων τῶν ἀδίκων. In Biblical
Hebrew, the act of wreaking vengeance (עשה משפט/שפטים) is expressed
with the preposition *beth* and not with *mem*, as in Exod 12:12 ובכל אלהי
מצרים אעשה שפטים "and I will execute judgements against all the gods of
Egypt".[168] Torrey (p. 25) very astutely indicated the use of the preposition
alien to Greek, employed here by the Greek translator in an uncharacteristic
moment of distraction, and suggested that the Greek originated in the
Aramaic expression דינה להוא מתעבד מנה (Ezr 7:26).[169] This is further born
out by texts which were subsequently discovered. See the Aramaic Book
of Enoch, 4QEn^e XXII, 3: דינא רבא די מנהון יתעבד, and the Bar-Kosiba
letters, n° 1: מנכן פרענותא תתעבד.[170] The Greek is even a more accurate
reflection of the formulations in *Qal*, such as עבד לי דין מנה in the Genesis
Apocryphon 20:14 (similarly Onkelos to Deut 33:7), and note the striking
resemblance between our text and 4QEn^g1 IV, 16: למעבד דין קשוט מן כול
רשיעין.

(4) 4:42 εὑρέθης σοφώτερος. Biblical Hebrew does not use נמצא
'found to be' in this manner, as an auxillary verb which acts as a copula in
the sentence,[171] but Biblical Aramaic does show this kind of usage; see
Dan 5:27 השתכחת חסיר "found wanting".

---

[168] Cf. also Num 33:4, Ps 149:19. See, however, Ps 119:84, where the preposition has
presumably been modified by the translator: מתי תעשה ברדפי משפט ≈ πότε ποιήσεις
ἐκ τῶν καταδιωκόντων με κρίσιν "when will You bring my persecutors to
judgement"; cf. also Judg 11:36 אחרי אשר עשה לך ה׳ נקמות מאויביך "seeing that the
Lord has vindicated you against your enemies". I thank Prof. T. Muraoka for these
references. These are hardly as straightforward an explanation as the Aramaic phrase.

[169] There, however, our translator found an adequate verb which replaces the entire
Aramaic phrase, i.e., κολαθήσονται, simply: they should be punished, 8:24.

[170] Kutscher (1977), pp. לח, מ.

[171] There seems to be a similar use in late Biblical Hebrew, Esth 6:2 וימצא כתוב, also
Dan 12:1, but the meaning of 'finding' is still apparent, as Neh 7:5 clearly shows. In
Rabbinic Hebrew, the use of נמצא as an auxiliary verb is already common, possibly
borrowed from Aramaic; see Sarfatti (1987), pp. 227-231.

The above-noted idioms stand out clearly in the translation, and constitute striking evidence of its reliance on Aramaic. These examples are little more than the tip of the iceberg, although, the others are less clear.

(5) 4:6 ἀναφέρουσι τοὺς φόρους. The word used to signify 'tax' in Official Aramaic is מנ(נ)דה (Ezr 4:13, 20; 6:8; 7:24), and in its wake the Hebrew מדה (Neh 5:4). Could this have been the term which stood before the translator, who chose to render it in the plural φόροι? This might be the case, considering the custom in II Esd. Only, in I Esd מנ(נ)דה is consistently rendered as φορολογία.[172] Hence, it is difficult to assume that מנ(נ)דה stood at the basis of φόροι. Moreover, the verb chosen here – ἀναφέρειν, is never used with φορολογία.[173] Instead, the verbs of δοῦναι and ἐπιβάλλειν are used, in keeping with נתן/יהב and רמי of the Aramaic original; whereas, ἀναφέρειν is the equivalent of להעלות (80 times). It seems, therefore, that ἀναφέρουσι τοὺς φόρους is a reflection of a different phrase. It betrays its Aramaic original in three different ways. 1) In Biblical Hebrew, מס like מס עובד means forced labor, corvée; 2) it is generally used in the singular;[174] 3) he who is said להעלות מס 'to raise the corvée', is the ruler who imposes the corvée. From the Targumim, however, we learn that the Aramaic usage was different: 1) מס was apparently not limited to corvée, but meant tax in general;[175] 2) the word is always in the plural (מסין); 3) and he who raises the taxes is not the recipient of the tax but the one who pays it.[176] To

---

[172] See 2:18; 6:27; 8:22 (Ezr 4:13; 6:8; 7:24) and cf. 2:23 (Ezr 4:20).

[173] We would usually expect the standard φέρειν (or another verb such as ἀπάγειν) on the subject of raising taxes, only ἀναφέρειν presumably takes the place of a causative verb in the source before him.

[174] In the phrase שרי מסים in Exod 1:11, the plural שרי drags the plural of מס along after it, as in לוחות אבנים, frequent in the Torah.

[175] As testified by the Palestinian Targumim to Gen 49:15.

[176] The following are telling examples. Deut 20:11 יהיו לך למס "they shall serve you at forced labor" was transmitted in the Jewish Targumim as מס (1): יהוו לך למסקי מסין was changed to מסין and (2) the מסקי מסין are none other than those who must pay

be sure, the Aramaic evidence is not derived from independently written literature, but in the Targumic literature the phrase is the translator's own formulation, independent of the exact wording of their source. Our text in I Esd is speaking about the taxes on agricultural products which the subjects owed the king rather than forced labor, and it therefore reflects in form and content an expression such as מנ(נ)סקין מסין.[177]

Let us briefly mention a few other such phrases:

(6) 4:5 καὶ τὰ ἄλλα πάντα may reflect the Aramaic ואחרן כלא. Support for this is found in the letter of the Jews of Elphantine to Bagohi (Cowley 30:11-12).[178] The phrase reoccurs in 6:4 (Ezr 5:3), without a direct parallel in the MT.

(7) 4:10, 31 πρὸς τούτοις. One wonders whether this is not a literal rendering of לקבל דנה, or the more frequent כל קבל דנה. The real significance of the Aramaic is 'at that time', 'then'; and as such fits the context.[179]

(8) 4:22 δεῖ ὑμᾶς γνῶναι. Torrey (p. 53) suggested that the translator chose this syntactical construction since the sentence hinged upon the Aramaic אריך; cf. Ezr 4:14 לא אריך לנא למחזא "and it is not right that we should see".

---

it. The author of Targum Jonathan to the Prophets was forced to change 1 Kgs 5:27 ויעל המלך שלמה מס מכל ישראל to: ומני מלכא שלמה מסקי מסין, such is to say, (1) he changed מס into מסין, (2) he supplies a verb not in his *Vorlage* (ומני) and, once again, (3) the מסקי מסין are those who provide the taxes.

[177] מעלי מסין mentioned in the Amoraic literature (Palestinian Talmud, Demai 22d; Shevi'it 36c) is apparently a loan-translation of the Aramaic מסקי מסין, since the Aramaic evidence precedes this by hundreds of years.

[178] The letter reads: ואחרן זי תמה הוה כלא באשה שרפו, which is generally translated as: "and (every thing) else, that was there, all of it they set on fire" (as if אחרן were an adj. and used elliptically, without the noun); however, it might have been used as a substantive, which acquired, through metonymy, the meaning of 'everything else'; cf. Dan 2:11; Kraeling 10:10.

[179] On Torrey's suggestions see above, note 163.

(9) Before turning to other matters, let us note the position of the verb at the end of the sentence, one of the trademarks of Official Aramaic.[180] There are several places in the story which would appear to testify to this Aramaic usage: 3:6; 4:42, 43, 44, 46, 50.

(b) Issues of Content

Often, baffling elements in the content of the story can be explained against the background of a misunderstood Aramaic *Vorlage*.

(1) 3:1 οἰκογενεῖς. In the beginning of the story mention is made of the guests summoned to the king's banquet, and among these the οἰκογενεῖς receive a place of honor. The meaning of the Greek word is 'houseḅorn slaves' which is highly incongruous under the circumstances. It seems that this infelicity is nothing more than a translation of בני ביתא. In Official and Middle Aramaic, בר ביתא is a high-ranking official in the royal court;[181] whereas, in Hebrew, בן בית is a slave that was born into the house of his master.[182] The translator must have found בר ביתא in his *Vorlage* and made

---

[180] Official Aramaic inherited it from Akkadian, which in turn inherited it from Sumerian; cf. Segert, p. 422. It is worth noting that this linguistic usage, alien to the Semitic languages, disappeared from the dialects which took the place of Official Aramaic; see the discussion on pp. 223ff.

[181] The list may possibly name the high-ranking officials according to their hierarchical importance, with the οἰκογενεῖς standing at the top. Indeed, בר ביתא is the title of Arsham, one of the senior officials of the Persian government (see Driver, letters 1, 2, 3, 5) and cf. Beyer's reading of the Genesis Apocryphon 19:24 תלתא גברין מן רברבי מצרי[ן] מן בני ביתא די פרעו צען "three men from among the nobles of Egypt of the princes of Pharaoh of Zoan", Bayer, p. 173; the text, however, is dubious. It is hard to accept Rundgren's position, which attributes the Aramaic meaning to the Greek on the basis of the word's usage here.

[182] In Gen 15:2-3 בן ביתי is a synonym for בן משק ביתי; unfortunately the meaning of the latter is dubious, but see Eccl 2:7 קניתי עבדים ושפחות ובני בית היה לי "I bought male and female slaves, and I acquired stewards". Zimmermann (1963/4), p. 199, was imprecise in this matter.

a literal translation of its different components; only, it is very out of context here.[183]

(2) 4:14 is something of a *locus classicus* to any discussion of this kind: οὐ μέγας ὁ βασιλεὺς καὶ πολλοὶ οἱ ἄνθρωποι καὶ ὁ οἶνος ἰσχύει. The usual meaning of πολλοί ill accords with the context, since one would expect the emphasis to fall on power, magnitude, and not on number. Rudolph (p. ix), as is his wont, plowed through the sources and found that the Greek word also carries a nuance of 'strong'. It is doubtful, however, whether a Greek author would have settled precisely on this word, when its primary meaning is 'numerous'. This is evidently nothing but a mistranslation. Torrey (p. 24) claims that the translator erred in translating the Aramaic word רברבין 'great men, nobles' in the sense of its Hebrew counterpart רבים 'numerous'. On the other hand, if we assume that the translator worked from an Aramaic text such as: שגיאין בני אנשא – everything slips into place, since שגיאין in Aramaic has connotations of both number,[184] and magnitude.[185] The translator chose the first of these meanings, when, in fact, he should have chosen the second.

(3) One wonders whether Zimmermann was correct in suggesting (pp. 187-188) that the ambiguous חבו in Aramaic led to a mistranslation in 4:27, since the translator preferred the nuance of 'to sin' over that of 'to owe'. The latter nuance seems to be no more in keeping with the verbs alongside it than the first.

(4) Another mistranslation much better explained against the background of Aramaic usage than against that of Hebrew can also be found in 4:49ff. Time and again, the Greek text gives the impression that the king is busy dashing off letters to the Judaeans about to leave his

---

[183] Admittedly, the term expected to underlie the title οἰκονόμος in 4:47, 49 is also בר-בית. In this case, it is not quite clear why he introduced an unsuitable term here.

[184] Cf. שנין שגיאן "many years", Ezr 5:11.

[185] Cf. צלם חד שגיא "a big statue", Dan 2:31; מתנן רב שגיאן "many great gifts", *ibid.*, v. 48; and a similar usage in the Palestinian Targumim, e.g., to Gen 4:13.

kingdom, the priests, the Levites and the guards of the city. Since על means 'to' as well as 'about', the translator erred in thinking that the king's letter was addressed to the Judaeans etc. In fact, the documents were designated for the authorities in Coelesyria and Phoenicia, as written in v. 48, and their content was <u>about</u> the Judaeans etc. The ambiguity of the word על is daily fare of Official Aramaic, but neither, it must be admitted, is it lacking in Hebrew (cf. Ezr 4: 6, 7).

(5) 4:36 καὶ οὐκ ἔστιν μετ' αὐτοῦ ἄδικον οὐδέν; 4:40 εὐλογητὸς ὁ θεὸς τῆς ἀληθείας. Many have noted the difficulty presented by the unexpected mention of God in the discourse about truth, 4:35, 36, 40. If we understand v. 35 οὐχὶ μέγας ὃς ταῦτα ποιεῖ as a continuation of the discourse on the subject of the sun and not as a definition of God, who is not explicitly mentioned in the verse, the fact that God does appear in vv. 36 and 40 can be explained as a mistranslation of the Aramaic *Vorlage*. Torrey (pp. 55-56) suggested a solution in this direction but contended that the translator's change was tendentious, and that he sought to glorify God in a speech which praised the superiority of the creation without mention of the creator. Only, had Torrey taken into account the masculine gender of the Aramaic קושטא, קשוט,[186] none of this would have been necessary. It is precisely because of the feminine gender of אמת and of ἀλήθεια, and the masculine gender of קשוט, that the Aramaic original of the story is revealed. Verse 36 revolves around the subject of truth, and it is thus quite reasonable for its ending to do just the same: καὶ οὐκ ἔστιν μετ' αὐτοῦ ἄδικον οὐδέν, that is, ולא איתי עמה כל עולה "it [the truth] has no iniquity.[187] In the *Vorlage*, the pronoun (עמּה) devolved not with reference

---

[186] Thus in all the Aramaic dialects קושטא, קשוט is masculine; and even in Syriac, in which the form is קושתא (through dissimulation of the emphatic consonants) and the *taw* could have been understood as denoting the feminine – Bar ʿAli says explicitly: "ודכרנאית ולא נקבאית – masculine and not feminine", Payne Smith (1901), p. 3773.

[187] עולה is the word contrasting קושטא both in the Aramaic Book of Enoch, see 4QEnᶜ1 V, 3, Milik, p. 189: ואכרת עולה מן [...] ותתחזא נ]צבת קושטא "and destroy iniquity... and let the plant of righteousness appear", and in Syriac (Payne Smith, *ibid.*).

to God but to קשוט; the translator should have switched to the feminine, in keeping with the Greek ἀλήθεια. However, he erred and did not make the change, thus leaving the masculine pronoun to refer to God. In v. 40 εὐλογητὸς ὁ θεὸς τῆς ἀληθείας, the translator might have had before him: מברך/בריך אלה קשטא, such is to say, "God-blessed is the truth", which he understood to mean as 'Blessed is the God of truth'.[188]

4. The Language of the Redaction

If we have succeeded in bringing sufficient evidence – and indeed the evidence has an accumulating importance – to show that the story was translated from a Semitic language, apparently from Aramaic, this still does not tell us how it came to form part of I Esd. It might have been included by an 'Aramaic' or 'Hebrew' redactor, but it might also have been in its Greek form that the story first reached the book. This is more than a hypothetical question since the answer has ramifications for the same traits which distinguish I Esd from the MT and which are connected to the inclusion of the Story of the Youths. If the story was first included in I Esd already in its Greek form, then the changes caused by the interpolation of the story must have first been written in Greek as well.

In the course of discussing I Esd's characteristics we noted a number of points which seemed to indicate intervention on the part of the translator, and which nevertheless conform with I Esd's unique redaction.[189] As a

---

[188] Perhaps the *Vorlage* read: בריך/מברך יהוה קשטא, such is to say: 'may the truth be blessed' and the translator understood the verb יהוה as the name of God. And cf.: להוה בריך דין קושטא in the Aramaic Enoch 4QEn[d]l XI, 2, Milik, p. 218.

[189] This is the case for 2:18 (Ezr 4:14), in which the expression מלח היכלא מלחנא is translated by καὶ ἐπεὶ ἐνεργεῖται τὰ κατὰ τὸν ναόν, introducing the work at the Temple into the complaint, together with the choice of equivalents for the root of יסד in 5:52-60 (3:6-12), as well as the attribution of the title פחה to Zerubbabel in 6:28 (6:8-9). Indeed, these changes are best explained on the assumption that the translator elaborated his *Vorlage*. But they also join two trends of redaction in

result, the question arose if these changes might not be indicative of similar elaborations: should they all be explained as originating from the hand of the translator, even though they would seem more indicative of a different *Vorlage*? This possibility we reject out of hand. Even if the translator was responsible for some significant changes, he probably did not author the redaction as a whole. Since the evidence presupposes relations between a source and its translator, the supposition that the redaction was Greek also forces us to conclude that the redaction was made by the translator, and that we are not dealing with the redaction of an existing Greek translation. This would mean that in order to include the Greek story he undertook quite a comprehensive piece of translation, and during the course of translation, he also changed its structure and adapted its content. This scenario, which places all the work squarely on the shoulders of the translator, is not entirely logical, to say the least. Even were we to say that this translator, who gave himself a free hand in everything concerning linguistic usage, also intervened in matters of content, we would still be a long way from explaining the evolution of I Esd in its entirety. To be sure, details always make for a certain skepticism and foster a greater readiness to attribute the change to the translator. Such is not the case, however, when the discrepancy is on a larger scale. When we come across a passage like 1:21-22 in I Esd, unparalleled in the MT, we do not tend to attribute the addition to the translator since the shadow of the Hebrew original is hovering over each and every word.

The major evidence that the inclusion of the story, and the changes in the book that it involved, did not take place at the level of Greek is found in the passage linking the Story of the Youths to the rest of the book (5:1-6). This passage could have been written in Aramaic, or it could have been written in Hebrew, but it is hard to believe that it was written in

---

I Esd: the first two changes adapt the text to the different place of the letter of complaint in I Esd, and the last accords with Zerubbabel's special role in the Story of the Three Youths.

Greek, if only for the reason that here, more than anywhere else in the book, the writing least fits the Greek pattern.[190]

Let us suffice by glancing at the following examples:

(1) Three consecutive main sentences begin with καί (5:2, 3, 4), evidence which is sufficient to cast strong doubt on the claim that the passage was originally written in Greek.

(2) Both μετὰ δὲ ταῦτα (5:1), which starts the first part of the passage, and καὶ ταῦτα τὰ ὀνόματα (5:4), which starts its second part, reflect Semitic patterns.

(3) The manner in which the groups of returning exiles are depicted: κατὰ πατριὰς αὐτῶν εἰς τὰς φυλὰς ἐπὶ τὴν μεριδαρχίαν αὐτῶν (5:4) is pure biblical formulation.

(4) The manner of noting the month by μηνὶ Νισὰν τοῦ πρώτου μηνός (5:6) is again a biblical formula, which a 'Greek' writer would not use.

(5) And finally, it would seem that at the bottom of the awkward Greek text in 5:5 stands a mistranslation of the *Vorlage*: οἱ ἱερεῖς υἱοὶ Φινεὲς υἱοῦ Ἀαρών Ἰησοῦς ὁ τοῦ Ἰωσεδὲκ τοῦ Σαραίου καὶ Ἰωακεὶμ ὁ τοῦ Ζοροβαβὲλ τοῦ Σαλαθιήλ. The opening with οἱ ἱερεῖς 'the priests' calls for more than one priest, yet only one priest is mentioned. Moreover, Joiakim was the son of Jeshua the son of Jozadak (Neh 12:26), while no son of Zerubbabel is known by this name. The leaders mentioned must have been the priests Jeshua and his son Joiakim, and Zerubbabel. It

---

[190] There is no logic in Fritzsche's assumption that the story was written originally in Hellenistic Greek, and that the ending (5:1-6) is a translation whose *Vorlage* has not come down to us. If the passage linking the story to its context was originally Hebrew or Aramaic, the story could not possibly have been written first in Greek. The Semitic nature of this passage also refutes a conjecture like that of Pohlman (1970), pp. 35-52, who argues that the story was included in I Esd only after the book reached its Greek form, as a translation of 2 Chr 35-36, Ezr 1-10, Neh 8, and that only the inclusion of the story within the book led to the changes, at the level of Greek, in its internal order.

can only be that the pronoun of בנו or ברה which defined Joiakim as the
son of Jeshua was overlooked, and Joiakim thus turned into Zerubbabel's
son. The words which the translator found before him, then, were: הכהנים
or [191]בני פינחס בן אהרן ישוע בן יוצדק בן שריה ויויקים בנ(ו ו)זרובבל בן שאלתיאל
similarly in Aramaic כהניא בני פינחס בן אהרן ישוע בר יוצדק בר שריה ויויקים
בר(ה ו)זרובבל בר שאלתיאל.

According to this, the interpolation of the story in the book, as well
as the changes made in the book in order to accommodate it, were
accomplished before the translator set to work on the book. Should this be
the case, the Greek of the entire book, both the Story of the Youths and
the other parts, is by one and the same hand. Indeed, the story and the
sections parallel to Chr-Ezr-Neh all bear the same stamp. In our discussion,
we noted a similar distribution of linguistic usage between the story and
the rest of I Esd. Let us illustrate the common style with a few examples:
the phrase καὶ τὰ ἄλλα πάντα comes both in 6:4 (Ezr 5:3) and in the
story 4:5; χρυσώματα serves both 3:5 and 8:56 (Ezr 8:27); and in 8:51
(Ezr 8:22), the escort along the road is described as προπομπή, and in the
story, 4:47, as ἵνα προπέμψωσιν αὐτόν; the region is called Κοίλη Συρία
καὶ Φοινίκη in both the story – 4:48, and numerous times throughout the
rest of the book; the Temple is called τὸ ἱερόν in the story – 4:51, 63, and
in numerous other places in the book. All of these are unusual expressions
in the corpus of the LXX.

In sum, it is not to the evolution of the Greek corpus which I Esd
attests, but rather to the evolution of a late redaction of a section of Chr,
Ezr and Neh.

---

[191] The omission of one or more *waws* before the letter *zayin* can be explained by the
similarity between the letters, cf. ובוזים in 2 Chr 36:16, as opposed to ובים in I Esd
1:49.

Conclusion

In view of the central problems that beset the formation of I Esd, it seems very likely that there existed a Hebrew-Aramaic work whose *raison d'être* was the Story of the Youths. The Story of the Youths is the core of the book; without it, all the rest of I Esd is pointless. Not only is it true that the book would not have survived – it would never have come into being at all, had not some author or redactor decided to weave the Story of the Youths into the history of the Restoration. The Story of the Youths is not just one of the differences between I Esd and the canonical books, but it is the reason for most of those differences. The Book of I Esd was created for the purpose of retelling the history of the Restoration in such a way that it revolved around the Story of the Three Youths and its hero Zerubbabel.

The author of I Esd does not select the material for his book autonomously, nor does he structure it independently. Although he clearly intends to create a new work, he relies heavily on materials at his disposal. He does not carefully pick and choose from the various books of the Bible, adding extrabiblical and originally written material, and then use all these building blocks to create a new, continuous work of his own. If that had been his procedure, one would have expected him to produce a properly structured entity. For example, had he not been constrained by his source, he would presumably have begun with Josiah but dropped the succeeding kings, as does Ben Sira, who, after praising Josiah (Sirach 49:1-3), dismisses the later chapter of history in a few words: לבד מדויד יחזקיהו ויאשיהו כלם השחיתו. ויעזבו תורת עליון מלכי יהודה עד תמם. ויתן קרנם לאחור וכבודם לגוי נבל נכרי. ויציתו קרית קדש וישמו ארחתיה "Except David and Hezekiah and Josiah they all sinned greatly for they forsook the law of the Most High; the kings of Judah came to an end; for they gave their power to others, and their glory to a foreign nation, who set fire to the chosen city of the sanctuary, and made her streets desolate" (49:4-6). However, the author of I Esd works in a different way: he begins at a certain point in a given continuous text, continuing from then on as in the original. The link between Chr and Ezr is not the personal contribution of the author of I Esd.

The book's beginning is in one respect logical, but in another, it is purely arbitrary. The author presumably intended to begin his account when the First Temple was still standing and the Davidic kings still reigned, leading on to the Destruction and the Restoration through Zerubbabel who was scion of the Davidic dynasty, and his efforts to rebuild the Temple. Josiah was probably chosen as a king who reigned not long before the fall of the kingdom of Judah and who had earned much praise both in the Bible and in postbiblical literature. However, the opening of the book with Josiah's celebration of the Passover, if not accidental, was not a good choice, as it resulted in the book lacking a clear-cut plan. Had the author begun with Josiah's succession to the throne, his discovery of the scroll of the Law, and the outcome of that event – religious reform and repairs to the Temple – then, going on to the celebration of the Passover, and finally ending with Ezra's reading of the Law and the festival of Booths, the book would have been well rounded. In that respect the decision to start with Josiah's Passover was in the nature of a technical, almost random, decision.

The linkage between Ezr 10 and Neh 10 is the invention of the author of I Esd. For his purposes, it was clearly natural to extract the whole episode of the reading of the Law (and probably also the celebration of the feast of Booths) from the story of Nehemiah and transplant it to the story of Ezra. The fact that the reading of the Law opens with a parallel to Neh 7:72 demonstrates that the link between Ezr 10 and Neh 8 is secondary.

The need to link up different parts of the Ezra narrative is also due to the omission of the story of Nehemiah. It seems probable that the author

of I Esd did not wish to give an account of Nehemiah. He therefore
removed the chapter relating to Ezra from the account of Nehemiah's time
and added it to the end of Ezr, thus, shifting the center of gravity from
Nehemiah to Zerubbabel and crediting the latter with Nehemiah's
achievements in the second part of the Story of the Youths. It was Zerubbabel
who, through his sagacity, secured permission to return to Judah and to
rebuild the Temple and Jerusalem: Zerubbabel, a representative of the
Davidic line, has thus become the standard-bearer of the Restoration.

The relationship between the Story of the Youths and Nehemiah's
life story raises the following considerations. If the author wrote the Story
of the Youths with his eye on the story of Nehemiah, one may well doubt
whether it was ever entirely independent of the canonical books. It does
not seem plausible that one author wrote the Story of the Youths
independently of its present context, using elements from the story of
Nehemiah, while another – the author responsible for the insertion of the
story in I Esd – realizing that Zerubbabel was in many respects a duplicate
Nehemiah, deliberately decided to omit the latter's story. The affinity
between the two stories strongly supports the theory that one author wrote
the Story of the Youths and created the setting of I Esd for its particular
convenience. The version of history conveyed in this book ascribes the
leadership of the Restoration to Zerubbabel and Ezra and not to Ezra and
Nehemiah.

The inclusion of the Story of the Youths made it necessary to rearrange
Ezr 1-6. The statement that the letter of complaint to Artaxerxes, Ezr
4:6-24, was removed from its problematic position in Ezr is not accurate.
The unit that was moved is the previous one, Ezr 2:1-4:5, featuring
Zerubbabel as the leader of the returnees. It has now been assigned a new
place after the Story of the Youths, which is the stage for the introduction
of Zerubbabel. The letter of complaint was left in place, but once the
previous unit had been moved away, the letter was left adjoining Ezr 1,

creating a well-nigh impossible juxtaposition – even worse than that in the canonical book. The end of the letter of complaint, I Esd 2:25, which states that the building was halted till Darius' reign, enabled the author to bring in the Story of the Youths. He chose an arrangement that enabled Zerubbabel to occupy the center of the stage, and the Story of the Youths functioned as a backdrop to that stage. Thus, the material in which there is no mention of Zerubbabel (Ezr 1, 4:6-24) was left together before the Story of the Youths, while the material in which Zerubbabel has a part (Ezr 2:1-4:5) was kept back until the story of Zerubbabel, i.e., the Story of the Youths, had been told.

The course of events thus created in I Esd is impossible. Events pertaining to the beginning of Darius' reign are described twice – and in two different, mutually exclusive, versions: construction work is renewed in Darius' second year (a) when Zerubbabel returns after winning the contest at Darius' court (Story of the Youths), (b) with the encouragement of the prophets and the renewed permission to build after the intervention of Tattenai, governor of Beyond the River, as related in the biblical version, which was also copied into I Esd. The inclusion of the Story of the Youths was an act of literary epigonism whose result lacks a proper backbone.

The Story of the Youths betrays the milieu in which I Esd was composed. The book was not forged in the same furnaces as the canonical books of the Bible. The author, or the redactor, who wove it into the history of the Restoration and fathered the impossible course of events described in I Esd, had nothing to do with the masters of the Chronicler's school. I Esd was born in a later generation, in a period that had already seen the creation of such Books as Esther and Daniel and, later, the additions to Esther and the apocryphal stories attached to Daniel. These books, as preserved in the LXX, open up a window to the Books of the Apocrypha. I Esd is a vestige of the intense literary activity, revolving around the Books of the Bible, of authors who wrote imaginary tales about biblical figures; they were a long way away from any living tradition or, surely, authentic history.

CHAPTER TWO

I ESDRAS' *VORLAGE*

COMPARED WITH

2 CHR 35-36, EZRA 1-10 AND NEH 8

Introduction

As we established in our discussion of its composition, I Esd presents itself as a later revision of a work not much different from that preserved in the parallel parts of Chr-Ezr-Neh. The main trends of this revision, as we argued, were first of all the interpolation of the Story of the Three Youths and the ensuing different order of events, as well as the omission of Nehemiah's Memoirs, thus enabling Zerubbabel and Ezra to become the only leaders of the restoration. This major revision of the work must have entailed smaller changes, such as the attempts to further enhance the image of Zerubbabel. Other differences may also derive from the hand of the same revisor, although their connection with the main themes that interest him is not obvious. However, the majority of variants have nothing to do with the revision and should be understood as part of the textual evolution. The text in front of the revisor who created I Esd must have been different from the MT to a certain extent. One may assume that his text was partly older and partly younger than the text-form which finally crystallized in the MT. We thus set out to evaluate the relationship between the *Vorlage* of I Esd and the parallel parts of the MT in regard to the history of the texts.

The questions surrounding I Esd's *Vorlage* have evoked entirely different answers. Some scholars do not even consider the possibility of a different *Vorlage*.[191] Other studies, eccentric as they may be, attribute every single difference between I Esd and the MT to I Esd's *Vorlage*.[192]

---

[191] Moulton (1899; 1900), who was the first to provide a list of differences between I Esd and the MT, set them all under the heading of translation technique.

[192] Especially Jahn (1909). His reconstruction is a model of how not to reconstruct a text. The following few examples, out of a multitude of similar ones, show his method, or rather lack of method. 8:45 (Ezr 8:17) καὶ τοῖς ἐν τῷ τόπῳ γαζοφύλαξιν which undoubtedly reflects MT's הנתו/ינים בכספיא המקום, is reconstructed by Jahn into: כל החרד בדברי אלהי ישראל אשר במקום (!) הכסף בית שמרי. Similarly, 8:69 (9:4) ≈

The more balanced studies recognize a certain amount of variants in I Esd, but still credit the translator with most of the differences, even with many of the omissions.[193] This reserved attitude towards I Esd's textual evidence was inspired by several reasons: 1) I Esd as a whole, being considered a later revision, affected, inappropriately, the judgment of the text proper. 2) Since the translation of I Esd goes far beyond the traditional literal translations characteristic of the LXX, it seemed right to attribute to the translator any changes which would not usually be considered under translation technique. 3) The general reluctance to accept the existence of divergent parallel texts prior to the flourish of Qumran studies also contributed to the rejection of a different text underlying I Esd. Torrey was not intimidated by such arguments. At the beginning of the century, he spoke of two text types underlying I Esd on the one hand, and the MT, the LXX (in his view, Theodotion), and the Vulgate on the other.[194] Klein (1966) eagerly joined the line set by Torrey and went on to prove – on the basis of differences in the length of the text – that I Esd is a faithful translation of a text-form different from the MT.[195]

In my view, while I Esd's *Vorlage* is indeed hidden under the heavy veil of a quite eccentric translation, it remains an acceptable witness to the history of the text. A thorough investigation of the translator's technique

---

5:43 .כל אשר יהמם (!) דבר הי... ,Jahn: ...ὅσοι ποτὲ ἐπεκινοῦντο τῷ ῥήματι κυρίου..., התנדבו לבית האלהים להעמידו על מכונו (2:68) ≈ εὔξαντο ἐγεῖραι τὸν οἶκον ἐπὶ τοῦ τόπου αὐτοῦ, Jahn: את הבית על מקומו (!) נדרו להעיר. On top of this absurd reproduction of a certainly non-existent *Vorlage* of the Hebrew parts, he also reconstructed those parts of I Esd which have an Aramaic counterpart in the MT into Hebrew! Batten (1913) also went much too far in reconstructions of this sort.

[193] Among these are the extensive studies by Bayer (1911) and Walde (1913), and the commentaries by Bewer (1922) and Rudolph (1949).

[194] Torrey (1910), pp. 82-90.

[195] Cross (1975), pp. 7ff, took into account Klein's conclusions regarding different text types represented in I Esd and the MT in reconstructing the different redactions of the work of the Chronicler. In my opinion, these issues pertain to different levels.

and a constant consideration of his tendencies and peculiarities as opposed to possible variants in his text, causes his *Vorlage* to become more and more accessible.

Although many cases remain ambiguous, we had to make a decision as to where a certain difference between I Esd and the MT belonged. Texts presented in the present chapter allegedly demonstrate the natural process of text transmission of I Esd's *Vorlage* on the one hand and the MT on the other. Consequently, they neither pertain, in the main, to the revision characteristic of I Esd, as described in the first chapter, nor do they belong with the cases which establish the image of the translator, described in detail in the following chapter.

Unlike Klein, I do not believe that the comparison of I Esd's *Vorlage* and the parallel parts in Chr-Ezr-Neh may lead us to the *Urtext* of this work. Rather, the comparison between the conjectured *Vorlage* of I Esd and the MT demonstrates the course of two texts which took different routes and underwent ongoing alteration. In our comparison of the texts, we concentrate on the given stages of the texts as reflected in the extant witnesses; the MT, on the one hand, and the text reflected in I Esd, on the other, have a large common basis but also a long and substantial separate history of transmission.

In this chapter we attempt to provide the full evidence which forms the variance between I Esd's *Vorlage* and the MT. The variants were gathered and classified after a careful analysis of the text, which will be presented in detail in the forthcoming commentary. In this framework, we cannot but offer random comments on certain difficult cases. Some examples remain disputable. Nevertheless, we believe that the grouped variants clearly establish parallel patterns and trends in the transmission of both the MT and I Esd's *Vorlage*.

The text used as basis for the reconstruction of I Esd's *Vorlage* is the impeccable text established by Hanhart in the Göttingen edition. This edition, although eclectic, is based primarily on the B-text and only seldom borrows meaningful variants from other text-groups. Indeed, only rarely did we find it necessary to refer to readings in MSS mentioned in the apparatus which may affect the *Vorlage*. In these few cases we specifically noted that the text which in our view represents the *Vorlage* of I Esd is not the text chosen by Hanhart as the original Greek text. The relationship between the Greek and its assumed *Vorlage* is noted by the sign ≈, which is meant to designate the doubts that accompany any reconstruction.

I. Variants

Under 'variants' we include all the details in which I Esd's conjectured *Vorlage* differs from the MT, except for omissions / additions and differences in word-order. The latter are dealt with separately since they are related to translation technique in too many ways. The issue of omissions and additions deserves individual treatment as it is an outstanding factor in the history of these texts. All the variants attest to the evolution of the texts, notwithstanding the originality of one text or the other.

a. Reading Variants

Since the text in front of the translator was naturally unvocalized, reading variants have to be described as the result of the interaction between the translator and the letters he found in his *Vorlage*. In fact, they are hardly variants at all since it is actually wrong to reconstruct a different vocalization assumed on the basis of the translation. Nevertheless, other variants too, e.g., a variant which constitutes an interchange between two similar letters, may also be only the result of what the translator imagined to see in his text, rather than an actual variant. In addition, the translator may, of course, preserve a genuine reading tradition. We note that while reading variants may seem trivial, in the majority of cases different vocalization entirely changes the meaning of the word.

1. 1:10 (2 Chr 35:10)

MT: כְּמִצְוַת (הַמֶּלֶךְ).   I Esd: ἔχοντες τὰ ἄζυμα ≈ בְּמִצּוֹת.

The context proves that the MT probably preserves the original (see pp. 139-140).

2. 1:10 (35:12)

MT: לַבָּקָר.   I Esd: τὸ πρωινόν ≈ לַבֹּקֶר.

The MT is the preferred reading, as suggested by the pair צֹאן-בָּקָר.

3. 1:30 (35:25)

MT: הַשָּׁרִים וְהַשָּׁרוֹת.   I Esd: καὶ οἱ προκαθήμενοι σὺν

γυναιξίν ≈ הַשָּׂרִים וְהַשָּׂרוֹת.

This is hardly a genuine variant. It rather seems to be the translator's interpretation envisaging the royal court instead of the singers.

4-5. 2:6, 8 (Ezr 1:4, 6)

MT: רכוש.   I Esd: μεθ' ἵππων / ἵπποις ≈ רֶכֶשׁ.

It may, however, be the translator's solution for the MT's רכוש, a word which he does not seem to know.

6. 9:10 (10:12)

MT: כִּדְבָרֶךָ.   I Esd: ὡς εἴρηκας ≈ כְּדָבָרְךָ.[196]

7. 9:53 (Neh 8:11)

MT: מַחְשִׁים.   I Esd: ἐκέλευον ≈ מְחִשִׁים.

In the MT the form is a derivative of חשה 'to silence', whereas, our translator derived it from חיש 'to urge'. The MT further develops the same

---

[196] Cf. 1:49 (2 Chr 36:16) דבריו - דְּבָּר הִי.

motif with הסו 'be silent', which remains unrepresented in I Esd. Hushing the weeping people perfectly fits the context, although urging the people at this point is not out of place.

8. 7:14 (Ezr 6:22)

MT: כִּי שָׂמְחָם הי.   I Esd: εὐφραινόμενοι ἔναντι τοῦ

                                          κυρίου ≈ כי שמחים לפני הי.

Different vocalization may have caused the introduction of the more common phrase in I Esd.

9. 9:20 (Ezr 10:19)

MT: וַאֲשֵׁמִים.   I Esd: καὶ εἰς ἐξιλασμόν ≈ אָשָׁם

                                          (cf. LXX).

We note that the reading variants adduced above do not necessarily illustrate the state of the *matres lectionis* in the compared texts.

b. Phonetic Variants

Unlike different vocalization, phonetic variants are more apprehensible as existent in the *Vorlage*.

In two cases, two gutturals presumably interchange:

1. 8:41 (Ezr 8:15)

MT: ואבינה בעם ובכהנים ומבני לוי לא מצאתי שם.

I Esd: καὶ κατέμαθον αὐτούς καὶ ἐκ τῶν υἰῶν τῶν ἱερέων καὶ ἐκ τῶν Λευιτῶν οὐχ εὑρὼν ἐκεῖ ≈

                      ואבינה בהם ומבני הכהנים ומן הלוים לא מצאתי שם.

Since Ezra is looking only for Levites, I Esd's formulation must be secondary.

2. 8:49 (8:21)

MT: ואקרא שם צום על הנהר אהוא.

I Esd: καὶ εὐξάμην ἐκεῖ νηστείαν τοῖς νεανίσκοις ≈

                      ואקרא שם צום על הנערים.

Mentioning, particularly, the young men in connection with the fast makes little sense. The corruption may be described in three stages: הנהר was mistaken for הנער; then, it was modified to read the plural, thus entailing the omission of the name of the river.[197]

3. 1:10 (2 Chr 35:12)

MT: לבני העם.   I Esd: ἔμπροσθεν τοῦ λαοῦ ≈ לפני העם.[198]

The variants may have been created either through interchange of the labials ב/פ, or because of the graphical resemblance between the letters and the entire words. Both variants are acceptable in the context.

c. Graphic Variants

Variants caused by the interchange of similar letters may illustrate the graphical quality of the translator's *Vorlage*. In those cases in which the variant reflected in the translation is secondary, it is impossible to tell whether the change first occurred in the process of translation or in the *Vorlage*.

First, the interchange ב/כ/מ/נ:

1. 1:48 (2 Chr 36:15)

MT: השכם ושלוח.   I Esd: μετακαλέσαι αὐτούς ≈ השבם.

The reading of השכם as השבם then caused the omission of the following ושלוח. The MT is to be preferred (see p. 139).

2. 2:1 (Ezr 1:1)

MT: מפי.   I Esd: ἐν στόματι ≈ בפי (Cf. 2 Chr 36:22).

---

[197] It is less plausible to argue that אהוא was missing in I Esd's *Vorlage*, independent of the change נהר/נערים.

[198] Cf. 1 Chr 26:15 ולבניו ≈ κατέναντι, possibly for לפני.

3. 5:47 (3:2)

MT: ויבנו (את מזבח אלהי ישראל).   I Esd: ἡτοίμασαν ≈ ויכנו.

I Esd is repetitive since the same statement occurs in the following verse: ויכינו המזבח על מכונתיו.

4. 9:2 (10:2)

MT: וילך.   I Esd: καὶ αὐλισθεὶς ≈ וילן.

I Esd preserves the original reading; the MT is repetitive: וילך אל לשכת יהוחנן בן אלישיב וילך שם לחם לא אכל ומים לא שתה.[199]

The common interchange of ר/ד occurs in examples which display further changes, such as metathesis:

5. 2:8 (1:6)

MT: לבד.   I Esd: ὡς πλείσταις ≈ לרב.

The Peshitta's reading דטב agrees with I Esd.

6. 8:66 (9:1)

MT: והאמרי.   I Esd: καὶ Ἰδουμαίων ≈ והאדמי.

The Ammorites at the end of the list of people is awkward in the MT, while the Edomites seem natural beside the Egyptians in accordance with Deut 23. Nevertheless, seeing that the author of the Story of the Three Youths shows interest in the Edomites, it is possible that it is part of the later revision.

d. Combined Graphic and Contextual Variants

Even in the comparatively simple cases of ר/ד + metathesis adduced above, it is obvious that the change is not strictly graphical but is initiated by the concept of the word as a whole and possibly also by reasons

---

[199] The same interchange occurs in Josh 8:9 וילן יהושע בלילה ההוא בתוך העם, as against v. 13: וילך יהושע בלילה ההוא בתוך העמק; also Jer 31 (38):9 αὐλίζων ≈ אוליכם.

beyond the mere graphical affinity. This is all the more obvious in the
following cases which are still unmistakably generated by a general graphical
similarity between the texts but entail further changes in the formulation
and meaning of the text:

1. 1:27 (2 Chr 35:23)

MT: וירו הירים.   I Esd: καὶ κατέβησαν οἱ ἄρχοντες

וירדו השרים. ≈

The MT's picture of the king being shot on the battlefield seems to
be the original one. While I Esd's variant may have originated from a
combined graphical error, it is not impossible that the change was intentional
to avoid Josiah's injury in battle (see notes 20, 36).

2. 1:49 (2 Chr 36:16)

MT: ובוזים דבריו.   I Esd: καὶ ᾗ ἡμέρᾳ ἐλάλησεν κύριος

וביום דִּבֶּר ה'. ≈

Here we have to take into consideration an interchange of ז/ו, a
different word division, and finally the confusion of the pronoun and the
divine name. Of course, the changes are not independent of each other.
The MT's range of verbs ומתעתעים... ובוזים... ויהיו מלעבים is more plausible.

3. 9:16 (Ezr 10:16)

MT: ויבדלו.   I Esd: καὶ ἐπελέξατο ἑαυτῷ ≈ ויבדל לו.

The MT is unclear; whereas, I Esd provides a smooth text: ויבדל לו עזרא
הכהן אנשים... וישבו.

4. 2:8 (1:6)

MT: בכלי כסף בזהב.   I Esd: ἐν πᾶσιν, ἀργυρίῳ καὶ χρυσίῳ

בכל בכסף ובזהב. ≈

I Esd is supported by other translations and is more plausible.

5. 1:16 (2 Chr 35:16)

MT: ‏ותכון כל‎.   I Esd: καὶ συνετελέσθη ≈ ‏ותכל‎
                                  (cf. Vulgate).

6. 1:53 (36:19)

MT: ‏וכל כלי‎.   I Esd: καὶ συνετέλεσαν πάντα
                                  ≈ ‏וכלו כל‎.

7. 1:3 (35:3)

MT: ‏הַקְּדוֹשִׁים‎.   I Esd: ἁγιάσαι ἑαυτοὺς
                                  ≈ ‏להקָדשם‎ (cf. LXX),
                                  or ≈ ‏הקָדשו‎ (cf. the Peshitta).

8. 1:6 (35:6)

MT: ‏והתקדשו והכינו‎.   I Esd: καὶ τὰς θυσίας ἑτοιμάσατε
                                  ≈ ‏והקדשים הכינו‎ (cf. LXX).

Below we briefly mention some additional possible variants. While there is a certain formal affinity between the readings, it is no easy matter to explain the interchange. The influence of the context seems to be the main reason for the change.

9. 1:3 (2 Chr 35:3) MT: ‏המבינים‎.   I Esd: ἱεροδούλοις ≈ ‏הנתינים‎.

10. 1:9 (35:9) MT: ‏שרי הלוים‎.   I Esd: χιλίαρχοι ≈ ‏שרי אלפים‎.

11. 1:19 (35:18)

MT: ‏ויושבי ירושלם‎.   I Esd: ἐν τῇ κατοικήσει αὐτῶν
                                  ἐν᾽ Ιερουσαλήμ ≈
                                  ‏במשבתם בירושלם‎

12. 1:25 (35:21) MT: ‏בית‎.   I Esd: τοῦ Εὐφράτου ≈ ‏פרת‎.

13. 1:28 (35:24) MT: ‏המרכבה‎.   I Esd: τῆς παρατάξεως ≈ ‏המערכה‎.

14. 1:31 (35:25) MT: ככתוב. I Esd: καὶ τῆς συνέσεως αὐτοῦ ≈ ובינתו.

15. 1:40 (36:8) MT: אשר עשה. I Esd: καὶ τῆς αὐτοῦ ἀκαθαρσίας. Presumably ≈ ?ורשעתו?.

16. 5:53 (Ezr 3:7) MT: ושמן. I Esd: ms B καὶ χαρα ≈ ?ושמחה?.

This is a very dubious example, especially since it may be a case of an inner-Greek corruption χρίμα-χαρα, which would suggest that I Esd's text was the same as the MT. Hanhart, rather unconvincingly, chose to print in his text the variant καὶ κάρρα. If ושמחה is indeed a variant, the MT seems preferable, since the context requires items payed in return for the work done by the Sidonians: ומאכל ומשתה ושמן לצדנים.

17. 5:60 (3:12) MT: ורבים. I Esd: καὶ ἤλθοσαν ≈ ויבאו.

The structure of the verse shows the MT to be the original: ...ורבים בכים... ורבים... בשמחה.

18. 6:17 (5:14).

MT: והיבל המו להיכלא I Esd: καὶ ἀπηρείσατο αὐτὰ ἐν τῷ ἑαυτοῦ ναῷ ≈ ויהב המו בהיכלא.

19. 6:21 (5:17) MT: דך. I Esd: τοῦ ≈ די.

20. 8:27 (7:28) MT: ראשים. I Esd: ἄνδρας ≈ אנשים.

21. 8:53 (8:23)

MT: ונצומה ונבקשה. I Esd: καὶ πάλιν ἐδεήθημεν ≈ ונשובה ונבקשה.

I Esd's ונשובה ונבקשה is out of place since there was no previous request.

22. 8:74 (9:7) MT: אנחנו. I Esd: τοῖς ἀδελφοῖς ἡμῶν ≈ אחינו.

23. 8:76 (9:8) MT: ‏מעט‏.   I Esd: ἐν τῷ καιρῷ ≈ ‏בעת‏.

The change sometimes involves more than one word producing an entirely different text; nevertheless, the interdependence between the texts is still visible:

24. 1:36 (2 Chr 36:4)

MT: ‏ויסב את שמו יהויקים ואת יואחז אחיו לקח נכו ויביאהו מצרימה‏

I Esd: καὶ ἔδησεν ᾿Ιωακεὶμ τοὺς μεγιστᾶνας, Ζάριον δὲ τὸν ἀδελφὸν αὐτοῦ συλλαβὼν ἀνήγαγεν ἐξ Αἰγύπτου ≈

‏ויאסר יהויקים את השרים ואת ?? אחיו לקח ויביאהו ממצרים‏.

25. 6:26 (Ezr 6:7)

MT: ‏שבקו לעבידת בית אלהא דך‏.   I Esd: ἔασαι δὲ τὸν παῖδα τοῦ
κυρίου Ζοροβαβέλ ≈
‏שבקו לעבדא די אלהא זרבבל‏.

I Esd's text complies with the general trend in the book which seeks to ennoble Zerubbabel.

26. 9:36 (10:44)

Against the MT's ‏ויש מהם נשים וישימו בנים‏, I Esd reads καὶ ἀπέλυσαν αὐτας σὺν τέκνοις "and they sent them away with their sons". It is difficult to reconstruct the *Vorlage*. The text may have read ‏וישלחום עם בניהם‏, thus providing a clear-cut ending which is definitely lacking in the MT.

The following variants are obviously intentional, although, the revisor tries to stay as close to the original text as possible:

27. 1:25 (2 Chr 35:21)

MT: ‏ואל ישחיתך‏.   I Esd: καὶ μὴ ἐναντιοῦ τῷ κυρίῳ ≈
‏ואל תשחית לאלהים‏.

28. 1:50 (36:17)

MT: ‏בבית מקדשם‏.   I Esd: περικύκλῳ τοῦ ἁγίου
αὐτῶν ἱεροῦ ≈ ‏סביב בית מקדשם‏.

Finally, texts which relate little to each other but, nevertheless, may have started from a simple interchange of similar words:

29. 1:24 (35:21)

MT: ‏וישלח אליו מלאכים.‏

I Esd: καὶ διεπέμψατο βασιλεὺς
Αἰγύπτου πρὸς αὐτὸν ≈
‏וישלח מלך מצרים אליו.‏

Klein (p. 105) argues that the original text was ‏וישלח אליו‏ which was expanded in the MT by an object, and in I Esd by the subject; and yet, one cannot overlook the connection between ‏מלאכים‏ and ‏מלך.‏

30. 1:25 (35:21)

MT: ‏לא עליך אתה היום.‏

I Esd: οὐχὶ πρὸς σε ἐξαπέσταλμαι
ὑπὸ κυρίου τοῦ θεοῦ ≈
‏?לא אליך שלחני ה׳ אלהים.‏

I Esd may reflect a completely different text. It may, however, be the translator's solution to a difficult text (other translators understood the word ‏אתה‏ as a verb 'to come').

31. 5:38 (Ezr 2:61)

The MT: ‏בני ברזלי אשר לקח מבנות ברזלי הגלעדי אשה ויקרא על שמם.‏
I Esd: υἱοὶ Ἰοδδοὺς τοῦ λαβόντος Αὐγίαν γυναῖκα τῶν θυγατέρων
Φαρζελλαίου καὶ ἐκλήθη ἐπὶ τῷ ὀνόματι αὐτοῦ.

I Esd provides a name for him who married a daughter of Barzilai's, as well as, a name for her whom he married. One wonders whether both Αὐγία and Ἰοδδους were not conceived from the surname ‏הגלעדי,‏ not represented otherwise in I Esd. The MT is the original since it specifies that he was renamed Barzilai on marrying a daughter of that family.

In sum, in quite a few of the variants which emerged through graphical resemblance, it is not exactly clear which variant is to be preferred (about 15 cases); in some (8 cases), I Esd seems to preserve the original text, while in others (about 15 cases) the MT is to be preferred. Both texts, then, have undergone their share of corruption or rewriting; although, the MT seems to be in a better condition. Moreover, if we do not count the cases, but, rather, weigh them, we may say that in conventional interchanges well-known in the process of text transmission, the MT and I Esd show the same amount of corruption. However, in the more complicated cases, which are on the verge of revision, the MT clearly appears to preserve the original text.

All the cases adduced above constitute variants which are similar in form, to a certain degree. One is, therefore, bound to assume that they are genetically connected, that is, one form is the original whereas the other emerged from it, either by sheer mistake or by intention. Finally, we have to remind ourselves repeatedly that, in many cases, there is no way of telling whether the reading in question existed as a real variant or was born in the mind of the translator.

e. Contextual Variants

In this group there is no formal connection between the variants. The variant was either directly borrowed from the context or more generally influenced by the content:

1. 1:2 (2 Chr 35:2)

MT: ויחזקם לעבודת בית ה׳.   I Esd: ἐστολισμένους ἐν τῷ ἱερῷ

τοῦ κυρίου ≈ מלבשים בבית ה׳.

I Esd pays attention to the clothing of the priests on other occasions also.

2. 1:4 (35:4)

MT: ובמכתב.   I Esd: καὶ κατὰ τὴν μεγαλειότητα

≈ וכיד (cf. LXX).

The MT's במכתב was borrowed from the context, replacing the original וכיד, reflected in both I&II Esd (see pp. 134-135, 189).

3. 1:26 (35:22)

MT: ‫ממנו‬.   I Esd: ἐπὶ τὸ ἄρμα αὐτοῦ ≈ ‫על רכבו‬.

4. 1:31 (35:25)

MT: ‫על הקינות‬.   I Esd: ἐν τῷ βυβλίῳ τῶν βασιλέων
                                    Ἰσραὴλ καὶ Ἰούδα ≈
                                    ‫על ספר דברי הימים למלכי יהודה‬.

The MT seems to preserve the original; I Esd's formula was borrowed by mistake from the context.

5. 5:41 (Ezr 2:64)

MT: ‫כל הקהל כאחד‬.   I Esd: οἱ δὲ πάντες ἦσαν Ἰσραὴλ
                                    ἀπὸ δωδεκαετοῦς ≈
                                    ‫כל ישראל מבן שתים עשרה‬.

I Esd introduces a post-biblical designation of the age-limit of adulthood.[200]

6. 7:6 (6:16)

MT: ‫חנכת בית אלהא דנה בחדוה‬.   I Esd: ἀκολούθως τοῖς ἐν τῇ
                                    Μωυσέως βίβλῳ ≈ ‫ככתב ספר משה‬.

The inauguration disappears in I Esd; instead, a phrase that appears in the context is introduced.

7. 8:17 (7:19)

MT: ‫לפלחן‬.   I Esd: εἰς τὴν χρείαν ≈ ‫לחשחות‬.

I Esd's presumed *Vorlage* ‫חשחות‬ appears again in the context.

8. 8:28 (8:1)

MT: ‫והתיחשם‬.   I Esd: καὶ τὰς μεριδαρχίας ≈ ‫?למפלגות?‬

---

[200] Mishna Nidda 5:6 ‫בן שתים עשרה שנה ויום אחד נדריו נבדקין‬ "he who is twelve years and one day old, his vows are checked".

9. 9:40 (Neh 8:2)

MT: מֵבִין.   I Esd: τοῖς ἱερεῦσιν ≈ הכהנים.

The following are characteristic of I Esd:

10. 5:46 (Ezr 3:1)

MT: ירושלם.   I Esd: τὸ εὐρύχωρον τοῦ πρώτου
                                        πυλῶνος τοῦ πρὸς τῇ ἀνατολῇ ≈
                                        הרחוב אשר לפני השער למזרח.

We assume an original text τὸ πρὸ τοῦ instead of τοῦ πρώτου.
Similarly:

11. 9:38 (Neh 8:1)

MT: הרחוב אשר לפני שער המים.   I Esd: τὸ εὐρύχωρον τοῦ πρὸς
                                        ἀνατολὰς τοῦ ἱεροῦ πυλῶνος ≈
                                        הרחוב אשר למזרח שער בית האלהים.

12. 9:41 (Neh 8:3)

MT: הרחוב אשר לפני שער המים.   I Esd: ἐν τῷ πρὸ τοῦ ἱεροῦ πυλῶνος
                                        εὐρυχώρῳ ≈
                                        ברחוב אשר לפני שער בית האלהים.

f. Stylistic Variants

As opposed to graphical variants which are close in form and quite
different in meaning, stylistic variants have little in common in respect to
their form, but they are very close in meaning. Contrary to other categories
in which the context is, in many cases, bound to suggest which variant is
to be preferred, in the following instances, we are usually unable to decide
which variant is the original one. The interchanges do not affect the meaning
of the text; only rarely do they offer a different interpretation, or introduce
a new idea. Hardly ever would the characteristic revision of I Esd find
expression in this sort of variant.

1. 1:23 (2 Chr 35:20)

MT: נכו.   I Esd: Φαραώ ≈ פרעה.

Note that 'Necho' disappears in I Esd altogether.

2. 5:48 (Ezr 3:2)

MT: בתורת.   I Esd: ἐν τῇ... βίβλῳ ≈ בספר.

3. 5:58 (3:11)

MT: תרועה גדולה.   I Esd: φωνῇ μεγάλῃ ≈ קול גדול (cf. LXX).

4. 6:16 (5:13)

MT: שם טעם.   I Esd: ἔγραψεν ≈ כתב.

5. 8:52 (8:22)

MT: לאמר.   I Esd: ὅτι ≈ כי.

6. 8:79 (9:11)

MT: צוית.   I Esd: ἔδωκας ≈ נתת (cf. LXX).

7. 8:82 (9:12)

MT: עד עולם.   I Esd: τὸν ἅπαντα χρόνον ≈ כל הימים.

8. 8:84 (9:14)

MT: מצותיך.   I Esd: τὸν νόμον σου ≈ תורתך.

9. 9:37 (Neh 7:72)

MT: ויגע (החדש).   I Esd: τῇ νουμηνίᾳ ≈ ביום אחד (לחדש).

Designations of the Temple:

10. 1:5 (2 Chr 35:5)

MT: בקדש.   I Esd: ἐν τῷ ἱερῷ ≈ בבית.

11. 6:17 (Ezr 5:14)

MT: היכלא.   I Esd: τοῦ οἴκου ≈ ביתא.

12. 6:25 (6:5)

MT: היכלא.

I Esd: τοῦ οἴκου ≈ ביתא.

13. 6:25 (6:5)

MT: להיכלא.

I Esd: εἰς τὸν οἶκον ≈ לביתא.

Designations of the people and the country:

14. 1:5 (2 Chr 35:5)

MT: בני העם.

I Esd: υἱῶν Ἰσραήλ ≈ בני ישראל.

15. 1:32 (36:1)

MT: עם הארץ.

I Esd: οἱ ἐκ τοῦ ἔθνους ≈ בני העם.

16. 1:34 (36:3)

MT: הארץ.

I Esd: τὸ ἔθνος ≈ העם.

17. 5:7 (Ezr 2:1)

MT: המדינה.

I Esd: τῆς Ἰουδαίας ≈ יהודה.

18. 5:41 (2:64)

MT: הקהל.

I Esd: Ἰσραήλ ≈ ישראל.

19. 8:16 (7:13)

MT: יהודה.

I Esd: Ἰσραήλ ≈ ישראל.

20. 8:88 (10:1)

MT: מישראל.

I Esd: ἀπὸ Ἰερουσαλήμ ≈ מירושלם.

21. 9:2 (10:6)

MT: הגולה.

I Esd: τοῦ πλήθους ≈ הקהל.

22. 9:1 (10:6)

MT: מלפני (בית האלהים).

I Esd: ἀπὸ τῆς αὐλῆς ≈ מחצר (בית האלהים).

The following variant, distinguishing between Jerusalem and the rest
of the province, is characteristic of I Esd; it is not impossible, however,
that the translator rephrased the *Vorlage* (see pp. 258-259).

23. 5:45 (2:70)

MT: בעריהם.   I Esd: ἐν Ἰερουσαλὴμ καὶ τῇ χώρᾳ

                                 ≈ בירושלם ובמדינה!?

24. 9:37 (Neh 7:72)

MT: בעריהם.   I Esd: ἐν Ἰερουσαλὴμ καὶ ἐν τῇ χώρᾳ

                                 ≈ בירושלם ובמדינה!?

The following variants constitute simple reformulations of phrases:

25. 1:40 (2 Chr 36:8)

MT: על ספר מלכי ישראל ויהודה.   I Esd: ἐν τῇ βίβλῳ τῶν χρόνων τῶν

                                 βασιλέων ≈ על ספר דברי הימים למלכים.

The formulation in the MT is the more common one.

26. 6:27 (Ezr 6:8)

MT: למבנא.   I Esd: μέχρι τοῦ ἐπιτελεσθῆναι ≈

                                 עד יתבנא.

27. 8:85 (9:14)

MT: עד כלה.   I Esd: ἀπολέσαι ἡμᾶς ἕως ≈ לכלותנו עד.

28. 8:84 (9:14)

MT: בעמי התעבות האלה.   I Esd: τῇ ἀκαθαρσίᾳ τῶν ἐθνῶν τῆς

                                 γῆς ≈ בתועבת עמי הארצות (cf. LXX).

29. 6:10 (5:9)

MT: כנמא אמרנא להם.   I Esd: λέγοντες ≈ לממר.

30. 8:25 (7:27)

MT: ברוך ה׳ אלהי אבותינו.   I Esd: Εὐλογητὸς μόνος ὁ κύριος ≈

                                 ברוך ה׳ לבדו.

31. 8:71 (9:6)

MT לההרים אלהי פני אליך.   I Esd: κατὰ πρόσωπόν σου ≈ לפניך.

32. 2:5 (1:3)

MT: הוא האלהים אשר בירושלם.   I Esd: οὗτος ὁ κύριος ὁ κατασκηνώσας

                                   ἐν᾽ Ἰερουσαλήμ ≈

                                   הוא האלהים השכן בירושלם.

I Esd's reference to God is more moderate.

Significantly, many of the variants introduced in this category are necessary components of the text. Therefore, they do not attest to a secondary growth of the parallel texts, each text being expanded by a different element. One of the variants must have been in the original text, only to be replaced by an equivalent at a later stage in the course of transmission.

The large number of stylistic interchanges, as well as the numerous contextual divergencies, lucidly demonstrate the intensive evolution of the texts before they were crystallized in their present form.

II. Word-Order

The data concerning the state of word-order in I Esd as compared with the MT are handled in the chapter which deals with translation technique. Although it may forward some interesting consequences in regard to the history of the text, we preferred to cite the entire material together, and the fact is that the majority of cases do indeed belong to translation technique.

We mention here briefly three categories of word-order which possibly belong here, that is to changes introduced in the process of transmission, not by the translator. They all seem to testify to revisions affecting the Aramaic material much more than the Hebrew sections:

1. The place of the verb in the sentence. The fact that in I Esd the verb is placed earlier in the sentence than it is in the MT may testify to a later revision which tends to replace the western Aramaic pattern by the eastern one (see pp. 223-229).

2. In I Esd, the title מלך precedes the name whereas in the MT it follows it; again, mainly in the Aramaic material. The usage in the Aramaic of Daniel supports our assumption that the change might have happened in the *Vorlage*, rather than in the process of translation (see pp. 221-223).

3. Another change of word-order which occurs in the Aramaic material is that of the components of כסף ודהב, which are replaced throughout I Esd with דהב וכסף (see pp. 219-220).

Other transpositions too probably occurred on the level of transmission, not translation, especially where entire passages are concerned (see pp. 231-233).

Assuming the mentioned transpositions indeed attest to the history of the text, they add substantial evidence and help define the nature of the evolution of the compared texts from a different angle: as we also argue in the case of additions/omissions, it is not only a matter of glosses added in the process of transmission, but rather, a variegated and intensive process of rewriting which affected both texts.

III. Additions / Omissions

The main discrepancy between I Esd and the MT lies in the length of the text. In his book, Klein (1966) described this phenomenon at length in an attempt to establish the existence of an original shorter text. His collection of items missing from I Esd as compared to the MT amounts to 400 words. I Esd, however, is not the reflection of this original shorter text. It too underwent changes including additions which amount to about the same number of the missing elements (pp. 18, 213). Consequently, there must have been an original shorter text which grew into I Esd on the one hand and the MT on the other (p. 273).[201] Klein gathers all the relevant details, explains them in a certain way, and, accordingly, classifies them into categories. He thus arrives at his conclusions. In my view, many details were misconstrued and, therefore, set in the wrong categories. The consequences drawn are, thus, inaccurate. Let us look at the first five examples in his first chapter which presents minuses in I Esd supported by other textual witnesses.

1. 1:1 (2 Chr 35:1)

MT: ויעש יאשיהו בירושלם פסח.

LXX: καὶ ἐποίησεν Ἰωσίας τὸ φάσεχ.

I Esd: καὶ ἤγαγεν Ἰωσίας τὸ πάσχα ἐν Ἰερουσαλήμ.

Klein argues that since בירושלם is not represented in the LXX and is transposed in I Esd, it must be a gloss inserted at a later stage in both the MT and I Esd; only, this was done at different points in the sentence. This is not necessarily the right conclusion: first of all, there is no evidence that I Esd's *Vorlage* was shorter. In addition, it is not self-evident that the shorter text is the original one. Generally speaking, independent additions of the same glosses are not very likely to occur. Apparatuses in critical editions show, rather, that there is a correlation between omissions and transpositions: while an item is missing in certain MSS, it is transposed in others. The technical condition of the text must have caused both the omission and the transposition.

2. 1:4 (35:4)

MT: ובמכתב.

LXX: καὶ διὰ χειρός.

I Esd: καὶ κατὰ τὴν μεγαλειότητα.

---

[201] The main discrepancy is between these two; although, the LXX also presents some pluses and minuses which show that its *Vorlage* did not suffer all the expansions characteristic of the MT, on the one hand, but attracted some expansions of its own, on the other (*ibid*).

As Klein himself notes, this is not a case of a shorter / longer text, but of variants: במכתב in the MT against ביד, which is reflected in both I Esd and the LXX (cf. pp. 126, 189). Since the text never existed without both elements there is no reason why it should appear in Klein's lists as a case among minuses in I Esd.

3. 1:6 (35:6)

MT: והתקדשו והכינו.

LXX: καὶ τὰ ἅγια ἑτοιμάσατε.

I Esd: καὶ τὰς θυσίας ἑτοιμάσατε.

Klein comments that the *waw* is missing before the second verb and the first word is read as והקדשים instead of והתקדשו. The moment the reading is והקדשים it becomes the subject of the following verb, which cannot, therefore, be preceded by a *waw*. At any rate, this is hardly a case of a shorter text, as suggested by Klein.

4. 1:7, 8 (35:8)

MT: אלה מרכוש המלך. ושריו לנדבה... הרימו... נתנו.

LXX: ταῦτα ἀπὸ τῆς ὑπάρξεως τοῦ βασιλέως. καὶ οἱ ἄρχοντες αὐτοῦ ἀπήρξαντο... ἔδωκεν... καὶ ἔδωκαν.

I Esd: ταῦτα ἐκ τῶν βασιλικῶν ἐδόθη κατ' ἐπαγγελίαν... καὶ ἔδωκεν.

The texts present syntactical difficulties and a different word-order, but there is scarcely any evidence of a shorter text, as suggested by Klein. The word ושריו is not missing in I Esd. It was taken together with the preceding words, and the entire phrase – מרכוש המלך ושריו – was translated as ἐκ τῶν βασιλικῶν. This assumption is corroborated by the similar equivalent in 1:51 (36:18) ואצרות המלך ושריו ≈ καὶ τὰς βασιλικὰς ἀποθήκας.

5. 1:13 (35:14)

MT: כי הכהנים בני אהרן.

LXX: ὅτι γὰρ ἱερεῖς.

I Esd: οἱ γὰρ ἱερεῖς.

This presentation of the texts, as proposed by Klein, is misleading.
The words בני אהרן are not missing in I Esd. They are transposed and even
expanded:

MT: ‎...ולכהנים כי הכהנים בני אהרן.

I Esd reflects: ‎...ולכהנים אחיהם בני אהרן כי הכהנים.

A detailed consideration of the remainder of the examples cited by
Klein shows that many have similar problems. Out of 49 cases of combined
evidence from I Esd and the LXX, adduced by Klein, there are 20 cases
(!) in which the shorter reading is clearly not attested in I Esd; and, there
are some others which are doubtful. In other, smaller categories adduced
by Klein: 15 cases in which I Esd is said to be corroborated by the
Peshitta and 7 cases backed up by the Book of Kings, we also find some
unacceptable examples. Additionally, in several cases the only missing
element is a *waw*, a כל, or a pronoun. Consequently, the figure of 70 cases
of combined evidence (p. 76) should be taken with a grain of salt. We
must also criticize the oversimplified presumption which underlies the
gathering of all the minuses in different textual witnesses, as if setting all
of them aside will leave us with the original shorter text.

We do accept Klein's main point that since, in some cases, I Esd is
supported by other textual witnesses we should accept I Esd's evidence
also in regard to other minuses which are not attested elsewhere. It is,
however, no easy matter to accurately determine the genuine cases of
minuses reflected in I Esd, especially considering the nature of this particular
translator. It is only natural that Torrey and Klein sought to define I Esd as
a faithful translation[202] in order to enhance its credibility as a textual
witness to a different text-type. Torrey (p. 83): "It is a faithful rendering,
of the kind to which we are accustomed in the older parts of the Greek
Old Testament". Klein (pp. 19-20): "In I Esdras... the translator followed
his *Vorlage* clause by clause, and his omissions follow no pattern... Unless

---

[202] See also Talshir's attempt to portray the translator as a literary translator (1982).

we suppose that the translator was faithfully rendering his *Vorlage*, it is difficult to see why he would copy so accurately and fully the various lists in the book... How can scholars reconcile the hypothesis that I Esdras tried to smooth out difficulties by abbreviating and translating freely with the fact that the translator often rendered a text which might have made no sense to him with great literal fidelity...". These arguments are not convincing. The fact that the translator keeps to the lists of names or that it so happens that he literally translates an obscure text does not prove a thing regarding his translation technique. General assumptions regarding the faithfulness of the translator do not suffice as a basis for the delicate task of textual criticism.

Since there is a constant interrelation between the evaluation of the text in front of the translator and his practice of representing it, the only way to accurately evaluate I Esd's *Vorlage* is to closely analyze the methods of the translator. The following chapter, devoted to the translation, forms the foundation of our evaluation of the *Vorlage* here. We shall have to leave a wide grey area of doubt over cases which may either be attributed to the translator or reflect a different text. A translator who produces equivalents such as 2:23 (Ezr 4:20) ומדה בלו והלך מתיהב להון ≈ φορολογοῦντες, or 8:24 (7:26) דינה להוא מתעבד מנה ≈ κολασθήσονται, is not the kind of translator who would spare every word in his *Vorlage*, and, thus, he should be constantly examined and re-examined. For example, in a case such as 2:18 (4:14) שלחנא והודענא ≈ προσφωνῆσαι, is it right to argue that והודענא is not reflected in I Esd (Klein, p. 85)? The Greek word means 'call or speak to, address, issue directions or orders, pronounce, utter, make a report' (Liddell & Scott). It therefore covers the range of meaning of both Aramaic verbs. It serves in similar contexts and formulations in the contemporary papyri, the language of which is close to our translator's, so that he is likely to introduce it in this context of official correspondence and give up the exact representation of the words in his *Vorlage*. Finally, while in 6:21 (5:17) προσφώνειν stands for שלח, in 6:6 (5:5), it again renders an entire phrase, though a different one: יתיבון נשתונא. This seems to prove that, in 2:18, we should consider προσφωνῆσαι as a counterpart of שלחנא והודענא, and not count והודענא as one of the minuses in the original short text.

We also have to reconsider the ultimate use of the rule of *lectio brevior*. Indeed is every shorter text the original text? We should not speak here of cases of haplography, homoioteleuton etc. which are undoubtedly secondary. Nevertheless, a word in reference to these technical omissions is also in order. Klein (pp. 148-162) adduces 47 (!) such cases. This does not really attest to an extremely corrupt state of the text, but rather, it shows the uncritical use of these phenomena by scholars. The larger part of these examples have nothing to do with haplography, homoioteleuton or the like. Thus, I would not define the omission of בית from the phrases במלאכת בית האלהים and עבידת בית אלהא 6:26, 7:15 (Ezr 6:7, 22), as cases of homoioteleuton considering that the phrases מלאכת ה׳ (cf. 2 Chr 26:30) and עבידת אלהא (cf. Ezr 6:18) are perfectly legitimate phrases. Generally speaking, the identification of cases of homoioteleuton – usually used for the omission of passages between similar words or phrases – as a skipping from one letter to a similar one (מלאכת - בית; עבידת בית) produces an inflation of such cases. In other cases collected by Klein in this category, the omitted elements are pleonastic ones, e.g. 8:69 (9:4-5) ראשי האבות לבית אבותם (10:16) 9:16, עד למנחת הערב. ובמנחת הערב. Is it not more plausible to explain the omission on this ground, as opposed to technical mishap?

Let us return to the more fundamental issue of *lectio brevior*. Is it not reasonable that the process of text transmission would include phenomena of reduction alongside expansion? For example, titles such as 'the king' could have been added to the name of the king as easily as omitted, or, similarly, an explicit noun could have been substituted by a pronoun as well as a pronoun expanded by the explicit noun. This is also true for more complicated cases such as 8:52 (8:22); the idea of ועזו ואפו על כל עזביו, not in I Esd, may be a later addition in the MT, but it also may have been omitted in I Esd.

A fine example of a longer text which is probably the original text is that of the introduction of the letter of complaint to Artaxerxes. Klein analyzes this text of 2:15-16 (Ezr 4:6-11) in detail (pp. 140-148) in an attempt to arrive at the original shorter text, yet he does not answer two questions: 1) How can we use I Esd as a witness to the secondary nature of the list of the inhabitants of Samaria (Ezr 4:9 דיניא וארפסתכיא etc.) when I Esd has a remnant of this very list, 2:16 κρίται which reflects דיניא? 2) Realistically, is the well-structured introduction in I Esd to be preferred in comparison with the cluttered double opening in the MT, 2:15 (4:7-8)? In the MT, the first letter is said to have been written by Bishlam, Mitredath and Tabel, the second by Rehum and Shimshai. I Esd combines all the names together as an introduction to the following letter; although, it clearly involves only Rehum and Shimshai, also according to I Esd, 2:21, 25 (4:17, 23). We do not argue that the MT is the original text, but I Esd revises a text already formulated as the MT (see pp. 36-38).

A simpler example would be that of 1:48 (2 Chr 36:15). The MT reads השכם ושלוח whereas I Esd has μετακαλέσαι αὐτούς. The following verse introduces several combined participles (ויהיו מלעבים...) which clearly advance a repeated action, thus advocating the reading of השכם ושלוח which initiates the iterative nature of the passage. The MT's וישלח... השכם ושלוח... ויהיו מלעבים... is, therefore, the original text. The different reading in I Esd resulted from misreading השכם as השבם, followed by the omission of ושלוח. The shorter text, then, is the secondary one. Similarly, 1:10 (2 Chr 35:10); after the king issued his orders regarding the work of the priests and Levites, the MT appropriately concludes with ותכון העבודה ויעמדו הכהנים על עמדם והלוים על מחלקותם כמצות המלך "When the service had been prepared for, the priests stood in their place, and the Levites in their divisions according to the king's command". In I Esd, כמצות was misread as במצות, and המלך was consequently omitted. Again, the longer text is the original one.

Our comments above were orientated towards the evaluation of the shorter text in I Esd, but they also pertain to the evaluation of longer texts in I Esd (Klein's fourth chapter). One wonders why certain expansions are attributed to the translator. Why would it be the translator who gave up the representation of the second verb in 1:46 (2 Chr 36:13) ויקש את ערפו ויאמץ את לבבו; whereas, the omission of the pleonastic והות בטלא in 2:25 (באדין בטלת עבידת בית אלהא... והות בטלא עד... Ezr 4:24) happened in the transmission of the *Vorlage* (p. 85)? Why is it the translator who added a verb before the second object in 1:4 (2 Chr 35:3 עבדו את ה׳ אלהיכם ואת עמו ישראל); whereas, ὁ κατασκηνώσας instead of אשר in 2:5 (Ezr 1:3 הוא האלהים אשר בירושלם) is an addition in the *Vorlage* (pp. 248, 256)? It is not only a matter of disagreement in details since the change in the evaluation of details causes a great shift in their classification. We adduced above the extreme example of many cases of homoioteleuton which have to be distributed in other categories. In this chapter, too, Klein adduces an overloaded category of 70 cases (!) of double translations (pp. 227ff), a third of which belong in other categories.

The starting point for Klein's classification of the many pluses-minuses is indicative of his method. He defines the pluses in the MT as follows: pluses caused by double readings; inclination to add nouns, adjectives and the word כל; elements borrowed from the context; or, on the other hand, omissions through haplography and stylistic omissions (chapter 2). The pluses in I Esd, however, he defines from a completely different angle; in his opinion, these either represent the original text, or are nothing more than double translations or stylistic additions by the translator or (later?) expansions (chapter 4). This classification manifestly shows that Klein *a priori* undertook to reduce the significance of the additions in I Esd as against the additions in the MT; even though, he repeatedly admits the fact that there are no fewer pluses in I Esd than there are in the MT. Moreover, he presents the material for the pluses in I Esd and the MT separately presuming no affinity between the parallel phenomena of expansion. Therefore, he may conclude in a later article (1969) as follows: "In a recent study of the Greek text of I Esdras we argued that it frequently reflected an old, often unexpanded Semitic *Vorlage* despite the many corruptions and secondary expansions peculiar to the 'apocryphal' text". The expansions are thus treated by separate standards: while in the cases where I Esd is shorter, it is the original, unexpanded text; in the cases where I Esd has the longer text, it represents a corrupted text or expansions characteristic of the apocryphal version. Is this, indeed, the case? Is there really such a fundamental difference between the types of expansion in I Esd and the MT? Certainly, there are some expansions characteristic of the apocryphal revision represented in I Esd, but the majority of pluses in I Esd hardly fit this category.

Our case of parallel texts, as reflected in I Esd and the MT, provides an outstanding opportunity to compare parallel processes in the growth of, more or less, the same text which took different routes. Aligning the pluses reflected in I Esd with the pluses in the MT actually demonstrates these parallel processes. In order to clearly demonstrate that the texts underwent similar additions/omissions, a certain classification is needed. It would be rewarding were it possible to classify the additions/omissions in light of the reasons which caused the discrepancy between the texts, e.g., pluses borrowed from similar texts, or from the context, omissions caused by stylistic considerations, or such that are ideologically motivated, or even accidental omissions. However, such classifications would end in a very large number of categories turning the comparison between the texts ineffective. Moreover, such categorizing is necessarily subjective. It involves presumptions such as whether a certain word was omitted or perhaps added, or whether the change was accidental or deliberate. In addition, a survey of the data shows that the majority of pluses, in both I Esd and the MT, simply serve to further define or elucidate the words to which they are added. Such items are best defined in syntactical categories which also have the advantage of an objective classification. We, therefore, adduce the data under headings such as 'adnominals', 'adverbs' etc., thus, demonstrating that the changes in the text of I Esd are not much different from those of the MT. The relation that emerges is hardly that of a later expansionist text, represented by the MT, as against an earlier shorter text, reflected in I Esd, but rather, two texts which absorbed a certain amount of additions and also experienced a number of omissions, whether accidental or deliberate. I Esd presents further changes in line with its characteristic revision.

We endeavor to provide the entire relevant data, so that the relation between the texts is presented in full. In this framework, we cannot but accompany the data with only general notes and evaluations. The pluses in the MT are presented in square brackets. Pluses reflected in I Esd are reproduced in Hebrew or Aramaic. They are set in curly brackets and are underlined in order to emphasize that they are conjectured readings.

a. Function Words

The difference between I Esd and the MT here lies in function-words, which mainly serve as linking words and only little effect the meaning of the text. It seems that I Esd, more than the MT, tends to add function-words, in order to improve the sequence of the text. Further, it is noticeable that in both the MT and I Esd, there are more pluses in the Aramaic material than in the Hebrew;[203] even though, the Hebrew material is by far the more extensive.

---

[203] The MT has 5 cases in the Aramaic material, 2 in the Hebrew; I Esd 9 cases *versus* 5.

Additional function-words in the MT	**Additional function-words in I Esd:**

Additional function-words in the MT

1. 2:18 (Ezr 4:14)

‫[כען] כל קבל די מלח היכלא מלחנא.‬

2. 2:20 (4:16)

‫[לקבל דנה] חלק בעבר נהרה.‬

3. 6:33 (5:3)

‫[וכן] אמרין להון.‬

4. 6:6 (5:5)

‫[ואדין] יתיבון נשתונא.‬

5. 7:2 (6:13)

‫[כנמא] אספרנא עבדו.‬

6. 8:90 (10:3)

‫[ועתה] נכרת ברית.‬

7. 9:14 (10:15)

‫[אך] יונתן... ויחזיה... עמדו.‬

Additional function-words in I Esd:

1. 1:25 (2 Chr 35:21)

‫ו{עתה} אלהים.‬

2. 1:50 (36:17)

‫{כי} הכל נתן בידך.‬

3. 2:19 (Ezr 4:15)

‫{עד} מן יומת עלמא.‬

4. 2:20 (4:16)

‫{וכען} מהודעין.‬

5. 2:21 (4:17)

‫{אדין} פתגמא שלח.‬

6. 6:17 (5:14)

‫{יתוב/תב וי} הנפק המו.[204]‬

7. 6:24 (6:3)

‫בית אלהא {די} בירושלם.‬

8. 6:29 (6:9)

‫{ואף?} חנטין.‬

9. 8:17 (7:19)

‫אלה {די ב}ירושלם.‬

10. 8:20 (7:22)

‫ו{ואף?} עד חנטין.‬

11. 8:44 (8:17)

‫על עדו הראש {די} בכספיא המקום.‬

---

[204] The Greek reads: πάλιν ἐξήνεγκεν αὐτά. The translator may have added πάλιν to make things clearer. In addition, it is difficult to figure out the *Vorlage*.

12. 8:73 (9:7)

מימי אבתינו {כִי}.[205]

13. 8:80 (9:11) {וּכִי?} לאמר

הארץ אשר אתם באים לרשתה.
14. 8:87 (9:15)

הננו {עַתָה} לפניך.

15. 8:87 (9:15)

כי אין לעמוד {עוֹד}.

b. Adnominals

1. Quantifiers

(a) כל

The word כל is frequently left out or added in the process of text-transmission. Although it is a minor element and usually insignificant, it is a good indicator of the parallel development of texts. In our case, there are 11 occurrences of כל in the MT which are not represented in I Esd, and, similarly, 10 cases of a כל probably reflected in I Esd without parallels in the MT. This does not mean that the original text lacked all 21 cases. In the course of textual transmission a trivial element such as כל can either be added or omitted. It should be noted that the additional כל in the MT are expansive by nature; whereas, in I Esd, the כל may have grown out of similar adjacent elements, such as אל and על, in five out of ten cases. Finally, we may ask whether some of the minuses in I Esd are not to be attributed to the translator who is not very attentive where small components are concerned; thus, we do not include cases such as 8:69 (Ezr 9:4) כל חרד

---

[205] The reconstruction is doubtful not only because ὅτι is a conjecture, but also because it is not represented in the B-text. See commentary *ad hoc*.

rendered with ὅσοι ποτὲ ἐπεκινοῦντο, or 2:3 (1:2) כל...הארץ presumably represented by τῆς οἰκουμένης, in a sentence which he chose to paraphrase. Nevertheless, we assume that the cases adduced as pluses in I Esd do indicate the growth of I Esd's *Vorlage*; although, the evidence is not supported by other textual witnesses.

Pluses in the MT	Pluses reflected in I Esd
1. 1:3 (2 Chr 35:3) ל{כל] ישראל.	**1.** 1:30 (2 Chr 35:25) על {כל} ישראל.
2. 1:30 (35:25) [כל] השרים.	**2.** 1:47 (36:14) ככל תעבות {כל} הגוים.
3. 1:47 (36:14) [כל] שרי.	**3.** 5:56 (Ezr 3:9) {כל} הלוים כאחד.
4. 1:52 (36:19) ו[כל] ארמנותיה.[206]	**4.** 5:58 (3:11) על {כל} ישראל.
5. 2:5 (Ezr 1:3) מ[כל] עמו.	**5.** 6:18 (5:15) אל {כל} מאניא.[207]
6. 2:8 (1:6) ו[כל] סביבתיהם.	**6.** 8:7 (7:10) ב{כל} ישראל.
7. 2:23 (4:20) ב[כל] עבר נהרה.	**7.** 8:7 (7:10) {כל} חק ומשפט.
8. 8:13 (7:16) ב[כל] מדינת.	**8.** 8:53 (8:23) על {כל} זאת.
9. 8:19 (7:21) ל[כל] גזבריא.	**9.** 9:3 (10:7) ב{כל} יהודה.
10. 8:50 (8:21) ול[כל] רכושנו.	**10.** 5:49 (3:3) מ{כל} עמי הארצות.[208]
11. 9:4 (10:8) [כל] רכושו.	

[206] The כל is lacking in the LXX as well.

[207] Most LXX-MSS represent כל instead of אל.

[208] The phrase is reflected twice in I Esd, the first time without the כל.

In 1:30, 47, the כל wandered from one phrase to another; similarly it
may wander between elements of the same phrase:

‎.ויהודה ו[כל] ישראל — ו[כל] יהודה וישראל (2 Chr 35:18) 1:19

‎.על מבקשיו ל[כל] טובה — על [כל] מבקשיו לטובה (Ezr 8:22) 8:52

(b) שאר

Out of 11 occurrences of שאר in our material in the MT, 4 are not
represented in I Esd:

1. 2:21 (Ezr 4:17) ‎ו[שאר] כנותהון.

2. 5:54 (3:8) ‎ו[שאר] אחיהם הכהנים.

3. 5:67 (4:3) ‎ו[שאר] ראשי האבות.

4. 8:16 (7:18) ‎ב[שאר] כספא ודהבה.

Only once does שאר appear in I Esd without parallel in the MT:

‎.וישובו לירושלם ו[שאר] יהודה (2:1) 5:8

2. Pronouns

(a) Pronominal suffixes

Considering the divergent linguistic patterns, differences in pronouns
pertain to translation technique rather than to the history of the text. Where
pronouns are indispensable in Semitic languages, they are inessential in
the Greek. Thus, 8:21 (Ezr 7:23) τοῦ βασιλέως καὶ τῶν υἱῶν probably
reflects MT מלכא ובנוהי, even though the pronoun remains unrepresented.
Of course, changes in pronouns may also occur in the original language;
however, I Esd's evidence is more seriously considered when supported
by other textual witnesses, e.g., 8:72 (9:6) כי עוונתינו רבו) למעלה ראש ὑπὲρ
τὰς κεφαλὰς ἡμῶν. In the last analysis, it seems purposeless to collect
the differences regarding pronominal suffixes.

(b) Demonstratives

While I Esd reflects only one additional demonstrative vis-à-vis the MT, the latter clearly has far more cases of demonstratives not represented in I Esd. Except for one (irregular) case in Hebrew, the rest of the cases are in the Aramaic material.

Demonstratives in the MT not represented in I Esd:

1. 2:24 (Ezr 4:21) [דך] וקריתא.

2. 5:41 (2:65) שבעת אלפים [אלה].

3. 6:15 (5:12) סתרה [דנה] וביתה.

4. 6:27 (6:8) [אלך] שבי יהודיא.

5. 6:27 (6:8) [דך] בית אלהא.

6. 7:6 (6:16) [דנה] בית אלהא.

7. 7:7 (6:17) [דנה] בית אלהא.

8. 8:14 (7:17) [דנה] בכספא.

In one case, there is an additional demonstrative in I Esd:
6:18 (5:15) καὶ τὸν ναὸν τοῦ κυρίου τοῦτον οἰκοδομηθῆναι ≈
ובית אלהא {דנה} יתבנא.

(c) Noun / Pronoun

This category is not strictly a matter of pluses/minuses, for the pronoun, rather, replaces the explicit noun or, *vice versa*, is expanded by the explicit noun. I Esd, more than the MT, tends to prefer the pronoun where the noun has already been mentioned.

1. 1:30 (2 Chr 35:25)
MT: על יאשיהו (...על יאשיהו).
I Esd reflects: עליו.

2. 1:49 (36:16)
MT: במלאכי האלהים.
I Esd reflects: במלאכיו (cf. LXX).

5. 8:26 (7:28)
MT: שרי המלך (...לפני המלך).
I Esd reflects: שריו.

6. 1:48 (2 Chr 36:15)
MT: על עמו (...עליהם).
I Esd reflects: עליהם.

3. 1:49 (36:16)

MT: ‏חמת ה׳‎.

I Esd reflects: ‏חמתו‎.

4. 8:25 (Ezr 7:27)

MT: ‏(ברוך ה׳...) את בית ה׳‎.

I Esd reflects: **‏את ביתו‎.**

Since the probability that a prepositional phrase was replaced by a pronoun is not greater than the probability that a pronoun was expanded to make things clearer, it is not possible to decide which variant is the original.

In the following cases where the change is not merely stylistic, it seems that the longer version preserved in the MT is the original one:

8. 8:11 (Ezr 7:14)

MT: ‏(מני שים טעם...) מן קדם מלכא‎.

I Esd reflects: ‏מן קדמי‎.

9. 8:13 (7:15)

MT: ‏די מלכא ויעטהי התנדבו‎.

I Esd ἃ ηὐξάμην ἐγώ τε καὶ οἱ φίλοι may reflect a different text such as ‏די התנדבת אנא ויעטי‎ (cf. the Peshitta). Since the king is the speaker, the reference to the king is replaced by a pronoun in the first person. The official language of the royal letters tends, rather, to explicitly refer to the king, even though, the king is the sender; thus, in the same letter, we read ‏מן בית גנזי מלכא... על מלכות מלכא ובנוהי... ודתא די מלכא‎ (Ezr 7:20, 23, 26; cf. also Ezr 6:8, 10).

10. 8:90 (10:3)

MT: ‏(ויאמר לעזרא...) כעצת אֲדֹנָי‎.

I Esd: ὡς ἐκρίθη σοι ≈ ‏כעצתך‎.

The vocalization that yielded this pronoun is rather: ‏אדֹנִי‎ (cf. LXX).

7. 6:25 (Ezr 6:5)

MT: ‏בבית אלהא‎.

I Esd reflects: ‏תמה‎.

In the following cases the pronoun is represented in the MT whereas I Esd is more explicit:

1. 2:25 (Ezr 4:23)

MT: ‏(אזלו... על יהודיא ובטלו) המו‏.

I Esd: τοὺς οἰκοδομοῦντας ≈ ‏לבניא‏.

2. 6:6 (5:5)

MT: ‏(על שבי יהודיא ולא בטלו) המו‏.

I Esd τῆς οἰκοδομῆς ≈ ‏לבנינא‏ I

In both cases, ‏המו‏ refers to ‏יהודיא/שבי יהודיא‏. Its substitution by 'the builders' or 'the building' changes the content of the pronoun. For this reason, one has to surmise that I Esd offers the secondary variants. Considering that these cases are located one beside the other in the MT, but not in I Esd, one wonders whether the changes had not been made before the material was rearranged to meet the special literary needs of I Esd (see also p. 153).

3. 8:78 (9:9)

MT: ‏(לרומם את בית אלהינו ולהעמיד את) חרבתיו‏.

I Esd rather reflects ‏חרבות ציון‏.

The introduction of the city, beside the Temple, is characteristic of I Esd (see pp. 49ff). Similarly, the Temple is inserted into the complaint letter which, in its original version, spoke of nothing but the building of the city:

4. 2:17 (4:12)

MT: ‏(קריתא... בנין ושוריא שכלילו) ואשיא (יחיטו)‏.

I Esd: καὶ ναὸν ὑποβάλλονται seems to reflect ‏ואשי היכלא‏, presumably replacing a form ‏ואשיה‏ (cf. the additional pronoun in the LXX: καὶ θεμελίους αὐτῆς).[209]

---

[209] It may, of course, be a case of interchange between a simple noun and a construct, cf. 5:51 (Ezr 3:5) MT: ‏מועדי ה׳‏, I Esd simply reflects ‏המועדים‏; 9:16 (10:16) MT: ‏ראשי האבות‏, I Esd has only an equivalent for ‏ראשים‏.

In sum, the pluses reflected in I Esd are later expansions probably connected with the book's special revision. Some of the minuses in I Esd, those which are not merely stylistic, also seem to be secondary. Where stylistic interchanges are concerned, there is no way to decide which variant is to be preferred.

(d) Appositions

Appositions, *per definitionem* components which do not change either the meaning or the structure of a text, are liable to be one of the elements which form the gap between longer and shorter texts. A writer who is more expansive in his writing will tend to use appositions frequently; whereas, a more concise writer will give them up. First, we adduce the titles which often serve as appositions in our text, such as 'king', 'prophet', and 'priest'.

Additional appositions in the MT	Additional appositions in I Esd
1. 1:43 (2 Chr 36:10)	**1.** 6:33 (Ezr 6:12)
נבוכדנאצר [המלך].	. אנא דריוש {מלכא}
2. 5:68 (Ezr 4:3)	**2.** 1:30 (2 Chr 35:25)
כורש מלך פרס [המלך].	. ירמיהו {הנביא}
3. 5:70 (4:5)	
ועד מלכות דריוש [מלך פרס].	
4. 6:7 (5:6) [מלכא] לדריוש.	
5. 6:1 (5:1)	**3.** 7:3 (Ezr 6:14)
חגי [נביא] וזכריה בר עדו נבייא.	. בנבואת חגי וזכריה בר עדוא {נבייא}
6. 7:3 (6:14)	
בנבואת חגי [נביה] וזכריה בר עדוא.	

7. 8:3 (7:11)

.לעזרא הכהן [הספר] ספר

8. 9:7 (10:10)

.עזרא [הכהן]

4. 9:39 (Neh 8:1)

.לעזרא {הכהן} והספר

5. 9:42 (Neh 8:4)

.עזרא {הכהן} וספר

In some of the cases in which the title is not represented in I Esd the MT is indeed pleonastic, thus, (2) המלך כורש מלך פרס; (3) ועד מלכות דריוש. Indeed, regarding לעזרא הספר ספר... (7); חגי נביא וזכריה... נבייא (5); מלך פרס. Indeed, regarding cases (2) and (3) other translations also leave out the title.

Proper names are added in the following cases, mostly in I Esd:

6. 1:32 (2 Chr 36:1) אביו {יאשיהו}.

7. 6:24 (Ezr 6:4) מלכא {כורש} מן בית .[210]

9. 7:3 (6:14) [בר עדוא] וזכריה.

8. 5:56 (3:8) {אחיו} קדמיאל {ו}.

10. 9:49 (Neh 8:9) התרשתא [הוא נחמיה].

9. 5:40 (2:63) התרשתא {ז!?}{נחמיה}.

The identification of the Tirshata as Nehemiah in the MT, on the one hand, and in I Esd, on the other, may have wider implications than the categories referred to here and should possibly be explained on other grounds than the natural growth of the texts (see note 14).

Other appositions, not connected with private names, may have been added or omitted for different reasons and they are not all of the same importance to the understanding of the growth of the text. We are mostly dealing with stylistic alternatives which are part of the natural course of a transmitted text.

11. 1:51 (2 Chr 36:18)

בבל הביא [הכל] ...כלי כל.

10. 8:56 (8:27)

עשר שנים {כלים} ...נחשת וכלי.

---

[210] The addition of the name seems to be secondary since the text means to say that the expenses are on the royal treasury, not specifically on King Cyrus.

12. 2:14 (Ezr 1:12)

.וכל כלים... [הכל] העלה

13. 8:63 (8:35)

הבאים מהשבי [בני הגולה].

14. 1:7 (2 Chr 35:7)

[צאן] כבשים ובני עזים.[211]

15. 9:48 (Neh 8:8)

[בספר] בתורת האלהים.

16. 1:44 (2 Chr 36:10)

צדקיהו [אחיו].[213]

11. 7:10 (6:19)

.ויעשו [בני ישראל] בני הגולה

12. 1:1 (2 Chr 35:1)

.בארבעה עשר [יום] לחדש

13-15. 8:47, 54 (Ezr 8:19, 24)

אחיו ובניהם עשרים [הזכרים].[212]

16. 5:8 (2:2)

.זרבבל וישוע... [ראשיהם]

17. 5:36 (2:59)

[ראשם] כרוב.[214]

18-19. 1:12-13 (2 Chr 35:14)

ולכהנים [אחיהם].[215]

20. 5:56 (Ezr 3:9) וקדמיאל [אחיו].[216]

21-27. 2:16-18, 20 (4:11-12, 14, 16),

6:8, 20-21 (5:8, 17) מלכא [מראן(נ)א].

---

[211] This may involve more than a mere apposition.

[212] This accords with the rest of the list.

[213] Note 2 Kgs 24:19 וימלך מלך בבל את מתניה דדו תחתיו.

[214] I Esd repeatedly emphasizes the leadership of the mentioned figures; in 5:8 (Ezr 2:2) it is specified again, when, against the MT מספר אנשי עם ישראל, I Esd probably reflects: מספר אנשי העם [וראשיהם].

[215] It may be an addition in I Esd, where the relationship between the priests and Levites is slightly revised, see pp. 175-176. The designation בני אהרן may also have caused the addition.

[216] The verse has many textual problems and the addition/omission may be one of them.

The last case mentions seven times in which the title of the king (מלכא) is expanded in I Esd (e.g., κύριε βασιλεῦ). It is, therefore, a somewhat different case from the regular line of appositions. The expansion occurs in two different parts of I Esd (though not necessarily so in the arrangement of the material according to the MT; see also p. 149). It is also worth mentioning that the expanded title also occurs in the epilogue to the Story of the Youths, 4:46, a fact that may connect the expansion with the layer of revision characteristic of the apocryphal book. At any rate, it is a rather systematic change wherever the King of Persia is addressed by his servants. One cannot be absolutely sure whether the change was indeed made in the *Vorlage* or should be attributed to the translator, considering that it is a regular appellation of gods and kings in contemporary Greek papyri. While the translator is sensitive to 'royal language', he is hardly expected to add such elements repeatedly. Indeed, the title is no less expected in Aramaic, cf. Dan 4:21 (RSV 4:24) (כת: דנה פשרא מלכא וגזרת עלאה היא דמטת על מרי) מראי) מלכא "this is the interpretation, O king: It is a decree of the Most High, which has come upon my lord the king" (see also Dan 4:16). It is a common sight in Imperial Aramaic, e.g., Cowley 16, line 8 קדם מראי שלחת לאמר "I before my lord I have sent saying", regularly in addressing Arsham; see also Cowley 30, line 1: אל מראן בגוהי פחת יהוד "To our Lord Bigvai, governor of Judaea". It seems more likely that the title was added in I Esd's *Vorlage* than omitted in the MT.

(e) Construct State

One way to define the significance of a word more clearly is to turn it into a construct by appending either a *nomen rectum* or a *nomen regens*. Usually, the annexed elements neither add new aspects to the word nor substantially change its meaning.

(1) *Nomen rectum*

Pluses in the MT	Pluses reflected in I Esd

Pluses in the MT

1. 1:7 (2 Chr 35:7)

ל[בני] העם.

2. 5:28 (Ezr 2:42)

[בני] השערים.

3. 1:51 (2 Chr 36:18)

ואצרות [בית] ה׳.

4. 5:56 (Ezr 3:8)

מלאכת [בית] ה׳.

5. 7:15 (6:22)

במלאכת [בית] האלהים.

6. 8:15 (7:17)

על מדבחה די [בית] אלהכם.

7. 8:21 (7:23)

יתעבד אדרזדא ל[בית] אלהא.

8. 9:52 (Neh 8:9)

כי [חדות] ה׳ היא מעזכם.

9. 1:43 (2 Chr 36:10)

כלי [חמדת] בית ה׳.

Pluses reflected in I Esd

1. 1:30 (2 Chr 35:25)

לחק על כל {זרע} ישראל.

2. 2:7 (Ezr 1:5)

ל{שבט} יהודה ובנימן.

3. 5:63 (4:1)

צרי {שבט} יהודה ובנימן.

4. 9:5 (10:9)

אנשי {שבט} יהודה ובנימן.

5. 6:16 (5:13)

די {מדינת} בבל.

6. 8:76 (9:8)

להאיר עינינו {בבית} אלהינו.

7. 1:46 (2 Chr 36:13)

השביעו ב{שם} אלהינו.

8. 1:46 (36:13)

משוב אל {תורת?} ה׳.[217]

9. 1:45 (36:12)

מלפני {דברי} ירמיהו.

---

[217] The expansion here may be attributed to the translator, who may have had to add τὰ νόμιμα after using his favorite verb παραβαίνειν.

10. 8:55 (Ezr 8:25)

הכלים [תרומת] בית אלהינו.

10. 5:70 (Ezr 4:5)

כל ימי {חיי} כורש.

11. 6:4 (5:4)

מן אנון [שמהת] גבריא.[218]

11. 6:14 (5:12)

מלך בבל {מלך} כסדאה.[219]

12. 7:5 (6:15) ל[מלכות] דריוש מלך פרס.

13. 8:59 (8:30) וקבלו... [משקל] הכסף והזהב.

14. 9:39 (Neh 8:1) להביא את [ספר] תורת משה.

15. 9:41 (Neh 8:3) אל [ספר] התורה.

16. 9:50 (Neh 8:9) את [דברי] התורה.

The additional elements do not have much in common; only a few may be grouped together. Thus, some specify the members of the collective noun (זרע ישראל, מדינת בבל, שבט, בני העם, בני השערים), others its character (יהודה ובנימן).[220] The divine name is repeatedly expanded, probably in order to avoid phrases directly linked to God (בית הי/אלהים, שם אלהים). The repeated creation of the phrase [בית] הי/האלהים 'the house of God' in the MT apparently breaks the balance between the two texts; otherwise, there seems to be no fundamental difference in the development of the parallel texts in respect to the creation of constructs.

---

[218] One would not expect שמהת near מן which refers to גבריא.

[219] While the MT refers to the Chaldean (adj.) king of Babylon, I Esd speaks of the king of Babylon, the king of the Chaldeans (noun; see the *Ketiv*: כסדיה).

[220] I Esd's repeated additional 'tribe' seems out of place, introducing, like other apocryphal books, tribal terminology into a period in which it was defunct. Note that I Esd traces Zerubbabel's descent to the tribe of Judah in the Story of the Three Youths, 5:3.

(2) Genitival Attributes

Pluses in the MT	**Pluses reflected in I Esd**
1. 1:3 (2 Chr 35:3) [ישראל] מלך.	**1.** 2:12 (Ezr 2:12) {כְּסֶף} מחלפים.
2. 5:43 (Ezr 2:68) [האלהים] בית.	**2.** 6:22 (6:1) בבית ספריא די גנזיא {דִי מַלְכָּא}.
3. 5:62 (3:13) [השמחה] קול תרועת.	**3.** 8:17 (7:19) {דִי בֵית אֱלָהָא} ומאניא.
4. 5:70 (4:5) [פרס] כורש מלך.	**4.** 9:42 (Neh 8:4) {הַתּוֹרָה} ספר.
5. 6:17 (5:14) [די בבל] להיכלא.	**5.** 9:45 (Neh 8:5) {הַתּוֹרָה} ה[ספר {אֶת}.
6. 8:69 (9:4) [הגולה] על מעל.	**6.** 9:48 (Neh 8:7) {הֵן} לתור[ה][ת].

In two cases, an internal-construct (*figura etymologica*) disappears from I Esd through the omission of either the *nomen regens* or the *nomen rectum*:

7. 5:40 (2:63) הקדשים [קדש]מ.

8. 8:9 (7:2) [מלכיא] מלך ארתחשסתא.

Some of the expansions may have been induced by the context, for example, {כְּסֶף} מחלפים, תרועת [השמחה], מעל [הגולה], others yield common phrases, such as {דִי בֵית אֱלָהָא} מאניא, בית [האלהים], מלך [ישראל]. The pattern of parallel expansion of the text becomes obvious with a case such as the repeated creation of the phrase ספר התורה, which occurs twice in I Esd with the addition of התורה, and twice in the MT with the addition of ספר (see above, under the additions of the *nomen rectum*).

(f) Relative Clauses

The *nomen* may be more expressly defined by supplemental relative clauses. These usually add little to the meaning of the text. In addition, their detached position in the sentence turns them into elements which are easily added or omitted.

Pluses in the MT	**Pluses reflected in I Esd**
1. 2:15 (Ezr 4:11)	**1.** 1:31 (2 Chr 35:26)
‏פרשגן אגרתא [די שלחו עלוהי].‏	‏דברי יאשיהו {אשר עשה}.‏
2. 8:55 (8:25)	**2.** 1:45 (36:12)
‏וכל ישראל [הנמצאים].‏	‏דברי ירמיהו {אשר דבר} מפי ה׳.‏
3. 8:13 (7:15)	**3.** 2:15 (Ezr 4:7)
‏לאלה... [די בירושלם משכנה].‏[221]	‏כנותיו {די יתבין בשמרין}.‏
	4. 2:19 (4:15)
	‏בספר דכרניא {די כתב על דנה}.‏
	5. 5:53 (3:7)
	‏כרשיון {אשר כתב עליהם} כורש.‏

And some shortened relative clauses:

‏בית אלהך {די בירושלם}.‏ **4.** 8:23 (7:25)   **6.** 8:17 (7:19) ‏כחכמת אלהך [די בידך].‏

‏ולטפנו {אשר עמנו}.‏ **7.** 8:50 (8:21)

‏נשינו {אשר מעמי הארצות}.‏[222] **8.** 8:90 (10:3)

---

[221] I Esd simply reflects ‏לירושלם‏ instead of the relative clause.

[222] Assuming that τὰς ἐκ τῶν ἀλλογενῶν is a defective rendering of ‏עמי הארצות‏ (usually translated as τὰ ἀλλογενῆ ἔθνη τῆς γῆς). It may, however, reflect ‏הנכריות‏, as attested by the Lucianic MSS in the LXX (although it will, again, be an unusual equivalent).

In all, there are only a few cases of additional relative clauses; nevertheless, I Esd seems to be more expansive in this regard than the MT.

(g) Varia

Pluses in the MT   **Pluses reflected in I Esd**

1. 1:7 (2 Chr 35:7)   **1.** 9:11 (Ezr 10:13)

[למספר] שלשים אלף.   .והמלאכה {עלינו} לא ליום אחד

2. 5:50 (Ezr 3:4) [במספר] ויום ביום ועלת.

3. 9:16 (10:16) [לבית אבתם] אנשים ראשי האבות.

Surprisingly, there is only one case of an additional attributive adjective:

4. 8:26 (7:26) [הגברים] שרי המלך   **2.** 1:34 (2 Chr 36:3) {אחד} וככר זהב

c. Verbal Complements

Similar to the adnominals, the verbal complements too are a main factor in the growth of the text; they serve to better define the limits of the verb.

1. Objects

The additional objects either derive from the context, or are strictly internal objects, or merely retrospective pronouns.

Pluses in the MT	**Pluses reflected in I Esd**

Pluses in the MT

1. 1:23 (2 Chr 35:23)

הכין יאשיהו [את הבית].[223]

2. 1:48 (36:15)

וישלח ה׳... [עליהם].

3. 2:25 (Ezr 4:23)

אזלו... [על יהודיא].

4. 5:49 (3:8)

ויכינו המזבח... ויעלו [עליו].

5. 5:69 (4:4)

עם יהודה ומבהלים [אותם].

6. 6:18 (5:15)

אל מאניא שא... אחת [המו].

7. 6:29 (6:9)

כמאמר כהניא... להוא מתיהב [להם].

8. 7:13 (6:21)

בני ישראל... וכל הנבדל... [אלהם].

9. 9:41 (Neh 8:3)

ויקרא [בו].

10. 9:48 (Neh 8:7)

מבינים [את העם].

11. 6:23 (Ezr 6:3)

אתר די דבחין [דבחין]

Pluses reflected in I Esd

1. 1:6 (2 Chr 35:6)

לעשות {את הפסח}.

2. 1:8 (35:8)

נתנו לפסחים {צאן}... ובקר.

3. 1:9 (35:9)

הרימו לפסחים {צאן}... ובקר.[224]

4. 1:27 (35:22)

נכו... ויבא להלחם {בו}.

5. 1:33 (36:3)

ויסירהו... {ממלך} בירושלם.[225]

6. 1:35 (36:4)

וימלך... {מלך} על יהודה.

7. 6:11 (Ezr 5:10)

להודעותך די נכתב {לך}.

8. 8:58 (8:29)

עד תשקלו {אותם}.

9. 9:40 (Neh 8:2)

לשמע {את התורה}.

10. 9:46 (Neh 8:5)

וכפתחו {את התורה}.

11. 9:54 (Neh 8:12)

ולשלח מנות {לאין נכון לו}.

---

[223] The omission here may have been induced by general issues of composition; see pp. 14-15.

[224] The addition of צאן in vv. 8-9 effaces the distinction intended by the MT.

[225] The text is in fact defective without ממלך, which is attested in the parallel text of 2 Kgs 23:33.

2. Adverbs

Pluses in the MT	Pluses reflected in I Esd

1. 1:7 (2 Chr 35:7)

.ויֵרם... [לפסחים]

2. 1:39 (36:7)

.הביא... [לבבל]

3. 1:44 (36:11)

.מלך [בירושלם]

4. 2:22 (Ezr 4:18)

.[מפרש] קרי קדמי

5. 5:50 (3:4)

.ויעשו... [דבר יום ביומו]

6. 5:56 (3:8)

.מבן... [ומעלה]

7. 5:60 (3:12)

.ראו... [בעיניהם]

8. 6:20 (5:17)

.יתבקר... [תמה]

9. 6:22 (6:1)

.מהחתין [תמה]

1. 1:5 (2 Chr 35:5)

.ועמדו... {יַעל עֻמדכם?}

2. 1:28 (35:23)

.העבירוני {מן המערכה}

3. 1:28 (35:24)

.ויעבירוהו {מהרה}

4. 5:40 (Ezr 2:63)

.עד עמוד כהן {?לבוש?}

5. 5:49 (3:3)

.עלות {למועד}

6. 5:50 (3:4)

.ככתוב {בתורה}

7. 6:29 (6:9)

.תהוא מתיהבא... {תמיד שנה בשנה}

8. 6:33 (6:12)

.{כדנה} יתעבד

9-10. 8:13 (7:16)

.די תהשכח... {לאלה לירושלם}

10. 7:6 (6:16)

.ועבדו... [בחדוה]

11. 8:70 (9:5) עד למנחת הערב. ו[במנחת הערב] קמתי.

12. 9:13 (10:14)

.ו[עמהם] זקני עיר ועיר

13. 9:48 (Neh 8:7) והעם [על עמדם].

14. 7:14 (Ezr 6:22)

.[בשמחה] כי שמחם ה׳

15. 8:76 (9:9)

.[כי עבדים אנחנו] ובעבדתנו

Some of the additional adverbs endow the text with a special meaning or atmosphere (e.g., מפרש, בחדוה) and are not expected to be left out or added casually. In the majority of cases, however, they are dispensable, repeating or expanding other elements in the text.

d. Subjects and Predicates

Similar to the subordinate elements adduced above, the texts also differ in subjects and predicates, but, again, without changing anything fundamental in the meaning of the text.

Pluses in the MT	Pluses reflected in I Esd
1. 1:46 (2 Chr 36:13)	**1.** 1:4 (2 Chr 35:3)
עבדו את ה׳ אלהיכם	ויקש את ערפו
{ושרתו} את עמו ישראל.	[ויאמץ] את לבבו.

The similarity between these two cases is striking. Nevertheless, the case of ויאמץ is merely stylistic, and may be either an addition or an omission; whereas, ושרתו seems to be an ideological addition meant to distinguish between serving the people and worshipping God.

2. 2:25 (Ezr 4:24) [והות בטלא] ...בטלת. **2.** 1:23 (35:20) להלחם {בבאו} ...עלה.

3. 5:56 (3:8) על מלאכת [לנצח] ...ויעמידו. **3.** 2:25 (Ezr 4:23) לבטלא {ושרין}.

4. 8:49 (8:21)	**4.** 5:57 (3:10)
ואקרא שם צום ...[להתענות].	להלל את ה׳ {ולהדות}.
5. 8:71 (9:6)	**5.** 6:12 (5:11)
בשתי... [להרים]... פני אליך.	שמיא וארעא {עבד} אלה.
6. 5:41 (2:65)	**6.** 6:15 (5:12)
[ולהם] משררים ומשררות.	וביתה דנה סתרו {ושרפו}.

7. 2:19 (4:15)

קריתא דך [קריא] מרדא.

7. 8:1 (7:1)

ואחר הדברים האלה... {עלה} עזרא.

8. 9:54 (8:12)

לאכל ולשתות {ולשמוח}.

Some of the additional verbs are synonyms to verbs already in the text (ולהדות... להלל); others are auxiliary verbs (ושריו) or complementary ones (להתענות). They derive from the context or answer the needs of the context (עלה עזרא), or they form a known phrase (...לנצח על מלאכת). Some may be either additions or omissions, others are better explained as intentional additions (e.g., עבד, שרפו).

While the following elements serve as subjects, they are nevertheless dispensable, being as they are repetitive or a substitute for an impersonal subject.

Pluses in the MT

Pluses reflected in I Esd

1. 2:12 (Ezr 1:10)

כפורי... [כפורי].

1. 2:19 (Ezr 4:15)

ו.{יהודיא} מרד ואשתדור עבדין.

2. 5:56 (3:1)

ובני ישראל... ויאספו [העם].

2. 2:23 (4:19)

ו.{גבריא} מרד ואשתדור...

3. 6:23 (6:3)

בית אלהא... [ביתא] יתבנא.

3. 6:9 (5:8)

ומצלח {עבדא?} בידהם.

4. 7:3 (6:14)

ומצלח[ין][ה] {עבידת בית אלהא}.

The pluses in the MT vis-à-vis I Esd are all repetitive. The pluses reflected in I Esd serve to clarify the subject; the first two examples are of the same sort and so are the last two.

e. Independent Components

Pluses in the MT

1. 2:21 (Ezr 4:17) ‏[שלם] וכעת.

2. 8:71 (9:6) ‏להרים [אלהי] פני אליך.

f. Multiple Parts

While the following additions/omissions belong to different syntactic categories, they all form a component of a multiple part.

Pluses in the MT	**Pluses reflected in I Esd**
1. 1:13 (2 Chr 35:14)	**1.** 2:19 (Ezr 4:15)
‏בהעלות [העולה ו]החלבים.	‏{ומרד} ואשתדור עבדין.[226]
2. 5:45 (Ezr 2:17)	**2.** 5:51 (3:5)
‏והמשררים והשוערים [והנתינים].	‏עלת תמיד {ועלת לשבתות} ולחדשים.
3. 8:8 (7:11)	**3.** 5:57 (3:10)
‏מצות ה׳ [וחקיו על ישראל].	‏מלבשים {בשירים} ובחצצרות.[227]
4. 8:13 (7:16)	**4.** 5:65 (4:2)
‏התנדבות עמא [וכהניא].	‏ויגשו אל זרבבל {וישוע}.[228]
5. 8:61 (8:33)	**5.** 6:13 (5:11)
‏הכסף והזהב [והכלים].[229]	‏ומלך לישראל רב {ותקיף}.

---

[226] Cf. 2:23 (Ezr 4:19).

[227] ‏בשירים could easily have been created or lost near ‏מלבשים.

[228] Cf. 5:67 (Ezr 4:3).

[229] Cf. 8:59 (Ezr 8:30).

6. 8:66 (9:1)

היבוסי [העמני] המאבי.

7. 9:37 (Neh 7:72)

הכהנים והלוים [והשוערים
והמשררים... והנתינים וכל ישראל].

6. 6:17 (5:14)

ויהיבו [לזרובבל ו]ששבצר.[230]

7. 8:66 (9:1)

ישראל [והשרים] והכהנים והלוים.

8. 8:74 (9:7)

ובעונתינו [ובעונות אבותינו].[231]

Although most of the elements gathered here add a new aspect to the text, it is difficult to decide whether they are omissions or additions. The text may have been extended by influence of the context or of stereotyped lists of items.

g. Divine Names

The discrepancy between the parallel texts in regard to the divine names is similar to that of other categories. Here, too, there is a balance of extra elements in both texts (around a dozen cases in each of them). Most changes remain within the regular process of text transmission (e.g., ה׳ turns into ה׳ אלהים or *vice versa*). One change, however, is peculiar to I Esd: the author is obviously reluctant to represent the phrase אלה שמיא, reformulating it or omitting שמיא altogether (see pp. 265-266). It is a complicated task to decide the part of the translator in these changes. Thus, he uses κύριος where either the Hebrew or Aramaic would take only אלהים/אלהא. Consequently, one wonders, for example, whether I Esd s κύριος Ἰσραήλ reflects a text other than MT s ה׳ אלהי ישראל (see p. 267). Finally, there are also interchanges within the Greek tradition to be taken into consideration.

---

[230] The addition of Zerubbabel is certainly due to later revision; see pp. 52-54.

[231] I Esd καὶ διὰ τὰς ἁμαρτίας ἡμῶν καὶ τῶν πατέρων ἡμῶν does not actually reflect ובעונות, but there is no other way to reconstruct the Hebrew.

h. Name Lists

The changes in name lists are caused either by accidental corruption or by well-planned revision. In the list of returnees, 5:7-40 (Ezr 2:1-63), there are far more names lacking in the MT than in I Esd. While in the MT 21 names or groups of names (מבני + name + number) are lacking, in I Esd only 10 names are not represented. Many of the additional names in I Esd concentrate at two points: in the list of 5:15-16 (2:16) ≅ five groups, and at the end of the list of Nethinim, 5:34 (2:57) ≅ 8 groups. The stereotyped structure of the list may have caused the omission of entire groups of names through homoioteleuton.

In the list of those returning with Ezra, 8:28-43 (Ezr 8:1-16) there are two names lacking in I Esd as compared with the MT, and *vice versa*. I Esd seems to preserve the original text all along. The pluses in the MT are obviously doublets: [ולייריב ולאלנתן] ...וליריב ולאלנתן, 8:43 (8:16). As for the pluses reflected in I Esd, one of the names lacking must have fallen out from the MT through haplography, {בניה} ומבני, 8:36 (8:10). The structure of the list proves that the second name, too, fell out by accident; although, the reason is not quite clear, {זתוא} מבני, 8:32 (8:5).

In the list of those who married foreign women, 9:19-35 (10:18-43), there are 14 names missing from I Esd as compared with the MT; whereas, only 2 names which appear in I Esd are not represented in the MT. The names not represented in I Esd are random and there is no clue to explaining the discrepancy, either technical or intentional.

i. Additional Phrases and Sentences

Unlike the material gathered above, the following passages could not have been casually added or omitted, since most of the cases concern more than a random word or phrase. Unless the passages concerned were repeated or omitted by mistake, there should be a good reason as to why they were added or omitted. Some of the passages are longer than the others, and some are more significant than the others. Some are repetitive, while others add new information.

Pluses in the MT

1. 1:7 (2 Chr 35:7) ‏[הכל לפסחים] צאן... וירם יאשיהו.‏

The additional words serve as some sort of a summary.

2. 1:40 (36:8) ‏הנם כתבים... [והנמצא עליו] ויתר דברי...‏[232]

3. 2:18 (Ezr 4:13) ‏די [כען ידיע להוא למלכא] מלכא... וכענת ידיע להוא ל.‏

4. 6:4 (5:4) ‏[אדין כנמא אמרנא להם]... וכן אמרין להם.‏

5. 6:7 (5:7) ‏[פתגמא שלחו עלוהי וכדנה] על דריוש... פרשגן אגרתא די שלח תתני...‏
‏[כתיב בגוה.‏

6. 9:51 (Neh 8:10) ‏[ויאמר להם]... ויאמר נחמיה.‏

7. 8:6 (Ezr 7:8)
‏[ויבא ירושלם] בחדש החמישי... ובאחד לחדש החמישי בא אל ירושלם‏[233]

8. 8:52 (8:22)
‏[ועזו ואפו על כל עזביו] יד אלהינו על כל מבקשיו לטובה.‏[234]

9. 8:56 (8:27) ‏[לאדרכנים אלף] וכפרי זהב עשרים.‏

---

[232] The additional element disturbs the formula and has no substantial contribution to the text.

[233] The text in I Esd, without a counterpart for ‏ויבא ירושלם‏, remains awkward since the year is repeated without any reason: καὶ συνανέβησαν ἐκ τῶν υἱῶν Ἰσραήλ... ἔτους ἑβδόμου βασιλεύοντος Ἀρταξέρξου ἐν τῷ πέμπτῳ μηνί (οὗτος ἐνιαυτὸς ἕβδομος τῷ βασιλεῖ).

[234] The idea of the fate of those who forsake God does not quite fit the context. It is not impossible, however, that it was left out on second thoughts.

10. 8:80 (9:11) [מפה אל פה בטמאתם] בתועבתיהם אשר מלאוה.

11. 8:90 (10:3) [וכתורה יעשה] והחרדים במצות אלהינו.[235]

12. 9:48 (Neh 8:8) [מפרש ושום שכל] ויקראו... בתורת האלהים.

13. 9:50 (Neh 8:9)

היום קדש הוא לה׳ אלהיכם [אל תתאבלו ואל תבכו] כי בוכים...[236]

14. 2:15-16 (Ezr 4:6-11) Considerable parts of the MT are not represented in I Esd. The omission seems to be part of the reformulation connected with the transposition of the entire letter of complaint (see pp. 36-38).

In some cases in which the MT has a longer text in comparison with I Esd, it seems that the omission occurred through homoioteleuton; these cases do not strictly belong with the material adduced here since they are not concerned with the evolution of the texts, either by expansion or reduction, but rather with a mistake somewhere in the process of transmission. Since our assumption as to the reason behind the difference between the texts may not be the right one, we mention them here:

1. 1:10 (2 Chr 35:11) [וישחטו הפסח ויזרקו הכהנים] על מחלקותם כמצות המלך...
למפלגות [מידם והלוים מפשיטים. ויסירו העלה לתתם...

Since the words כמצות המלך are not represented in I Esd at this point, one may consider an homoioteleuton מחלקותם/לתתם. Without the omitted words the account does not mention the actual slaughtering of the Passover sacrifice (וישחטו הפסח). It is not impossible, however, that the detailed rite was added or omitted by intention.

---

[235] I Esd καὶ ὅσοι πειθαρχοῦσιν τῷ νόμῳ τοῦ κυρίου seems to reflect והחרדים בתורת אלהינו.

[236] The text is not clear without these words.

2. 1:37 (36:5) ‏[במלכו [ואחת עשרה שנה מלך]...

While the formulas are often reformulated in I Esd, probably by the translator, this seems to be a case of homoioteleuton since the information omitted is indispensable.

3. 8:20 (Ezr 7:22) ‏[ועד חמר בתין מאה [ועד בתין משח מאה].

These words must have fallen out through homoioteleuton; cf. Ezr 6:9.

Pluses reflected in I Esd:

1. 2:18 (Ezr 4:15) ‏[שלחנא... ל... מלכא די [הן עלך טב] יבקר...

The phrase occurs in the similar context of Ezr 5:17.

2. 5:53 (3:7) ‏[להביא מן הלבנון עצי ארזים [להעביר רפסדות] אל ים יפוא.

Probably borrowed from 2 Chr 2:15.

3. 5:55 (3:8)

‏[ויסדו את היכל האלהים באחד לחדש השני בשנה השנית בבואם ליהודה וירושלם].

This text may have fallen out of the MT through homoioteleuton ‏ירושלם-ירושלם; however, it does not say anything not said in the context.

4. 5:63 (4:1) ‏והקול נשמע עד למרחוק וישמעו צרי... יהודה

‏[ויבאו לדעת מה קול התרועה] וידעו כי...

I Esd supplies a nice literary transition. There is no obvious reason why it would have been omitted.

5. 5:70, 6:1 (Ezr 4:5, 5:1) ‏[וישביתו המלאכה שנים ‏להפר עצתם כל ימי... כורש...

‏שתים] עד מלכות דריוש... [ובשנת תרתין למלכות דריוש] התבני...

In I Esd' sequence of events, the date provided by Ezr 4:24 disappears and is supplied here – twice.

6. 6:8 (5:8)   די אזלנא ליהוד מדינתא {ואתינא לירושלם קריתא והשכחנא לשבי יהודיא בירושלם קריתא}

The words שביא אלך in the following verse seem to presuppose this additional verse. It must have fallen out from the MT.

7. 6:26 (6:6)   {ושם טעם ?אספרנא יתעבד?}.

A link between the quotation of the words of Cyrus and the words of Darius is indeed needed, but these additional words hardly serve as such. Cf. also the following case.

8. 6:27 (6:8)   ומני שים טעם {אספרנא יתעבד וזהירין הוו?}.

It is difficult to reconstruct the *Vorlage*; even though, it is clear that the addition uses official language.

9. 7:9 (6:18)   והקימו כהניא... ולויא... ככתב ספר משה {ותרעיא לתרעא ותרעא}.

10. 8:69 (9:4)   ואלי יאספו כל חרד בדברי אלהי ישראל {ואני מתאבל} על מעל הגולה.

11. 1:21-22 (2 Chr 35:19) I Esd presents a large addition over the MT, probably a late expansion connected with the composition of the apocryphal book (see pp. 15-21).

In the following case, there is a possibility of an accidental omission in the MT:

7:11 (6:20)   כי הטהרו הכהנים והלוים כאחד {וכל בני הגולה לא הטהרו כי הלוים כאחד} כלם טהורים.

The additional words probably fell out in the MT through homoioteleuton, as suggested by the context (see also no. 3 above).

The accidental omissions (through homoioteleuton), on the one hand, and the additions which are clearly part of the later revision characteristic of I Esd, on the other, are only a marginal segment in the material of pluses/minuses. Even if the text has a long history, there is no basis to Klein's theory that it suffered such a large number of accidental omissions.

Similarly, although I Esd is clearly a revision, the traces of this peculiar revision are evident only in a very limited number of cases. The majority of additions/omissions adduced here do not but attest the process of regular text transmission, as reflected in other parts of the material, which comprise a discrepancy between the MT and I Esd's *Vorlage*.

j. Double Readings

As opposed to double translations, double readings pertain to the history of the text, although the border between the two phenomena is not clear-cut.[237] For example, the double representation of a word such as שבי (יהודיא) in I Esd, as once with a *shin* and once with a *śin*, is recorded as a double translation since there is no way to represent it in the *Vorlage*. On the other hand, when the doublet is caused by a difference in one letter, we tend to attribute it to the *Vorlage*, although it may as easily be a double translation again.[238]

Such are the following cases:

1. 2:17 (Ezr 4:12) ושוריא paralleled by τάς τε ἀγορὰς αὐτῆς καὶ τὰ τείχη, possibly ≈ ‏{ושוקיה?} ושוריה.

2-3. 6:24 (6:4) ונדבך די אע חדת paralleled by καὶ δόμου ἐγχωρίου καινοῦ ἑνός, possibly ≈ ‏{חדא} חדת ‏{?די ארעא} ונדבך די אע.[239]

It is more characteristic of double readings, as opposed to double translations, that there is little difference between the repeated words or passages. Thus, in the following cases the doublet does not convey two different things; rather, it conveys the same thing in two different places or ways. Sometimes the doublet, though repetitive, is a reformulation of its counterpart, or introduces a new element:

---

[237] See Talmon (1960), pp. 144-184; (1961), pp. 335-383.

[238] See pp. 238ff.

[239] On another possible double reading (הגולה/הגדול) see 9:2 (Ezr 10:6).

4. 7:8 (6:17)

MT: על כל ישראל <u>תרי עשר</u> למנין שבטי ישראל

I Esd παντὸς τοῦ Ἰσραηλ <u>δώδεκα</u> πρὸς ἀριθμὸν ἐκ τῶν φυλάρχων τοῦ

Ἰσραὴλ <u>δώδεκα</u> ≈ {<u>תרי עשר</u>} למנין שבטי ישראל <u>תרי עשר</u> על כל ישראל.

5. 5:41 (2:64)

MT: כל הקהל כאחד ארבע רבוא אלפים שלש מאות ששים. מלבד <u>עבדיהם ואמהתיהם</u>

אלה שבעת אלפים...

I Esd: οἱ δὲ πάντες ἦσαν Ἰσραηλ ἀπὸ δωδεκαετοῦς χωρὶς <u>παίδων καὶ</u>

<u>παιδισκῶν</u> μυριάδες τέσσαρες δισχίλιοι τριακόσιοι ἑξήκοντα. <u>παῖδες</u>

<u>τούτων καὶ παιδίσκαι</u> ἑπτακισχίλιοι τριακόσιοι τριάκοντα ἑπτα ≈

כל ישראל מבן שתים עשרה מלבד <u>עבדיהם ואמהתיהם</u> ארבע רבוא אלפים שלש מאות

ששים. {<u>עבדיהם ואמהתיהם</u>} שבעת אלפים....

6. 5:38 (2:61-62)

MT:

ומבני הכהנים בני חביה... אלה בקשו כתבם <u>המתיחשים ולא נמצאו</u> ויגאלו מן הכהנה.

I Esd: καὶ ἐκ τῶν ἱερέων οἱ ἐμποιούμενοι ἱερωσύνης καὶ οὐχ εὑρέθησαν

υἱοὶ Ὀββία... καὶ τούτων ζητηθείσης τῆς γενικῆς γραφῆς ἐν τῷ

καταλοχισμῷ καὶ μὴ εὑρεθείσης ἐχωρίσθησαν τοῦ ἱερατεύειν ≈

ומבני הכהנים {<u>המתיחשים לכהנה ולא נמצאו</u>} בני חביה... אלה בקשו כתבם <u>המתיחשים</u>

<u>ולא נמצאו</u> ויגאלו מן הכהנה.

7. 6:11 (5:10)

MT: ואף שמהתהם <u>שאלנא להם</u> להודעותך די נכתב שם גבריא <u>די בראשיהם</u>.

I Esd ἐπηρωτήσαμεν οὖν αὐτοὺς εἵνεκεν τοῦ γνωρίσαι σοι καὶ γράψαι

σοι τοὺς ἀνθρώπους τοὺς ἀφηγουμένους καὶ τὴν ὀνοματογραφίαν

ᾐτοῦμεν αὐτοὺς τῶν προκαθηγουμένων ≈

ואף <u>שאלנא להם</u> להודעותך די נכתב לך גבריא <u>די בראשיהם</u> ושמהתהם {<u>שאלנא להם</u>

<u>די בראשיהם</u>}.

The following double, or as some would have it, triple reading, involves both a variant and a new function of the sentence in the context:

8. 5:49 (3:3)

MT: כי באימה עליהם מעמי הארצות

I Esd: καὶ ἐπισυνήχθησαν αὐτοῖς ἐκ τῶν ἄλλων ἐθνῶν τῆς γῆς... ὅτι ἐν ἔχθρᾳ ἦσαν αὐτοῖς καὶ κατίσχυσαν αὐτοὺς πάντα τὰ ἔθνη τὰ ἐπὶ τῆς γῆς ≈

‏{ויבאו עליהם} מעמי הארצות... כי באיבה עליהם {ויבאו עליהם כל עמי הארצות}.

In two cases, it seems that I Esd has conflated two readings:

9. 1:3 (2 Chr 35:3) MT's ארון הקדש is paralleled by τῆς ἁγίας κιβωτοῦ τοῦ κυρίου, which is possibly a conflation of a double reading: ‏ארון הקדש/ ‏ארון האלהים.

10. 5:44 (Ezr 2:69) For the MT's לאוצר המלאכה I Esd reads εἰς τὸ ἱερὸν γαζοφυλάκιον τῶν ἔργων, possibly a conflation of אוצר המלאכה and אוצר ‏בית הי/האלהים.

Against all these cases there is only one possible example of a doublet in the MT not represented in I Esd:

1:5 (2 Chr 35:5)

MT: ‏ועמדו בקדש לפלגות בית האבות... וחלקת בית אב ללוים

I Esd: καὶ στάντες ἐν τῷ ἱερῷ κατὰ τὴν μεριδαρχίαν τὴν πατρικὴν ὑμῶν τῶν Λευιτῶν ע ≈ ‏ועמדו בקדש לפלגות בית האבות ללוים.[240]

---

[240] There are other double readings in the MT, but they are also recorded in I Esd, e.g., ‏ואחר הכינו להם ולכהנים כי הכהנים בני אהרן בהעלות העולה (2 Chr 35:14) 1:12-13 ‏והחלבים עד לילה והלוים הכינו להם ולכהנים בני אהרן.

k. Additions and Omissions Generated by Other Changes

In the following cases we assume that a certain element was added or omitted because of another change or a different understanding of the text.

Pluses in the MT   **Pluses reflected in I Esd**

1. 1:7 (2 Chr 35:7)   **1.** 1:25 (2 Chr 35:21)

MT: לן בני ה]עם... [לכל] הנמצא.   MT: ואל ישחיתך.

I Esd: לעם הנמצא.   I Esd: {ואל תשחית [לאלהים[.[241]

2. 1:10 (35:10) MT: [המלך] כמצות.   **2.** 1:26 (35:22) MT: [נכו] דברי.

I Esd: במצות[242].   I Esd: {דברי [ירמיהו הנביא[.[243]

3. 1:36 (36:4)

MT: ויסב את שמו יהויקים ואת... אחיו לקח [נכו] ויביאהו מצרימה.

I Esd: ויאסר יהויקים את השרים ואת... אחיו לקח ויביאהו מצרים[244].

4. 1:48 (36:15) MT: [ושלוח] השכם.   **3.** 7:14 (Ezr 6:22) MT: כי שמחם ה'.

I Esd: השבם.   I Esd: כי שמחים {לפני[ה'.

5. 5:56 (Ezr 3:9) MT: [בני] חנדד...[.

In I Esd, the entire passage moves to another place; therefore, the name receives a different function in the context.

---

[241] This is probably a theological change in I Esd.

[242] The introduction of the unleavened bread is out of place here.

[243] The substitution of Necho with the prophet as carrier of God's message is undoubtedly secondary.

[244] The picture drawn in I Esd is quite awkward and irrational. The disappearance of Necho is characteristic of I Esd.

6. 8:49 (8:21)

MT: ‏על הנהר [אהוא].

I Esd: ‏על {הנערים}.

Mistaking הנהר for הנער/הנערים must have caused the omission of the river's name.

7. 9:53 (Neh 8:11)

MT:

‏והלוים [מַחשים] לכל העם לאמר [הסו כי]   היום קדש ואל תעצבו.

I Esd:

‏והלוים {מְחשים} לכל העם לאמר   היום קדש ואל תעצבו.

The reading of מְחשים 'urging' instead of מַחשים 'silencing' may have caused the further omission of הסו כי "be silent since".

This category does not comply with most of the categories outlined above. Unlike the balance in the growth of the texts characteristic to shorter and longer texts, here, the MT seems to preserve the original text in the majority of cases.

Conclusion

The substantial discrepancy in the length of the text reflected in I Esd as compared with the MT does not single out I Esd as a witness to a shorter text-type, but rather underlines the parallel evolution of both texts.

In the majority of categories, there is no clear tendency of one text towards a certain type of addition or omission. Only rarely is there an unbalanced development in the texts. Thus, I Esd displays a more frequent use of function words than the MT (15 cases versus 7); whereas, in the MT, there are more additional demonstratives than in I Esd (8 cases versus 1). Sometimes the balance is disturbed by a certain detail, such as the repeated addition of בית before the divine name in the MT, or the reiterated מרא to describe the king in I Esd. But in the main body of minuses / pluses, that of adnominals and adverbs, as well as in other syntactical categories, it is an almost symmetrical two-way movement.

The content of the additional elements is multifarious. Some of the additions in I Esd show the writer's sensitivity towards theological matters, e.g., 1:4 (2 Chr 35:3) {וישרתו} את עמו ישראל; 1:46 (36:13) עבדו את ה' {וישרתו}; 6:12 (Ezr 5:11) {עבד} שמיא וארעא {אלה; the repeated omission of שמיא from the phrase אלה שמיא belongs to the same trend, 6:28, 8:9, 21 (6:9; 7:12, 23). Other variants, which are not strictly omissions or additions, also join the same tendency, e.g., 2:5 (1:2) {השכן} בירושלם האלהים for the MT's {תשחית לאלהים} (2 Chr 35:21) {אשר} האלהים; 1:25 for the MT's {סביב} בית מקדשם (36:17) 1:50 {ישחיתך} ואל; instead of {ב}בית מקדשם in the MT. Twice the priests are defined as the Levites' brothers in I Esd, 1:12-13 (35:14). On several occasions, I Esd seeks to avoid the distinction between priests and Levites, 1:10 (35:10) I Esd reflects: ויעמדו הכהנים והלוים על מחלקותם..., instead of the MT: ויעמדו; 8:42 (Ezr 8:15) I Esd reflects: הכהנים [על עמדם] והלוים על מחלקותם... ואבינה, where the MT reads: ואבינה בעם ומבני הכהנים ומן הלוים לא מצאתי שם; 7:9 (6:18) I Esd must have read: ובכהנים ומבני לוי לא מצאתי שם כהניא ולויא

במחלקתהון {מלבשין}, as against כהניא בפלגתהון ולויא במחלקתהון in the MT. In
the latter case, the garments of the priests and Levites are specifically
noted in I Esd; this is the case also in 1:2 (2 Chr 35:2), 5:40 (Ezr 2:63).
Such variants are probably deliberate. The majority of variants, however,
are random and pertain to the natural growth of the texts.

Indeed, the mass of additional elements in both I Esd and the MT, as
well as other variants which distinguish between the texts, do not have
much in common, except for the wish to retouch the text in order to better
define it, or, on the other hand, to avoid repetitious elements. In many
cases the meaning is barely changed, the variants being rather a matter of
a different style of writing. This is obvious in a great number of cases in
which the extra element is nothing more than a repetition of an existant
one, e.g., the following words, not represented in I Esd: 1:39 (2 Chr 36:7)
2:25; כפורי זהב... [כפורי] כסף (Ezr 1:10) 2:12; להליכו בבלה.. הביא... [לבבל]
ועלת יום ביום... [דבר יום (3:4) 5:50; באדין בטלת עבידת... [והות בטלא] (4:24)
פרשגן אגרתא (5:7) 6:7; והתנבי חגי [נביא] וזכריה בר עדוא נבייא (5:1) 6:1; ביומו]
והיבל (5:14) 6:17; די שלח... על דריוש מלכא [פתגמא שלחו עלוהי וכדנה כתיב בגוה]
שם טעם (6:3) 6:23; המו להיכלא [די בבל] הנפק המו כורש מלכא מן היכלא די בבל
ותנדע די קריתא דך [קריא] מרדא (4:15) 2:19; בית אלהא בירושלם [ביתא] יתבנא
אלהי בשתי... להרים (9:6) 8:71 ;...עד למנחת הערב. [ובמנחת הערב]... (9:5-6) 8:70
אנשים ראשי האבות [לבית אבתם] (10:16) 9:16; [אלהי] פני אליך.

In the following three texts, the introducion to the words spoken is
repeated in the MT; although, the words spoken are not interrupted: 2:17-18
וכן אמרין להם... (5:3-4) 6:3-4; ידיע להוא למלכא... [כען ידיע להוא למלכא] (4:13)
ויאמר נחמיה... [ויאמר להם] (Neh 8:9-10) 9:51; [אדין כנמא אמרנא להם] In
these last cases, the impression is that the repetitive text is rather the
original text while I Esd shows a tendency to shorten apparently pleonastic
texts. This, however, is not necessarily the general conclusion regarding
the relationship between the texts since there are cases in which the pleonastic
text is that of I Esd and the MT offers the more concise version. Thus, 1:6
ועבידתא דך אספרנא (Ezr 5:8) 6:9; ושחטו הפסח... לעשות {הפסח} (2 Chr 35:6)

התנדבו לאלה ישראל לירושלם... וכל... (7:16) 8:13; מתעבדא ומצלח {עבדא} בידהם
9:40; וכלי נחשת... {כלים}... שנים עשר (8:29) 8:58; די תהשכח... {לאלהא לירושלם}
ויפתח עזרא (Neh 8:5) 9:46; ויביא... את התורה... לשמע {את התורה} (Neh 8:2)
את. {ה]ספר {התורה}... וכפתחו {את התורה}. Expansive writing is expressed in
many other ways, but the repetitive texts adduced here best illustrate the
development of the texts through reduction and expansion.

As for the amount of pluses/minuses, it is not possible to arrive at an
accurate number of elements which are added or omitted in one text as
compared with the other, or to fix the percentage of missing elements in
relation to the bulk of elements which constitute the entire work under
discussion. Are minor elements such as *waws*, pronouns and prepositions
counted separately? Is a text which replaces an explicit noun by a
retrospective pronoun shorter or just different? Is a variant such as MT על
הקינות, as opposed to על ספר דברי הימים למלכי יהודה reflected in I Esd,
shorter by four words or just deviant? Is an addition of one word counted
as one plus whereas an additon of a phrase counted according to the
number of words which constitute the phrase? Is an addition of two verses
– the case of 1:21-22 – counted as an addition of the total of the extra
words? Separating a longer addition into its elements distorts the data.
Thus, there are 360 additional <u>words</u> in the MT (seven percent of the
relevant material in the MT), which constitute 200 lacking <u>units</u> in I Esd
as compared with the MT. The telling information is that the MT, too,
lacks about the same amount of words or units as compared with I Esd.[245]

---

[245] This is the main difference between the result of the comparison between I Esd and
the MT and the result of the study of Jeremiah-LXX versus the MT. While I Esd
and its parallel parts in the MT have approximately the same amount of pluses,
Jeremiah-LXX is shorter than the MT in a ratio of 1:7, but is longer than the MT
only by 1:70; see Min (1970), who concludes that Jeremiah-LXX represents the
original short text, later expanded in the MT. At any rate, they certainly represent
two diachronically different stages in the transmission of the text; whereas, in our
case, we speak of two parallel processes in the evolution of the text.

The comparison between the pluses in I Esd and the MT shows little difference in the quality of text evolution represented in both texts. Some changes are characteristic of the unique revision of I Esd, but these constitute only a minority. Others seem to indicate that the text reflected in I Esd was not as well-preserved as the MT: it shows more cases of omission through homoioteleuton as well as doublets. Some omissions and additions, which probably ensue from other changes, seem to indicate that the text reflected in I Esd was treated more loosely than the MT. On the whole, however, the balanced comparison beween I Esd and the MT shows that the same processes are characteristic of both texts.

It is impossible to arrive at the *Urtext* by a comparison of I Esd and the MT. It seems incorrect to take the parts common to both texts as the original text. The fact is, that besides the minuses/pluses, there are about one-hundred variants between the texts, not counting the differences in word-order, which may have occurred in the *Vorlage*. These variants are not later additions to one earlier common text; rather, the text existed in one form and was modified into another since many of the variants are significant in the context. This is also true, at least partly, in regard to the main issue of minuses/pluses. One is reluctant to accept the simplistic conclusion that the original text is the one which emerges after the omission of all pluses from both I Esd and the MT. We are not in a position to describe the condition of the texts at the point at which they took separate routes, that is, the starting point of a long process during which they developed into representatives of different, recognizable text-forms.

Describing I Esd as a representative of a separate group of texts, or of a text-type,[246] is a matter of speculation. Indeed, I Esd is supported in several cases by the LXX and sometimes also by the Lucianic Mss of the LXX, the Peshitta and the Vulgate, and, in the appropriate parts, by the counterpart in the Books of Kings and by the parallel list of Neh 7; but, there is no substantial evidence to tie the text-form reflected in I Esd to

---

[246] See the terminology of Cross (1975), as against the looser terms used by Tov (1992).

that of the other extant textual witnesses, which are incomparably closer to the MT. From the evidence we have, I Esd's *Vorlage* represents only itself. It must have departed from the main text at an early stage, on the one hand, and undergone a substantial process of transmission, on the other. This text came into the hands of the revisor, who created I Esd and who must have contributed his own share to the modification of the text in general, not just along the main lines which characterize the apocryphal book.

It is complicated to distinguish between the changes that already existed in the version used by the revisor and those introduced by him, or between possible changes which entered the text in the course of transmission of the apocryphal book. It is quite clear, however, that the majority of variants do not carry the distinctive stamp of the main revision, but agree with the standard processes of textual transmission. The gap between the texts preserved in I Esd and in the MT stands out only in that it is unconventionally deep, much more than the ordinary amount of changes which affect texts. On the whole, including the activity of the revisor, the relationship between I Esd and the MT complies with the kind of textual and literary activity which emerges from the comparison between the MT and the LXX in the books of Esther and Daniel.

Finally, we must take into consideration the translator's contribution to the design of the text since he is certainly no conventional translator. In this matter, too, it is not always possible to determine between variations which go back to the translator and variants in the *Vorlage*.[247]

The main impression created by the detailed comparison between the conjectured *Vorlage* of I Esd and the parallel parts in the canonical books is that of a continued and intensive course of change. The discrepancy is not the result of a defined line of revision in one text or the other, but rather, it results from a fluid, though outstanding, growth of both texts.

---

[247] The continuity in the processes of textual transmission is emphasized by Talmon (1975), pp. 321-400.

CHAPTER THREE

THE TRANSLATION

I. Translation Technique

In this chapter we will seek to evaluate the translation through which I Esd has come down to us.[248] The study of translation techniques ranges from general assessments to a more precise and detailed analysis of the data. Today's research tends to lean in the latter direction, and indeed much has changed since Thackeray first mapped the Greek translations in his now classic study.[249] Though many of Thackeray's general conclusions have since been replaced by the results of more detailed research, the overall picture remains basically the same. Only now hard facts and figures support it. Even so, it seems doubtful whether the study of translation technique will ever become an exact science, when neither the *Vorlage* nor the original translation has come down to us. Yet another obstacle to this goal is the difficulty of establishing precise criteria of translation technique.

A number of scholars, of whom Barr and Tov are the foremost representatives,[250] have advanced various criteria for defining the literal translation. In doing so they seek to refine both the study of translation technique and the use of translations in textual criticism. It should be noted that Barr (p. 281) is reluctant to speak of 'free' translations, arguing that there is no such species in the world of the LXX. Indeed, it seems far more appropriate to speak of a translation as being more or less literal, than to define it as 'free'. The latter can imply a philosophy of translation foreign to the milieu of translators in which we are concerned. It might also be wise to relinquish the characterization of translations as 'free' for another reason, namely, the relatively few limits as to what a free translation

---

[248] Since Nestle (1893), no one has questioned that I Esd is indeed a translation rather than a revision of some other, certainly unknown Greek translation; see Tedesche (1938), pp. 12-15.

[249] Thackeray (1909); on I Esd see pp. 13, 15.

[250] Barr (1979); Tov (1981), pp. 50ff.

can be. The literal translation, on the other hand, can be defined in more exact terms, with the work of a translator such as Aquilas setting the standards. In order to determine the extent to which a translation is literal, let us apply two sets of criteria: (1) the degree to which all elements are faithfully represented, in both quantity and word-order; (2) the adequacy of the equivalents and the consistency with which they are used. Of these criteria, it is no doubt the former which most characterizes the translation.

If we understand 'literal' in its most basic sense, we would expect a literal translation to reflect every word of its *Vorlage* down to the smallest particle. The technique behind this kind of translation is highly systematic with each element retaining its strict autonomy. It requires the translator to direct his attention to only one item at a time, and to faithfully represent it in its original order and through a standard equivalent. Needless to say, such a technique makes short shrift of idiomatic phrases and does not lend itself to the kind of translation which syntactical or logical units demand. Were it possible to actually measure the units on which a translator based his translation, we would be closer to finding precise standards of literalism. In other words: the larger the unit, the less literal the translation. The following examples, taken from I Esd and the LXX, graphically show the difference between literal and non-literal translations:

כל ממלכות הארץ נתן לי (1:2) 2:1
     5   4   3   2   1
LXX: Πάσας τὰς βασιλείας τῆς γῆς ἔδωκέν μοι
     1   2   3   4   5
I Esd: Ἐμὲ ἀνέδειξεν βασιλέα τῆς οἰκουμένης
     5   2 + 4   1 + 3
Or,

ובשנת אחת לכורש מלך בבל (1:1) 2:1
     8   7   65   4   321
LXX: Καὶ ἐν τῷ πρώτῳ ἔτει Κύρου τοῦ βασιλέως Περσῶν
     1   2   3   4   3   5+6   7   8
I Esd: Βασιλεύοντος Κύρου Περσῶν ἔτους πρώτου
     5+7   6   8   1+2+3   4

In sum, the translator of I Esd takes the entire syntactical unit as his starting point while the LXX generally strives for a word for word translation (only in the case of לכורש is the preposition taken together with the name: Κύρου).

There are many cases in which our translator obviously considered entire syntactical units before translating them. To cite one characteristic phenomenon, we find that a tendency to form subordinate clauses results in linking verbs which were separated by a string of words in his *Vorlage*, e.g., 1:1-2 (2 Chr 35:1-2): וישחטו (הפסח בארבעה עשר לחדש הראשון) ויעמד (הכהנים...) ≈ καὶ ἔθυσεν... στήσας... (similarly 1:5-6). To cite another, the translator often reformulated the syntax in order to change clauses from active to passive, an act which caused him to treat the entire clause and not just the individual words. The frequent changes in word-order so characteristic of our translator also imply a concern for units of logic, rather than a blind adherence to the individual elements. Interestingly enough, considering the relative size of the translation units, the respective equivalents are generally easy to identify.

In summary, the method of translation reflected in I Esd is a far cry from other translations in this corpus of literature which failed to distinguish between content and form and thus transmitted words at the expense of their meaning. With these comments in mind, let us now turn to a more detailed examination of our translator's working techniques.

a. Adequacy of Equivalents

1. Consistency in Choice of Equivalents

In principle one could argue that the literal translation does not necessarily require consistent word choices. Theoretically speaking, a translator could render the same word differently each time it occurs and still be considered a literal translator as long as he adequately represents his *Vorlage*. The translator of I Esd, for example, does not have a fixed equivalent for a simple term such as שרים. When the שרים appear in conjunction with the king, they are called οἱ μεγιστᾶνες,[251] and as the head of their people or clans either οἱ ἡγούμενοι,[252] or οἱ προηγούμενοι, and at times οἱ προκαθήμενοι.[253] שרי הכהנים, on the other hand, were found worthy of their own term: οἱ φύλαρχοι τῶν ἱερέων.[254] What does this flexibility in word-choice mean for the nature of the translation as a whole? Does the translator's sensitivity to the changing context ultimately produce an unfaithful translation? If the goal is to try to recover I Esd's *Vorlage*, inconsistent word-choices obviously make our task more difficult. This is especially true when we consider yet another angle of the problem: does the translator use these terms exclusively for שרים? Unfortunately, he does not, as shown by the fact that some of them also double as ראשים, specifically in the term ראשי האבות.[255] Therefore, if a phrase such as οἱ ἡγούμενοι τῶν πατερῶν appears in I Esd without a parallel in the MT, any hypothetical reconstruction can only submit both ראשי/שרי האבות, similar to שרי האבות in 8:58 (Ezr 8:29), or ראשי האבות in 5:63 (2:68). In this case, the latter equivalent should be preferred, since it occurs with more frequency. If reconstruction is the goal, then, fixed equivalents can obviously play a major role.

In actual fact, the literal translation assumes a one-to-one relationship with its *Vorlage*, with any given word in Greek automatically referring to

---

[251] 8:26, 55 (Ezr 7:28; 8:25); cf. also 1:36 (2 Chr 36:4). In 1:27 (35:23) he presumably read שרים (MT ירים) and rendered with ἄρχοι.

[252] 1:47 (2 Chr 36:14), 8:48, 58, 65 (Ezr 8:20, 29; 9:1).

[253] 8:67; 9:12 (Ezr 9:2,;10:14); 9:4 (10:8).

[254] 8:54, 58, 92 (Ezr 8:24, 29; 10:5), and cf. 1:9 (2 Chr 35:9) שרי הלוים ≈ χιλίαρχοι (שרי האלפים?).

[255] Thus οἱ ἡγούμενοι, οἱ προηγούμενοι, οἱ προκαθήμενοι, 5:63, 65, 67 (Ezr 2:68; 4:2, 3), cf. also 9:16 (10:16); 8:28 (8:1); 5:60 (3:12).

a standard counterpart in the original. It seems safe to say that a translator who is consistent in his choice of equivalents is likely to be more literal in other aspects of the translation as well; however, this would require a survey well beyond the purview of the present study. Generally speaking, however, it seems that our specific translator did not view consistency in word-choice as a top priority.

This is not to say, however, that our translator is totally inconsistent. He consistently renders (חג) לעשות by ἄγειν (10 times), גולה is rendered on all but one occasion by αἰχμαλωσία, אספרנא by ἐπιμελῶς, ענה by φωνεῖν, derivatives of קדש are paralleled by ἁγι-, and צלח by εὐοδ-, etc. This trend is especially noticeable in relation to technical terms. Words such as משוררים, שוערים, נתינים, סופר, etc. are kept fairly consistent. Yet even in these cases, consistency is not a matter of primary importance since the translator only used a term when convinced that it was best suited to the context. At times, he was only partially consistent, as in his handling of שים טעם. In this case, he chose the stem τάσσειν, usually as προστάσσειν (7 times), but he also variegates the prefix: ἐπιτάσσειν (3 times) and συντάσσειν (once). All three equivalents occur in the same chapter. A good deal of thought seems to have gone into his choice of equivalents for words such as נדבה, נדב. Though he generally rendered these words as εὐχή (3 times) and εὐχεσθαι (3 times), he called the noun ἐπαγγελία the first time it appeared in the text, and, possibly, ὁ νοῦς ἠγέρθη the first time it appeared in verb form. Verses 8:10, 13 (Ezr 7:13, 15, 16) are noteworthy for their sheer variety of equivalents: מתנדבים ≈ τοὺς βουλομένους... αἱρετίζοντας; התנדבו ≈ ηὐξάμην; התנדבות ≈ τῷ δεδωρημένῳ. This technique clearly shows that far from being committed to consistency, the translator was consciously striving for variation. Such variation is not only a stylistic device but also a way of giving a word different shades of meaning, as seen in his use of double translations.

Examples of this are many:

1. 1:54-55 (2 Chr 36:21) למלאות... למלאות ≈ ἀναπλήρωσιν... συμπλήρωσιν.

2. 5:49 (Ezr 3:3) עלות... עלות ≈ θυσίας... ὁλοκαυτώματα.

3. 6:31 (6:11) ביתה... ביתה ≈ τῶν ἰδίων αὐτοῦ... καὶ τὰ ὑπάρχοντα αὐτοῦ.

4. 7:4 (6:14) מן טעם... ומטעם ≈ διὰ προστάγματος... καὶ μετὰ τῆς γνώμης...

5. 8:16 (7:18) למעבד... תעבדון ≈ ποιῆσαι... ἐπιτέλει.

6. 9:48 (Neh 8:7, 8) מבינים... ויבינו ≈ ἐδίδασκον... ἐμφυσιοῦντες.

The phenomenon is even more striking when a rare word is involved, such as אשתדור:

7. 2:19 (Ezr 4:15) ואשתדור עבדין בגוה ≈ καὶ πολιορκίας συνιστάμενοι ἐν αὐτῇ; 2:23 (4:19) ואשתדור מתעבד בה ≈ καὶ πολέμους ἐν αὐτῇ συντελοῦντες.

2. The Level of Semantic Parallelism between Equivalents

The above examples make it clear that the translator of I Esd supplied some rather extraordinary equivalents. Far from feeling obligated to create a translation that could be easily retroverted into its *Vorlage*, our translator felt free to imbue the text with something of his own spirit. He translated in the manner which he deemed best able to convey the meaning of a word in a given context. Thus, he repeatedly chose equivalents which conveyed only one particular nuance of the original words; as in:

1. 2:17 (Ezr 4:12) שכללו ≈ θεραπεύουσιν.
2. 7:15 (6:22) לב ≈ βουλήν.

3. 2:25 (4:23) אזלו ≈ ἀναζεύξαντες.

4. 9:3 (10:7) קול ≈ κήρυγμα.

5. 5:50 (3:4) ככתוב ≈ ὡς ἐπιτέτακται.

6. 9:42 (Neh 8:4) מגדל ≈ βῆμα.

7. 5:53 (Ezr 3:7) ים ≈ λιμένα.

His equivalents for יד are particularly noteworthy. For example, in 1:4 (2 Chr 35:4), his text presumably read (וכ(י)ד (שלמה which he rendered with μεγαλειότης (MT ובמכתב, cf. LXX διὰ χειρός). This is perhaps not too far-fetched, considering his treatment of יד throughout the book. The word occurs 27 times in his *Vorlage*, but I Esd uses the standard equivalent of χείρ only in 10 of them. The LXX, on the other hand, uses χείρ almost 27 times. This discrepancy is due to the fact that יד is used as a preposition as well as in idioms, two categories which are subject to reformulation by translators. The preposition was rendered either by a simple διά or by derivatives of δίδωμι. The idiomatic phrases changed almost beyond recognition, as in 8:67 (Ezr 9:2) ויד השרים והסגנים היתה במעל הזה ≈ μετεῖχον, which preserves the meaning, but retains little of the formal components. We could also mention 8:6 (7:9) בא אל ירושלם כיד אלהיו הטובה עליו ≈ κατὰ τὴν δοθεῖσαν... εὐοδίαν; again a perfect match in terms of content, but not in form.[256] While it is quite easy to draw parallels between the MT and I Esd, it would be almost impossible to retrieve the *Vorlage* in such cases, were it not for the MT.

b. Changes in Morphemes

Of all the factors involved in the comparison between source and translation, the linguistic data remain among the most elusive. Chr provides a good case in point. Had the text come down to us in its Greek version alone, we could probably assume that no one would ever have given much

---

[256] See further Talshir (1982), pp. 50-52.

thought to the language of its *Vorlage*. Most of the valuable material deduced from the comparison of the parallel texts of Chr and Samuel-Kings would be subsumed under the category of translation technique. Thus, even significant differences such as expansions, abbreviations and exegesis, not to mention differences which can be explained as reformulation, syntactic modification, and certainly secondary or small elements, would be attributed to the translator.

Changes in morphemes have been suitably defined as variants/non-variants.[257] A translator who tends to recast his source according to the standards of the target-language is likely to unintentionally neglect the smaller elements. However, parallel Hebrew texts are rife with differences in these elements which often provide important evidence for textual transmission, and even for linguistic development. I Esd may, therefore, preserve differences in the *Vorlage*.

1. *Waws*

The differences between textual witnesses concerning copulative *waws* are to be found at every stage of textual transmission. This is the easiest element to retrovert, yet at the same time one of the least certain. There is really no way of knowing whether differences in conjunctive elements originated with the translator, or were to be found already in his *Vorlage*.

The differences in the use of *waws* can be quite instructive. Gerlemann, for example, concluded on the basis of *waws* in the lists of the Book of Genesis, that Chr has an affinity with the Samaritan Pentateuch, and not the MT.[258] Kutscher adduced more than 200 cases in which the *waw* in 1QIsaᵃ has no parallel in the MT, but only 70 cases in the opposite direction. The scroll, then, reflects the later tendency towards syndesis, just as Chr

---

[257] Tov (1981), pp. 217ff.

[258] Gerleman (1948), pp. 10, 12.

does too, when compared with its sources.[259] Since both texts continued to develop independently once the contact between them ended, it is noticeable that the later tendency is not restricted to only one of the witnesses. It would seem, then, that the tendency towards syndesis can serve as a means of dating parallel texts relative to each other. However, we are naturally reluctant to make the same conclusions on the basis of translations.

The translator of I Esd would have had little compunction when it came to dealing with something as minor as a *waw*. He was quick to drop it when turning paratactic sentences into hypotactic ones, or when making units appear asyndetically beside tens, a construction impossible in the *Vorlage*. On the other hand, in places where καί is used for emphasis, we can assume this to be his own addition, e.g., 2:19 (Ezr 4:15) על דנה קריתא דך החרבת ≈ δι᾽ ἣν αἰτίαν καὶ ἡ πόλις αὕτη ἡρημώθη. Generally, however, we cannot rule out the possibility that the change originated in the *Vorlage*, especially where other textual witnesses back up I Esd's evidence. Moreover, were the translator responsible for the changes we would expect him to follow a given pattern, but this is not the case. His indifference is especially apparent in lists which are replete with *waw*s and which call for changes in respect to syndesis or asyndesis. There are lists of names connected by *waw*s in the MT which turn asyndetic in I Esd, while in other cases, the names remain unconnected in the MT but joined by καίs in I Esd. This is clearly demonstrated by the list in 9:21-33 (10:20-43). Our translator was obviously unconcerned about repeating the καί in accordance with the syndetic list in the MT in 9:26 (10:25) ויזיה ומלכיה ומימן ואלעזר ומלכיה ובניה ≈ καὶ Ἰεζίας καὶ Μελχίας καὶ Μιάμινος καὶ Ἐλεάζαρος καὶ Ἀσιβίας καὶ Βανναίας, or in following the partly asyndetic list in 9:28 (10:27) אליועני אלישיב מתניה וירמות וזבד ועזיזא ≈ Ἐλιαδᾶς Ἐλιάσιμος Ὀθονίας Ἰαριμὼθ καὶ Σάβαθος καὶ Ζερδαίας. Therefore, the translator is hardly to blame for the addition of καίs in 9:29, 31 (10:28, 30), or for the

[259] Kutscher (1974), pp. 414-429.

omission of *waw*s in v. 34 (10:34-42). The same is true of other lists as
well, whether of names, e.g., 9:43, 44, 48 (Neh 8:2, 4, 7), or of other
items, e.g., 7:7-8 (Ezr 6:17) ‏תורין... דכרין... וצפירי עזין...‏ 1:7 (2 Chr 35:7)
‏...ובקר ‏כבשים ובני עזים...‏, where the *waw* is not represented in I Esd (or in
the Peshitta), or 6:29 (Ezr 6:9) ‏חנטין מלח חמר ומשח‏ and 5:56 (3:8) ‏ישוע בניו‏
‏ואחיו‏ which are preceded by καί s in I Esd. There are some cases which
would almost seem to demand the addition of a connective element during
the process of transmission or translation, e.g., when only two items stand
by each other asyndetically; thus, 1:4 (2 Chr 35:4) ‏לבית אבותיכם‏
‏כמחלקותיכם‏ (connected by καί also in the LXX), or 8:8, 9 (Ezr 7:11, 12)
‏הכהן הספר; כהנא ספר דתא‏. All in all, the translator seems to have followed
his *Vorlage*, not necessarily from any sense of obligation, but because he
worked quite automatically when it came to lists. Since the changes go
both ways, it seems that the MT and I Esd's *Vorlage* each experienced
their share of rewriting, more likely attracting *waw*s in the course of
transmission and linguistic development than dropping them.

Sometimes the addition or omission of a *waw* has deeper implications
since it changes the meaning of the text. Thus, the omission of the *waw* in
9:4 (Ezr 10:8) ‏השרים [ו]הזקנים‏ turns two categories into one, while the
addition of a καί turns the settlers of Samaria into an entity in its own
right in 2:21 (4:17) ‏כנותהון [ו]די יתבין בשמרין‏; cf. also 2:15 (4:8). Another
group is similarly divided in two in 8:45 (8:17) ‏אחיו [ו]הנתונים (הנתינים)‏
‏בכספיא המקום‏, and the omission of the *waw* in 7:13 (6:21) ‏בני ישראל השבים‏
‏מהגולה [ו]כל הנבדל מטמאת גוי הארץ‏ turns ‏כל הנבדל...‏ into a description of the
Israelites. Once again, we have no way of knowing whether the translator
or his *Vorlage* is to blame.

Though we might have expected a more frequent use of δέ, the
translator once again shows himself reluctant to use conjunctions where
his *Vorlage* has none. Thus, out of 40 δέs, only 10 are unparalleled in the
MT. We can probably assume that some of these cases represent free

additions on the part of the translator, others reflect a different text. The same goes for οὖν, which is used twice for a *waw* and once for וּאן, in addition to four times without parallel in the MT. The conjunction most conspicuously used in I Esd without counterpart in the MT is ὁμοίως δέ, which has the effect of separating the offerings from the rest of the Temple needs, 6:29 (6:9) ואמרין לעלון לאלה שמיא חנטין מלח חמר ומשח ≈ εἰς ταύρους καὶ κριοὺς καὶ ἄρνας, ὁμοίως δὲ καὶ πυρὸν καὶ ἅλα καὶ οἶνον καὶ ἔλαιον; similarly 8:20 (7:22).

In summary, the translator tended to follow his *Vorlage* in the matter of conjunctions. The results are inconclusive and give us no evidence that would point to a clear-cut preference for either syndetic or asyndetic constructions in I Esd's *Vorlage*.

2. Singular / Plural

Another phenomenon generally treated in the category of variants/non-variants is the difference between singular and plural.

The difference between singular in the MT and plural in I Esd is quite conspicuous when it comes to nouns in the *status constructus* or *status pronominalis*, with the feminine ending *taw*:

1. 1:14 (2 Chr 35:15) כְּמִצְוַת ≈
κατὰ τὰ... τεταγμένα (cf. LXX).

2. 1:52 (36:19) חוֹמַת ≈
τὰ τείχα (cf. Peshitta).

3. 5:50 (Ezr 3:4) וְעֹלַת ≈
καὶ θυσίας.

4. 5:51 (3:5) וְעֹלַת ≈
καὶ θυσίας.

7. 8:4 (Ezr 7:6) בְּקָשָׁתוֹ ≈
τὰ ἀξιώματα αὐτοῦ.

8. 8:72 (9:6) וְאַשְׁמָתֵנוּ ≈
αἱ γὰρ ἁμαρτίαι ἡμῶν.

9. 8:83 (9:13) וּבְאַשְׁמָתֵנוּ ≈
καὶ τὰς... ἁμαρτίας ἡμῶν.

10. 8:87 (9:15) בְּאַשְׁמָתֵינוּ ≈
ἐν ταῖς ἀνομίαις ἡμῶν.

5. 5:56 (3:8) מְלֶאכֶת ≈
τῶν ἔργων.

11. 9:7 (10:10) אַשְׁמַת ≈
ἁμαρτίας.

6. 7:13 (6:21) מֻטמְאַת ≈
ἀπὸ τῶν βδελυγμάτων.

Only in one instance do we find a change in the opposite direction:
1:40 (2 Chr 36:8) וְתֹעֲבֹתָיו ≈ καὶ τῆς αὐτοῦ ἀκαθαρσίας.

The differences can easily be attributed to the translator's manner of
rendering general nouns such as מצוה 'orders', or עולה 'offerings' in the
plural. It is possible, however, that he read a defective *ḥolem,* instead of a
pataḥ (e.g., וְעֹלַת for וְעֹלַת), or that he had a text with more *matres lectionis,*
i.e., that his source already tended to give the plural. Some support for this
latter possibility is the reading in Ezr 9:15 בְּאַשְׁמָתֵינוּ, in which the *yod*
points to the plural, but is vocalized as though it were singular.

I Esd has other examples in which the transition to the plural requires
more than a change in vocalization:

13. 1:49 (2 Chr 36:17) מלך ≈
τοὺς βασιλεῖς.

17. 8:7 (7:10) חק ומשפט ≈
τὰ δικαιώματα καὶ τὰ κρίματα.
(cf. LXX; Peshitta).

14. 5:56 (Ezr 3:9) עשה ≈
ποιοῦντες.

18. 8:45 (8:17) אָחִיו ≈
τοῖς ἀδελφοῖς αὐτοῦ.

15. 5:69 (4:4) עם הארץ ≈[260]
τὰ δὲ ἔθνη τῆς γῆς.

19. 8:90 (10:3) והנולד ≈
σὺν τοῖς τέκνοις αὐτῶν.
(cf. LXX).

16. 7:4 (6:14) מלך ≈
βασιλέων Περσῶν (cf. LXX).[261]

20. 9:20 (10:19) איל ≈
κριοὺς.

---

[260] עמי הארץ is regular, see below.

[261] In this case, the plural is required by the context, since three kings are mentioned,
      so that the change cannot be considered purely linguistic.

In addition, we encounter the recurring interchange of singular-plural with the word יד:

21-23. 1:50 (2 Chr 36:17); 6:14 (Ezr 5:12); 9:20 (10:19).

There are remarkably fewer examples in the opposite direction, that is, plural in the MT for singular in I Esd:

1. 1:29 (2 Chr 35:24) בקברות ≈
ἐν τῷ... τάφῳ.

4. 6:28 (Ezr 6:9) לעלון ≈
εἰς θυσίαν.

2. 1:31 (35:26) וחסדיו ≈
καὶ τῆς δόξης αὐτοῦ.
(cf. LXX)

5. 8:69 (9:4) בדברי ≈
τῷ ῥήματι.

3. 1:48 (36:15) מלאכיו ≈[262]
τοῦ ἀγγέλου αὐτοῦ.

6. 8:74 (9:7) (מלכי) הארצות ≈
τοῖς βασιλεῦσιν τῆς γῆς.

7-9. We further note the construct עמי הארצות 8:66, 67, 80 (9:1, 2, 11), in which the genitival attribute is rendered in the singular (τῆς γῆς). The translator might have had in his *Vorlage* a form such as עם הארץ 5:69 (4:4), or עמי הארץ 8:89, 9:9 (10:2, 11). In this case, the text reflected in I Esd is older since the doubly marked plural of attributive constructs is characteristic of later stages in the development of the language.[263] However, it is possible that the translator was more concerned with clarifying the meaning of his text than in preserving its outer form. The phrase does refer to the people who dwelled in the land, not to people of different lands.

If the translator tended to read the plural or, better, if his source already reflected it, this may show the tendency of Late Hebrew to prefer the plural over the singular for collective or abstract nouns, such as

---

[262] The singular here is awkward since the verse goes on to speak about the messengers of God in the plural, in both the MT and I Esd.

[263] Hurvitz (1982), p. 38; Polzin (1976), p. 42; Qimron (1986), pp. 74-75.

בקר-בקרים, גורל-גורלות, פסח-פסחים, and many others.[264] This tendency is
particularly evident in I Esd, though sporadically attested in the MT as
well.

c. Changes in the Syntax of the Verb

Changes which occurred in the syntax of the verbal clause provide us
with one of the richest mines of information concerning the way in which
the translator regarded his source. We cannot always know when the
change was due to the translator rather than the *Vorlage* itself, but I Esd
evinces two striking phenomena which clearly pertain to translation
technique. Both are grounded in the nature of the Greek language itself,
i.e. its tendency towards passive formulations and hypotactic constructions.
Our translator showed himself more than eager to conform with his target
language on both of these accounts. He rarely missed an opportunity to
turn a paratactic construction into a hypotactic one, and at times even
made them up freely. Similarly, he frequently replaced the active voice for
the passive one.

1. The Voice

(a) Active / Passive

Biblical Hebrew tends to use active constructions whenever the
sentence has a well-defined subject. The use of the passive is generally
restricted to sentences in which the subject is indefinite. Even then, however,
one can see a definite trend away from the passive in Chr, the Qumran
scrolls and much of Rabbinic literature.[265] The fact of different developments
within Hebrew itself raises the possibility of a different *Vorlage*.
Nonetheless, the differences between source and translation in this respect

---

[264] Kropat (1909), p. 8ff; Polzin (1976), p. 42f; Hurvitz (1982), pp. 43-46.
[265] Kutscher (1974), p. 400.

can usually be chalked up to the translators.[266] This is true for our translator as well, since the introduction of passive forms is the rule rather than the exception in I Esd. There is little difficulty in identifying the active constructions which lay behind his use of the passive.

Only in a few cases would a possible change in vocalization warrant the consideration of a variant reading:

1. 1:7 (2 Chr 35:8) נָתַנ (read as נִתְּנוּ?) ≈ ἐδόθη.

2. 1:16 (35:16) וְהַעֲלוֹת...לַעֲשׂוֹת (read as וְהֵעָלוֹת...לְהֵעָשׂוֹת?) ≈ ἀχθῆναι... καὶ προσενεχθῆναι.

The next example seems to suggest a different text:

3. 2:22 (Ezr 4:19) (ומני שים טעם ובקרו) והשכחו (די קריתא דך) ≈ καὶ εὑρέθη.

Cf. the Lucianic mss of II Esd, and 6:22 (6:2) באדין דריוש מלכא שם טעם ובקרו... והשתכח באחמתא... (though this sentence is structured differently).

In the main, however, the changes can safely be attributed to the translator. Thus, he tends to introduce the passive for constructions which involve verbs in the Hiphᶜil:[267]

4. 1:29 (2 Chr 35:24) (ויולכהו...וירכיבהו) ≈ (καὶ ἀνέβη)... καὶ ἀποκατασταθείς.

5. 1:46 (36:13) אשר השביעו ≈ καὶ ὁρκισθείς... (ἐπιορκήσας).

6. 1:47 (36:14) אשר הקדיש ≈ τὸ ἁγιαζόμενον.

7. 8:22 (Ezr 7:24) ולכם מהודעין ≈ καὶ ὑμῖν δὲ λέγεται.

---

[266] Rabin (1962), pp. 60-76. Rabin examined the practice of translators in 242 cases of indefinite subjects reaching the conclusion that the differences are without meaning to the history of the text and attributable to the individual habits of the translators alone.

[267] See Tov (1982), § iv.

8. 8:75 (9:8) להשאיר לנו פליטה ≈ καταλειφθῆναι ἡμῖν ῥίζαν.

9. 5:57 (3:10) ויעמידו הכהנים ≈ καὶ ἔστησαν οἱ ἱερεῖς.
There is strong evidence from other witnesses in favor of a different reading (וַיַּעֲמְדוּ) here.

10. 7:9 (6:18) והקימו כהניא ≈ καὶ ἔστησαν οἱ ἱερεῖς.

The passive is introduced for constructions other than the Hiphᶜil, the change sometimes involving the verb alone, though more frequently entire clauses:

11. 1:41 (2 Chr 36:9) במלכו ≈ ὅτε γὰρ ἀνεδείχθη.

12. 1:30 (35:25) ויתנום ≈ καὶ ἐξεδόθη τοῦτο.

13. 9:42 (Neh 8:4) אשר עשו לדבר ≈ τοῦ κατασκευασθέντος.

14. 9:55 (8:12) אשר הודיעו להם ≈ οἷς ἐδιδάχθησαν.

15. 5:39 (Ezr 2:62) ואלה בקשו כתבם ≈ καὶ τούτων ζητηθείσης τῆς... γραφῆς.

16. 6:6 (5:5) ולא בטלו המו עד טעמא (לדריוש) יהך (ואדין) ≈ καὶ οὐκ ἐκωλύθησαν τῆς οἰκοδομῆς... τοῦ ὑποσημανθῆναι... καὶ προσφωνηθῆναι.
Sometimes the translator shifts to a complete passive construction, introducing the agent through a preposition (mainly ὑπό). Considering the changes involved, it must have taken no little effort to make such complicated reformulations:

17. 2:11 (Ezr 1:8) ויספרם ≈ διὰ δὲ τούτου παρεδόθησαν.

18. 2:13-14 (1:11) העלה ששבצר ≈ διεκομίσθη... ἀνηνέχθη δὲ ὑπὸ Σαναβασσάρου.

19. 7:1 (6:13) די שלח דריוש מלכא ≈ τοῖς ὑπὸ τοῦ βασιλέως Δαρείου προσταγεῖσιν.

20. 8:3 (7:6) אשר נתן ה׳ אלהי ישראל ≈ τῷ ἐκδεδομένῳ ὑπὸ τοῦ θεοῦ τοῦ Ἰσραήλ.

21. 8:76 (9:9) לא עזָבָנו אלהינו ≈ οὐκ ἐγκατελείφθημεν ὑπὸ τοῦ κυρίου ἡμῶν.

22. 9:39 (Neh 8:1) אשר צוה ה׳ ≈ τὸν παραδοθέντα ὑπὸ τοῦ κυρίου.

At times, he even replaced simple nominal phrases with passive clauses, when he could easily have dismissed them with a literal equivalent:

23. 1:14 (2 Chr 35:15) כמצות דוד ≈ κατὰ τὰ ὑπὸ Δαυὶδ τεταγμένα.

24. 1:31 (35:27) ודבריו הראשנים ≈ τά τε προπραχθέντα ὑπ' αὐτοῦ.

25. 8:13 (Ezr 7:16) עם התנדבות עמא ≈ σὺν τῷ δεδωρημένῳ ὑπὸ τοῦ ἔθνους.

We find three cases in I Esd where the passive construction has no obvious counterpart in the MT. In view of all the above, one tends to reconstruct them into active forms, as following:

26. 1:25 (2 Chr 35:21) לא עליך אתה היום ≈ οὐχὶ πρὸς σὲ ἐξαπέσταλμαι ὑπὸ κυρίου τοῦ θεοῦ.

Were it not for the MT, one would readily suggest a simple *Vorlage* such as לא אליך שלחני ה׳ אלהים. It is not impossible, however, that the translator derived אתה from the root אתה 'to come' (LXX ἥκω), and formulated it in the passive voice, as he was wont to do. In that case, one would have to say that he also supplied the agent ὑπὸ κυρίου τοῦ θεοῦ, despite the fact that it seems somehow connected with the MT's היום.

27. 1:45 (2 Chr 36:12) לא נכנע) מלפני ירמיהו הנביא מפי ה') ≈ ἀπὸ τῶν ῥηθέντων λόγων ὑπὸ 'Ιερεμίου τοῦ προφήτου ἐκ στόματος τοῦ κυρίου.

The translator may have had a more expansive text such as מלפני דברי ירמיהו הנביא אשר דבר מפי ה'. Other versions also add a verb at this point, a fact which tends to suggest reformulation on the part of the translators.

28. 5:53 (Ezr 3:7) כרשיון כורש... עליהם ≈ κατὰ τὸ πρόσταγμα τὸ γραφὲν αὐτοῖς παρὰ Κύρου.

This is again a passive formulation which might go back to an active אשר כתב, but it could also be a free, wholly characteristic construction on the part of our translator (the Peshitta and the Vulgate also turned כרשיון into a verbal clause).

(b) Passive / Active

Changes in the opposite direction, i.e., from passive to active, are few and insignificant.

1. 2:22 (Ezr 4:18) קרי קדמי ≈ ἀνέγνων.

2. 8:66 (9:1) לא נבדלו העם... והכהנים... מעמי הארצות ≈ οὐκ ἐχώρισαν τὸ ἔθνος... καὶ οἱ ἱερεῖς... τὰ ἀλλογενῆ ἔθνη.

Altogether, we found some 30 cases of active/passive interchanges, or a ratio of 1:11 for I Esd's 340 verses.[268] Though verses obviously make for an inadequate unit of measure, they do provide us with a reliable basis for comparing the situation in the parallel portions of the LXX where no such interchanges occur. It is also difficult, if not impossible, to offer any other basis for comparing translations in respect to syntactical reformulations of this kind.

---

[268] It is also worth noting that more than a third of the cases are concentrated in the first chapter.

2. Parataxis – Hypotaxis

The frequent use of subordinate clauses is one of I Esd's most outstanding features.[269] The translator repeatedly used hypotactic constructions, either as a replacement for paratactic constructions in his *Vorlage* or as a substitute for various other formulations. The pattern typically used by the translator calls for a combination of the participle and finite verb.

(a) Hypotactic Clauses / Paratactic Clauses

This group of examples best illustrates the issue at hand, since it shows the tendency of Hebrew and Aramaic towards paratactic constructions versus the tendency of Greek towards the hypotactic. This group is also important since it provides us with a ready standard of literalism clearly demonstrating the difference between translators who follow the genius of the original language and those who try to bend it to suit the target language. In this context let us also remember that the translator was obliged to deal with a relatively large chunk of his *Vorlage* before deciding whether to subordinate one verb to another, a step which in itself calls for paraphrase.

The trend toward hypotactic clauses is thus a well-established characteristic of our translator. Had the original text been lost, one might be tempted to theorize about the presence of subordinate clauses in I Esd's *Vorlage* on the basis of texts such as Neh 8:5 וכפתחו עמדו כל העם and Ezr 9:3 וכשמעי את הדבר הזה קרעתי את בגדי. But with the MT to guide us, there is little doubt as to the original equivalents.

---

[269] Walde (1913), pp. 18-19. In seeking to prove that I Esd is not based on the LXX, Walde cites this fact somewhat clumsily as evidence of the profound difference between I Esd and the LXX regarding their treatment of the parallel material. Cf. Hanhart (1974*), p. 109: "Partizipiale Formulierungen sind dem Stil von Esdr I in einer Weise eigentümlich, dass ihr Verhältnis zur hebräischen Vorlage nur noch von geringer Bedeutung ist". See also Aejmelaeus (1982), and the discussion above.

1. 1:1-2 (2 Chr 35:1-2) וישחטו... ויעמד ≈ καὶ ἔθυσεν... στήσας.

2. 1:5-6 (35:5-6) ושחטו... ועמדו ≈ καὶ στάντες... θύσατε.

3. 1:10 (35:10) ותכון... ויעמדו ≈ καὶ τούτων γενομένων εὐπρεπῶς ἔστησαν (gen. abs. + finite verb).

4. 1:26 (35:22) התחפש ולא שמע ≈ ἐπιχειρεῖ οὐ προσέχων.

5. 1:29 (35:24) ימת... ויוליכהו ≈ καὶ ἀποκατασταθεὶς... μετήλλαξεν τὸν βίον αὐτοῦ.

6. 1:32 (36:1) וימליכהו... ויקחו ≈ καὶ ἀναλαβόντες... ἀνέδειξαν βασιλέα.

7. 1:36 (36:4) ויביאהו... לקח ≈ συλλαβὼν ἀνήγαγεν.

8. 1:39 (36:7) ויתנם... הביא ≈ λαβών... καὶ ἀπενέγκας ἀπηρείσατο.

9. 1:44 (36:10) ויביאהו... שלח ≈ ἀποστείλας... μετήγαγεν αὐτόν.

10. 2:5 (Ezr 1:3) ויבן... ויעל ≈ καὶ ἀναβάς... οἰκοδομείτω.

11. 2:17 (4:12) בנין... אתו... די סלקו ≈ ἀναβάντες... ἐλθόντες... οἰκοδομοῦσιν.

12. 2:25 (4:23) ובטלו... אזלו ≈ ἀναζεύξαντες... ἤρξαντο κωλύειν.

13. 5:39 (2:62) ויגאלו... ולא נמצאו... בקשו ≈ ζητηθείσης... εὑρεθείσης ἐχωρίσθησαν (gen. abs. + finite verb).

14. 5:46 (3:1) ויאספו... ויגע ≈ ἐνστάντος δὲ... συνήχθησαν.

15. 5:47 (3:2) ויבנו... ויקם ≈ καὶ καταστὰς... ἡτοίμασαν.

16. 5:65 (4:2) ויאמרו... ויגשו ≈ καὶ προσελθόντες... λέγουσιν.

17. 6:2 (5:2) ושריו למבנא... קמו ≈ στάς... ἤρξαντο οἰκοδομεῖν.

18. 6:19 (5:16) אתא יהב ≈ παραγενόμενος ἐνεβάλετο.

19. 6:19 (5:16) מתבנא ולא שלם ≈ οἰκοδομούμενος οὐκ ἔλαβεν συντέλειαν.

20. 8:42-43 (8:15-16) מצאתי... ואשלחה ≈ εὑρών... ἀπέστειλα.

21. 8:44-45 (8:17) ואוצאה (ואצוה) אותם... ואשימה בפיהם דברים ≈ καὶ εἶπα αὐτοῖς ἐλθεῖν... ἐντειλάμενος αὐτοῖς.

22. 8:70 (9:5-6) קמתי... ובקרעי... ואכרעה... ואפרשה... ואמרה ≈ καὶ ἐξεγερθείς... διερρηγμένα ἔχων... κάμψας... καὶ ἐκτείνας... ἔλεγον.

23. 8:82 (9:12) תחזקו ואכלתם ≈ ἰσχύσαντες φάγητε.

24. 8:89 (10:2) ויען... ויאמר ≈ καὶ φωνήσας... εἶπεν.

25. 8:92 (10:5) ויקם... וישבע ≈ καὶ ἀναστάς... ὤρκισεν.

26. 9:1 (10:6) ויקם... וילך ≈ καὶ ἀναστάς... ἐπορεύθη.

27. 9:2 (10:6) וילך... אכל ≈ καὶ αὐλισθείς... ἐγεύσατο.

28. 9:7 (10:10) ויקם... ויאמר ≈ καὶ ἀναστάς... εἶπεν.

29. 9:47 (Neh 8:6) ויקדו... וישתחוו ≈ προσπεσόντες... προσεκύνησαν.

30. 9:48 (8:8) ויקראו... ויבינו ≈ ἀνεγίνωσκον... ἐμφυσιοῦντες.

31. 9:51 (8:10) לכו אכלו ≈ βαδίσαντες οὖν φάγετε.

Such an abundance of data argues for the reconstruction of paratactic clauses in those cases where the *Vorlage* has not come down to us:

32. 5:63 (Ezr 4:1) וישמעו (צרי יהודה ובנימן) ≈ καὶ ἀκούσαντες... ἤλθοσαν ἐπιγνῶναι.

Presumably, וישמעו... ויבאו לדעת.

33. 6:8 (5:8) ‫(ליהוד מדינתא)‬ ‫אזלנא‬ ≈ παραγενόμενοι... καὶ ἐλθόντες... κατελάβομεν.

Presumably, ‫אזלנא... ואתינא... והשכחנא...‬.

34. 8:91 (10:4) ‫(כי עליך הדבר)‬ ‫קום‬ ≈ ἀναστὰς ἐπιτέλει

Presumably, ‫קום עשה‬.[270]

In spite of this clear and well-documented pattern, the interchange of parataxis and hypotaxis cannot serve as a fail-proof measure of literalism. There are any number of ways in which hypotactic constructions can be made and diverse degrees of rewriting may be involved. For example, the way in which the translator linked non-contiguous verbs is far more indicative of his method, than when the verbs are adjacent to each other. Then, too, there are verbs which are natural candidates for hypotactic treatment, such as ‫ויען/ויקם... ויאמר‬, and thus require a slight change only. In more complicated cases, the translator had to completely rewrite his *Vorlage*. One general, though obviously inaccurate, way of seeing the difference between translators is to actually count the number of verses in which such cases occur. In I Esd, we find a total of 35 cases out of 285 verses (excluding the lists), a ratio of 1:8.[271] In the parallel material of the LXX, on the other hand, we find not even one. It seems that the translators of I Esd and II Esd (and, in this case, also LXX-Chr) represent two extremes, one feeling free, or even compelled, to adapt the *Vorlage* to his target language, the other blindly adhering to the original.

---

[270] This may, however, be an expansion by the translator, since he sometimes uses two words to express a given verb in order to better convey its meaning; see below.

[271] The distribution is uneven. Chapters 2, 5 and 6 show an average of one change for every eight verses, Chapters 1 and 9 a ratio of 1:6, while in Chapters 7 and 8 the ratio drops to 1:14. There is no apparent reason for the differences. In the Aramaic parts, the ratio is 1:10, in the Hebrew – 1:8. This may only signify that both languages were similarly treated.

(b) Reformulation of Subordinate Clauses

In places where a finite verb + infinitive served as a condensed complex sentence, the translator replaced them with his favorite combination of finite verb + participle.

1. 5:57 (Ezr 3:10) ויעמידו... להלל ≈ καὶ ἔστησαν... ὑμνοῦντες.

2. 5:58 (3:11) ויענו (בהלל) ובהודת ≈ καὶ ἐφώνησαν... ὁμολογοῦντες.

3. 5:59 (3:11) הריעו... בהלל ≈ ἐσάλπισαν... ὑμνοῦντες.

4. 7:13 (3:10) הנבדל... לדרש ≈ οἱ χωρισθέντες... ζητοῦντες.

The following examples are particularly interesting because the verbs change their role: the infinitive assumes the role of the finite verb, while the finite verb is replaced by a participle.

5. 1:38 (2 Chr 36:6) ויאסרהו... להליכו ≈ καὶ δήσας αὐτὸν... ἀπήγαγεν.

6. 1:46 (36:13) ויקש... משוב ≈ καὶ σκληρύνας... παρέβη.

7. 6:4 (Ezr 5:4) שם... טעם... לבנא ≈ συντάξαντος... οἰκοδομεῖτε.

8. 6:10 (5:9) שם... טעם... למבניה ≈ προστάξαντος οἰκοδομεῖτε.

9. 8:59 (8:30) וקבלו... להביא ≈ καὶ οἱ παραλαβόντες... εἰσήνεγκαν.

10. 8:60 (8:31) ונסעה... ללכת ≈ καὶ ἀναζεύξαντες... εἰσήλθομεν.

A finite verb + participle is introduced for a variety of other hypotactic formulations in the *Vorlage*:

11. 1:46 (2 Chr 36:13) מרד אשר השביעו... ≈ ὁρκισθείς... ἐπιορκήσας ἀπέστη.

12. 5:54 (Ezr 3:8) לבואם... החלו ≈ παραγενόμενος... ἤρξατο.

13. 8:88 (10:1) וכהתפלל... וכהתודתו ≈ καὶ ὅτε προσευχόμενος... ἀνθωμολογεῖτο.

14. 9:45 (Neh 8:5) ויפתח... כי... היה ≈ καὶ ἀναλαβὼν... προεκάθητο γάρ...

(c) Participle / Noun

At times, the translator replaces a noun with a hypotactic clause:

1-6. 1:20 (2 Chr 35:19) נעשה ...למלכות ≈ βασιλεύοντος ... ἤχθη.

In five other cases which indicate the year of reign, the translator replaces the nouns מֶלֶך and מלכות with a participle: 2:1 (Ezr 1:1), 6:16 (5:13), 6:23 (6:3), 8:5 (7:7), 8:1 (7:1).

7. 7:3 (6:14) ומצלחין בנבואת ≈ καὶ εὔοδα ἐγίνετο ... προφητευόντων.

Two nominal phrases are replaced by a participle:

8. 8:4 (7:6) כיד ה' ...ויתן ≈ καὶ ἔδωκεν ... εὑρόντος χάριν.

9. 8:6 (7:9) בא ...יסד המעלה ≈ ἐξελθόντες ... παρεγένοντο.

(d) Participle / Finite Verb

1. 5:60 (Ezr 3:12) אשר ראו ...(ורבים) ≈ οἱ ἑωρακότες.

2. 8:25 (7:27) אשר נתן ...(ברוך ה') ≈ ὁ δούς.

3. 2:7 (1:5) לכל העיר ...) ויקומו ≈ καὶ καταστάντες.

The participle was probably used in the first two cases because of the relative pronoun, while in the third, because of the usual function of קום as an auxiliary verb.

Altogether, the hypotactic pattern of finite verb + participle appears nearly 70 times without being formally paralleled in the *Vorlage* (i.e., one for every four verses). Not one of the parallel passages in the LXX used the participle.

Were it not for the MT, this eminently Greek characteristic might have caused us to say that I Esd was originally written in Greek. Fortunately for research, however, there is no doubt in this case that we are dealing with an issue of translation technique.[272]

3. Other Changes in the Status of the Verb

Though other changes in verbal syntax are less-well established, they are probably best attributed to the translator's idiosyncrasies. Let us mention three small groups:

(a) Finite verbs replaced by infinitives, as demanded by the syntax, e.g., an imperative which governs the following verb:

1. 1:49 (2 Chr 36:17) ויעל ≈ προστάξαι ἀναβιβάσαι.

2. 2:22 (Ezr 4:19) ובקרו ≈ ἐπισκέψασθαι.

3. 2:24 (4:22) וזהירין הוו ≈ καὶ προνοηθῆναι.

4. 5:44 (2:69) נתנו ≈ καὶ δοῦναι.

5. 6:11 (5:10) נכתב ≈ γράψαι.

6. 6:22 (6:1) ובקרו ≈ ἐπισκέψασθαι.

(b) Infinitives replaced by finite verbs:

1. 1:6 (2 Chr 35:6) לעשות ≈ καὶ ποιήσατε.

2. 1:13 (35:14) בהעלות ≈ καὶ ἀπήνεγκαν.

3. 8:12 (Ezr 7:14) לבקרה ≈ ὅπως ἐπισκέψωνται.

(c) Participles rendered in various ways, in accord with the changing context; e.g., in the past tense:

---

[272] Black (1967), pp. 61-69, points out the frequent use of idiomatic hypotactic clauses in the Gospels (except for Mark) and Acts, but suggests that they were translated from the Aramaic.

1. 1:30 (2 Chr 35:25) מתאבלים ≈ ἐπένθησαν.

2. 6:3 (Ezr 5:3) אמרין ≈ εἶπαν.

3. 9:48 (Neh 8:7) מבינים ≈ ἐδίδασκον.

4. 9:50 (Neh 8:9) בוכים ≈ ἔκλαιον.

5. 9:53 (Neh 8:11) מחשים ≈ ἐκέλευον.

In conclusion, we have to acknowledge the diversity and complexity of changes in verbal syntax, and hence, the difficulty in turning them into a criterion for comparative evaluation of translation techniques. Even keeping a simple tally of the changes can be problematic, seeing that some alterations are random, others systematic, some affect more than one verb, or even all of the surrounding text. As regards our translator, the mere knowledge of his work enables us to make more accurate use of the text for purposes of reconstruction.

d. Word-Order

The differences in word-order dramatically show the relationship between the study of translation technique and the attempt to determine the *Vorlage*.[273] Changes in word-order can basically be divided into three groups:

First, there are changes which evidently relate to the nature of the target language and obviously come from the hand of the translator. In placing the adjective before the noun, for example, an order which Hebrew does not permit, the translator is clearly striving to give his work an authentic Greek flavor.

---

[273] See Marquis (1986), pp. 59-94. Marquis offers a mathematical formula for measuring the literalism of a given translator based on deviations in word-order, so that he might take issue with our classifications below.

Second, there are changes which clearly go beyond the level of translation. This is the case when entire passages, sentences, phrases, sometimes even single words, appear in a different order but the rearrangement is not due to any considerations of the target language and is hence best attributed to the source from which the translator worked. On the whole, there are few differences of this kind between I Esd and the MT.

Finally, there are changes which fall between these two groups, and are difficult to determine. In such cases, it is hard to know whether it was the *Vorlage* or the translator who first initiated the change, especially in cases where the translator was not committed to strict accuracy.

I Esd offers dozens of examples where the change in word-order undoubtedly originated with the translator, seeing that they could not have happened in Hebrew or Aramaic. While we can theorize that the translator was responsible for other differences as well, ones which are not strictly 'Greek', we cannot rule out the possibility of a variant source.

1. Changes of Word-Order by the Translator

Our translator, sensitive as he was to the target language, made changes in word-order not only in order to avoid usages unacceptable in Greek, but also to try to endow his text with a certain grace and natural fluency.

Since Greek case-endings allow for a variegated word-order impossible in languages where the order determines a word's function in the sentence, the majority of changes which may safely be attributed to the translator are in noun phrases.

(a) Particles

One hardly expects the translator of I Esd to adhere to word-order when particles are concerned. He makes free use of particles such as γάρ

(24 times), οὖν (12 times) etc.; though, their parallels *waw*, כי, etc. would suggest another place in the sentence. Sometimes he inserts the particle between two elements which represent one word in his *Vorlage*, a characteristically Greek formulation; e.g., 5:66 (Ezr 4:2) כי ככם ≈ <u>ὁμοίως</u> γὰρ <u>ὑμῖν</u>; 8:7 (7:10) כי עזרא ≈ <u>ὁ</u> γὰρ Ἔσδρας.

(b) Noun Phrases

(1) Noun + Demonstrative

1. 6:28 (Ezr 4:2) לגבריא אלך ≈ τούτοις τοῖς ἀνθρώποις.

2. 8:62 (8:34) בעת ההיא ≈ αὐτῇ τῇ ὥρᾳ.

3. 8:84 (9:13) פליטה כזאת ≈ τοιαύτην ῥίζαν.

(2) Noun + Adjective

4. 2:12 (Ezr 1:10) כלים אחרים ≈ καὶ ἄλλα σκεύη.

5. 8:73 (9:7) באשמה גדלה ≈ ἐν μεγάλῃ ἁμαρτίᾳ.

6. 8:83 (9:13) ובאשמתנו הגדלה ≈ καὶ τὰς μεγάλας ἁμαρτίας ἡμῶν.

7. 9:10 (10:12) קול גדול ≈ μεγάλῃ τῇ φωνῇ.

8. 9:18 (10:18) נשים נכריות ≈ ἀλλογενεῖς γυναῖκας.

Month / year + ordinal:

9-16. 5:52 (Ezr 3:1) החדש השביעי ≈ τοῦ ἑβδόμου μηνὸς; similarly, 5:52 (3:6); 7:10 (6:19); 8:6 (7:8, 9), 8:60 (8:31); 9:37 (Neh 7:72), 9:40 (8:2).

17. 6:16 (Ezr 5:13) בשנת חדה ≈ ἐν δὲ τῷ πρώτῳ ἔτει.

18. 7:5 (6:15) שנת שת ≈ τοῦ ἕκτου ἔτους.

(3) Construct State

Our translator was eager to rewrite phrases in the construct state (*nomen rectum + nomen regens*), a practice unacceptable in Greek syntax. He first introduces an equivalent of the *nomen regens*, and that of the *nomen rectum* only after. In its new position, the *nomen regens* is either expressed by an adjective or else functions as one.

(a) The *Nomen Regens* expressed by an Adjective

19. 1:3 (2 Chr 35:3) ארון הקדש ≈ τῆς ἁγίας κιβωτοῦ.

20. 1:29 (35:24) בקברות אבתיו ≈ ἐν τῷ πατρικῷ τάφῳ.

21. 1:51 (36:18) ואצרות המלך ושריו ≈ καὶ τὰς βασιλικὰς ἀποθήκας.

22. 8:2 (Ezr 7:5) הכהן הראש[274] ≈ τοῦ πρώτου ἱερέως.

23. 8:18 (7:20) בית גנזי מלכא ≈ τοῦ βασιλικοῦ γαζοφυλακίου.

24. 8:24 (7:26) לענש נכסין ≈ ἀργυρικῇ ζημίᾳ.

25. 8:64 (8:36) אחשדרפני המלך ≈ τοῖς βασιλικοῖς οἰκονόμοις.

26. 8:69 (9:4) למנחת הערב ≈ τῆς δειλινῆς θυσίας.

27. 9:42 (Neh 8:4) מגדל עץ ≈ τοῦ ξυλίνου βήματος.

28-34. In his translation of כלי בית הי/אלהים only part of the *nomen regens*, that is, בית, is rendered by an adjective and placed before the *nomen rectum*; whereas, the parallel of הי/אלהים retains its place and function, as in 1:39 (2 Chr 36:7) ומכלי בית הי ≈ καὶ ἀπὸ τῶν <u>ἱερῶν</u> σκευῶν τοῦ κυρίου, and six additional cases.

35. 8:17 (Ezr 7:19) For the MT's מאניא, I Esd reads τὰ ἱερὰ σκεύη τοῦ κυρίου. On the basis of the above material, we believe that here, too, the Greek reflects: מאני בית אלהא, or possibly מאניא די בית אלהא (cf. examples 53-56).

---

[274] This is not a proper construct; the regular form is indeed כהן הראש (5 times).

(β) The *nomen regens* functions as an adjective

The *nomen regens*, which continues to act as a noun, is introduced in between the elements which stand for the *nomen rectum*, and thus assumes the functions of an adjective:

36. 1:14 (2 Chr 35:15) <u>כמצות</u> דוד ≈ <u>κατὰ</u> τὰ ὑπὸ Δαυὶδ <u>τεταγμένα</u>.

37. 1:16 (35:16) <u>מזבח</u> הי ≈ <u>τὸ</u> του κυρίου <u>θυσιαστήριον</u>.

38-41. 2:15 (Ezr 4:7) <u>מלך</u> פרס ≈ <u>τοῦ</u> Περσῶν <u>βασιλέως</u>; similarly, 2:25 (4:24); 5:53 (3:7); 8:1 (7:1).

42. 2:15 (4:7) <u>ובימי</u> ארתחשׁשׁתא מלך פרס ≈ 'Ἐν δὲ <u>τοῖς</u> ἐπὶ 'Αρταξέρξου τοῦ Περσῶν βασιλέως <u>χρόνοις</u>.

43. 5:48 (3:2) <u>בתורת</u> משׁה ≈ <u>ἐν τῇ</u> Μωυσέως <u>βίβλῳ</u>.

44. 5:50 (3:4) <u>את חג</u> הסכות ≈ <u>τὴν</u> τῆς σκηνοπηγίας <u>ἑορτήν</u>.

45. 5:53 (3:7) <u>אל ים</u> יפוא ≈ <u>εἰς</u> τὸν 'Ιόππης <u>λιμένα</u>.

46. 5:70 (4:7) <u>מלכות</u> דריושׁ ≈ <u>τῆς</u> Δαρείου <u>βασιλείας</u>.

47. 6:29 (6:9) <u>כמאמר</u> כהניא די בירושׁלם ≈ <u>καθὼς ἂν</u> οἱ ἱερεῖς οἱ ἐν 'Ιερουσαλὴμ <u>ὑπαγορεύσωσιν</u>.

48. 7:9 (6:18) <u>ספר</u> משׁה ≈ <u>τῇ</u> Μωυσέως <u>βίβλῳ</u>.

49. 8:3 (7:6) <u>בתורת</u> משׁה ≈ <u>ἐν τῷ</u> Μωυσέως <u>νόμῳ</u>.

50. 8:21 (7:23) <u>טעם</u> אלה ≈ <u>τὸν</u> τοῦ θεοῦ <u>νόμον</u>.

51. 9:13 (10:14) <u>ועמהם זקני</u> עיר ועיר ≈ <u>καὶ ἑκάστου δὲ</u> τόπου <u>τοὺς πρεσβυτέρους</u>.

52. On the basis of this pattern – example 48 in particular – we reconstruct the unparalleled text of 7:6 (6:16) <u>ἐν τῇ</u> Μωυσέως <u>βίβλῳ</u> by <u>בסֵפר</u> משׁה.

(4) Other Possessive Compounds

A sequence of genitives is sometimes broken up by the particle די;
these cases met with the same treatment accorded to simple constructs:

53. 2:18 (4:15) בְּסְפֵר דָכְרָנַיָא די אֲבָהָתָךְ ≈ ἐν τοῖς ἀπὸ τῶν πατέρων σου
βιβλίοις.

54. 2:25 (4:23) אַרְתַּחְשַׁשְׁתְּ מַלְכָּא די פַּרְשֶׁגֶן נִשְׁתְּוָנָא ≈ τῶν παρὰ τοῦ βασιλέως
Ἀρταξέρξου γραφέντων.

The following two examples are mutually instructive:

55. 6:21 (5:17) די מַלְכָּא בֵּית גִּנְזַיָּא ≈ ἐν τοῖς βασιλικοῖς βιβλιοφυλακίοις
τοῦ·κυρίου βασιλέως.

Βιβλιοφυλακίοις probably reflects בבית ספריא די גנזיא, as in the
following verse. This example is further complicated by a double translation
of די מלכא; the first (βασιλικοῖς) corresponding to the pattern described
here, the second (τοῦ κυρίου βασιλέως) to the *Vorlage*. Elsewhere, as
well, the translator readily replaced the noun מלך with the adjective
βασιλικός (see examples 21, 23, 26).

56. 6:22 (6:1) בבית ספריא די גנזיא ≈ ἐν τοῖς βασιλικοῖς βιβλιοφυλακίοις.
Βασιλικοῖς probably reflects an additional די מלכא, in accordance with the
previous verse.

In sum, phrases in the construct state were apt to stimulate changes
in word-order. It is worth noticing that our translator found other ways to
evade constructs, especially by simply turning the *nomen regens* into an
adjective.

The above-noted data can be characterized by two points: One, the
desire to change the word-order is rooted entirely in the fundamental
difference between the original language and the target language. Not one
of these cases makes us think that a different word-order existed in the

Vorlage. Two, there are more than enough cases to prove the characteristic work habits of the translator. Time and again we find him attentive to the needs of the target language, and not the least reluctant to rework his *Vorlage* into a natural sounding Greek text.

In the following cases, the Greek is less transparently different from the Hebrew and the categories involved less well-defined. The evidence is therefore too inconclusive to claim that the translator preferred one kind of construction over another; even though, the changes can probably be attributed to his hand.

(5) Appositions

57. 2:3 (Ezr 1:2) כרש מלך פרס ≈ ὁ βασιλεὺς Περσῶν Κῦρος.

The Greek word-order cannot possibly reflect a variant, nor did the translator choose to use it on other occasions.

58. 8:44-45 (8:17) בכספיא המקום... הנתונים בכספיא המקום ≈ τὸν ἐν τῷ τόπῳ τοῦ γαζοφυλακίου... καὶ τοῖς ἐν τῷ τόπῳ γαζοφύλαξιν.

The translator changed both the order and sense of the words, taking the place name to mean 'the place of the treasury'.

59. 2:7 (1:5) For the MT's ליהודה ובנימן, I Esd reads: τῆς 'Ιουδα καὶ Βενιαμὶν φυλῆς. This presumably stands for יהודה ובנימן (לשבט); cf. 5:63 (4:1); 9:5 (10:9), where φυλή comes first, retaining the order of our conjectured *Vorlage*.

While these examples are instructive in themselves, they do not allow us to draw further conclusions in regard to changes in the word-order of appositions.

(6) Numbers

The differences relating to numbers can be even trickier because in both Hebrew and Greek numbers can come either before or after the noun. The data point to a clear trend. When the noun precedes the number I Esd, always retains the order. But when the noun comes after the number, the order is usually reversed.[275]

60. 1:17 (2 Chr 35:17)
.שבעת ~ ימים

61. 1:33 (36:2)
.שלוש ועשרים ~ שנה

64. 1:37 (36:5)
.עשרים וחמש ~ שנה

65. 1:41 (36:9)
.שמונה ~ שנים

66. 1:42 (36:9)
.ושלשה ~ חדשים

67. 1:42 (36:9)
.ועשרת ~ ימים

62. 1:33 (36:2)
.ושלשה ~ חדשים

63. 1:34 (36:3)
.ומאה ~ ככר כסף

68. 1:44 (36:11)
.עשרים ואחת ~ שנה

69. 1:44 (36:11)
.ואחת עשרה ~ שנה

70. 1:55 (36:21)
.שבעים ~ שנה

71-80. 8:31-40 (Ezr 8:4-14)
.הזכרים ~ מאתים

81-82. 8:56 (8:26)
.מאה ~ לככרים, מאה ~ ככר

The question is how many of these cases can be attributed to the *Vorlage*, and thus, to a preference known in Late Biblical Hebrew.[276] In our own opinion, such cases are probably best attributed to the translator himself. First of all, in some of the cases adduced from Chapter 1 a different word-order in the *Vorlage* is impossible. Moreover, many of them come from the concluding formulae which were reformulated by the translator in other respects. Finally, we have already seen the changes of

---

[275] The order is left untouched in שבעת יעטהי, 8:11 (Ezr 7:14).

[276] Polzin (1976), pp. 58ff.

word-order in regard to ordinals (examples 9-18 above), changes which must surely originate with the translator. It seems, therefore, that the translator is at least partly responsible for the changes, although, not because the Greek requires them.[277] It is worth noticing that the translator of Daniel did not bother to change the order and left the number before the noun when it appeared that way in his *Vorlage*, e.g., Dan 7:2, 3, 5, 17; 8:8, 22.

(7) The Word כל

Quite unexpectedly we find only two random examples of a different word-order in relation to the place of כל / πᾶς, probably another free reformulation on the part of the translator:

83. 5:51 (Ezr 3:5) ולכל מועדי ה' המקדשים ≈ καὶ ἑορτῶν πασῶν ἡγιασμένων.

84. 9:53 (Neh 8:11) לכל העם ≈ τῷ δήμῳ παντί.

In sum, there is a wealth of noun phrases which lured the translator into changing the word-order of his *Vorlage* in order to achieve a more stylized Greek.

(c) Nominal Clauses

The nominal clause presented the translator with a number of ways to change the word-order of his *Vorlage*.

Considering his liberal use of εἶναι, there is little wonder that he sometimes moved the copula around. In the first two cases below, the Hebrew does not permit the word-order implied by the Greek, in which the copula comes between the noun and its adjectival predicate:

1. 8:80 (Ezr 9:11) ארץ נדה היא (...הארץ) ≈ ἡ γῆ... ἐστιν γῆ μεμολυσμένη.

2. 9:49 (Neh 8:9) היום קדש הוא ≈ ἡ ἡμέρα αὕτη ἐστὶν ἁγία.

---

[277] Blass-Debrunner (1961), §474(1): "Numerals are more often placed first in the Gospels. But in lists, statements of date and distance... they usually come after".

Similarly, we would not expect the predicate to come first in possessive sentences:

3. 2:20 (Ezr 4:16) לא איתי לך ≈ σοι οὐκέτι ἔσται.

4. 8:75 (9:8) (ועתה כמעט רגע) היתה (תחנה) ≈ ἡμῖν ἐγενήθη.

While this last example would suggest a reading of היתה לנו, which our translator chose to invert, such a reading is testified in ms B alone. All the other mss read ἐγενήθη ἡμῖν.

In the following examples, we can easily discern the hand of the translator as he uses one of his favorite methods: the insertion of an equivalent of one word between the elements which form the equivalent of another:

5. 8:3 (7:6) והוא סופר מהיר ≈ ὡς γραμματεὺς εὐφυὴς ὤν.

6. 5:48 (3:2) ככתוב בתורת משה איש האלהים ≈ ἀκολούθως τοῖς ἐν τῇ Μωυσέως βίβλῳ τοῦ ἀνθρώπου τοῦ θεοῦ διηγορευμένοις.

7. 2:24 (4:22) להנזקת מלכין ≈ εἰς τὸ βασιλεῖς ἐνοχλῆσαι.

8. 2:19 (4:15) ומהנזקת מלכין ומדנן ≈ καὶ βασιλεῖς καὶ πόλεις ἐνοχλοῦσα.

(d) Relative Clauses

The relative clause, though comprised of more than one word, is sometimes treated by the translator in the same way as an adjective or a *nomen regens*. Such is to say that he places the relative clause before its antecedent. Naturally, this would not be possible in either Hebrew or Aramaic.

1. 6:7 (Ezr 5:6) אפרסכיא די בעבר נהרא ≈ οἱ ἐν Συρίᾳ καὶ Φοινίκῃ ἡγεμόνες.

There seems to be a similar case in 6:26 (6:6), but the double translation involved there makes it unclear whether there is indeed a change of order.

2. 8:17 (7:10) (ונשאר) חשחות בית אלהך די יפל לך ≈ ὅσα ἂν ὑποπίπτῃ σοι εἰς τὴν χρείαν τοῦ ἱεροῦ τοῦ θεοῦ σου.

In the following example we again encounter our translator's favorite practice, i.e., the insertion of a relative clause between the components of the antecedent:

3. 8:41 (8:15) אל הנהר הבא אל אהוא ≈ <u>ἐπὶ</u> τὸν λεγόμενον Θερὰν <u>ποταμόν</u>.

On the basis of this pattern we may reconstruct the following readings:

4. 8:50 (8:21) ולטפנו ≈ <u>τε καὶ τοῖς</u> συνοῦσιν ἡμῖν <u>τέκνοις ἡμῶν</u>.
Reconstructed as: ולטפנו {אשר עמנו}.

5. 1:45 (2 Chr 36:12) מלפני ירמיהו הנביא ≈ <u>ἀπὸ τῶν</u> ῥηθέντων <u>λόγων</u> ὑπὸ Ἰερεμίου τοῦ προφήτου.
Reconstructed as: מלפני {דברי} ירמיהו הנביא {אשר דבר}.

6. 1:46 (36:13) וגם במלך נבוכדנאצר מרד אשר השביעו בשם אלהים ≈ καὶ ὁρκισθεὶς ἀπὸ τοῦ βασιλέως Ναβουχοδονοσὸρ τῷ ὀνόματι τοῦ κυρίου ἐπιορκήσας ἀπέστη.

The variant word-order might have originated in the *Vorlage*, seeing that in the MT the antecedent and relative clause are awkwardly separated by מרד. However, since the entire sentence was rewritten by the translator in order to form a passive construction, the change in word-order may have come from his hand as well.

A different *Vorlage* may account for the following example:

7. 8:13 (Ezr 7:15) (ולהיבלה כסף ודהב) די מלכא ויעטהי התנדבו לאלה ישראל ≈ τῷ κυρίῳ τοῦ Ἰσραὴλ ἃ ηὐξάμην ἐγώ τε καὶ οἱ φίλοι.

2. Changes of Doubtful Attribution

In view of all the above-noted material which clearly shows the translator's interference in matters of word-order, it is difficult to ascribe other changes in word-order to the *Vorlage* with any degree of confidence. At the same time, however, we cannot ignore the possibility that the translator found the inverted word-order in his source to begin with, in cases where the *Vorlage* would permit such an order. It should be noted that there may be a difference between Hebrew and Aramaic in reference to word-order.

(a) Nominal Phrases

(1) Silver and Gold / Gold and Silver

Hurvitz employed the word-pair זהב וכסף/כסף וזהב as proof of the phenomenon he termed 'diachronic chiasmus'; that is, the changed order of word-pairs testifies to the development of language patterns over time.[278] According to this view, a change of this sort is not merely a stylistic feature, but also a diachronic linguistic development proven by the distribution of data.[279] Indeed, of the forty times the pair 'gold-silver' appears in the Bible, thirty of them occur in late biblical books, a ratio which seems to speak for itself. The factor of linguistic development must be at work here.[280]

The same tendency is mirrored in I Esd. While in the MT, the pair occurs 9 times in the classical order 'silver and gold', and 4 times – 'gold and silver'; in I Esd, the ratio is 5 to 8, as we see in the table below:[281]

---

[278] Hurvitz (1971), pp. 248-255.

[279] Avishur (1974), pp. 253ff, questioned this analysis in his study of word-pairs, claiming that the change in order is a general stylistic phenomenon that has nothing to do with diachronic development.

[280] The shifting value of the metals may have affected the linguistic change; see Hurvitz, *ibid*, p. 250, note 14.

[281] Cases in which the two words appear several words apart are not included, since

	Hebrew		Aramaic	
	כסף וזהב	זהב וכסף	כסף ודהב	דהב וכסף
MT	6	2	3	2
I Esd	5	3	---	5

Though sparse, the data are highly instructive: (a) I Esd changes MT's 'silver-gold' into 'gold-silver' four times. There is no change in the opposite direction; (b) In the Hebrew sections, the order is changed only once; (c) In the Aramaic sections, 'silver-gold' gives way to 'gold-silver' on all three occasions; 'silver-gold' thus disappears from the Aramaic sections. The data clearly show that the differences do not originate with the translator since it is hard to imagine that he would insist on changing the order in the Aramaic sections but leave the Hebrew sections almost untouched. The evidence of Daniel is as always instructive: the data are almost evenly distributed in both the Hebrew and Aramaic sections, and rendered in the same order in the LXX. Considering the affinity between the translators of I Esd and LXX-Daniel,[282] we may conclude that neither reveal a preference in either direction, and that both of them faithfully rendered that which they found in their sources. A possible linguistic development in the *Vorlage* is supported by the distribution of the phrases in Aramaic documents. Indeed, we find כסף ודהב in the Old Aramaic inscriptions of Br-Rkb and Pnmu; whereas, the Elephantine documents, like Biblical Aramaic, make use of both כסף ודהב and דהב וכסף.[283] Finally, it is worth noting that in the Story of the Three Youths, the order is 'gold and silver' both times it occurs.

---

they are less likely to be rewritten. Indeed, 'silver' and 'gold' are used on four separate occasions in relation to various utensils, all in the Hebrew sections, twice in both ways. I Esd preserves the order of the MT.

[282] Their similar method of translation was recognized long ago. Some scholars even took them to be one and the same author; see Riessler (1899), pp. 52-56; Torrey (1910), p. 84.

[283] See Hurvitz, *ibid*, p. 251.

(2) The King X (title-name) / X the King (name-title)

Another expression which is used in a different order in the MT and in I Esd, again predominantly in the Aramaic sections, is the apposition composed of the king's name and title. Here too a factor of linguistic development comes into play.

In biblical Hebrew, titles such as כהן 'priest' or נביא 'prophet' are commonly preceded by the name. The title מלך, however, may either precede or follow the name, and the distribution is of interest: In Samuel-Kings, the prevailing order is title-name, as opposed to the order of other titles; whereas, in Chr, both patterns appear with equal frequency. It seems, therefore, that in later biblical Hebrew the usual order name-title influenced the use of מלך. This is also the customary order in Rabbinic Hebrew.[284]

In the Aramaic sections of Ezr and Daniel, the name ordinarily precedes the title.[285] In respect to the title of מלכא, however, we do find some fluctuation. Ezr is the more consistent, with the order being name-title (x מלכא) in all 14 cases. This is also the number of times it appears in Daniel as well, but here the reverse order (מלכא x) also appears on 6 occasions. The title-name order is unexpected in Aramaic since in both Ancient and Egyptian Aramaic the proper name precedes the title. It could have been borrowed from the common Greek pattern as found in the papyri and inscriptions of the last centuries B.C.E. Such borrowing, however, is not characteristic of the development of Aramaic in general, since in Late Aramaic the name-title pattern still holds sway.[286]

---

[284] Peretz (1968), pp. 129-133.

[285] רחום בעל טעם and the like (13 times in all in Ezr), or בלטשצר רב חרטומיא (3 times, and another 5 with an apposition that is not an official title, e.g., עבדוהי די אלהא in Daniel). Bauer-Leander (1927), p. 93, say only that the two types are interchangeable.

[286] Muraoka (1972), p. 23, counted 45 appositional phrases beginning with the proper name, and only one case in the opposite order.

Let us take a closer look at the way the data are distributed throughout I Esd and the MT:

	x מלכא βασιλεὺς χ	x מלכא χ βασιλεύς	x המלך βασιλεὺς χ	x המלך χ βασιλεύς
MT	---	14	7	2
I Esd	10 (+2)[287]	2	6 (+1)	1 (+1)
Story	1	5		

The dominance of the βασιλεὺς χ pattern (19:4) may be attributed to the translator's own preference, given his affinity to contemporary epigraphic sources. There are, however, several indications that he might simply have translated what he found in his *Vorlage*: (a) If the translator bothered to change his source on ten occasions, why did he leave the reverse order another four? (b) The interchange in 8:8 (Ezr 7:11) is particularly interesting, with I Esd reading χ βασιλεύς against both the MT and the dominant order in I Esd; (c) In the Story of the Three Youths, we find the title-name pattern only one out of six times, a ratio which fits the general Aramaic preference of Ezr, rather than the Greek of I Esd;[288] (d) The data for Daniel, which may serve as a control-group, also point in the same direction. There the normal order is χ βασιλεύς (22:7), unlike that which we find in I Esd. Apparently, the translator of Daniel also left his *Vorlage* unchanged; (e) The fact that both patterns appear in equal proportion in 2-4 Macc shows that neither dominated the Greek of their authors.

In view of these considerations, it would seem safe to conclude that the translator of I Esd had little reason to change the order in his source time and again. Given the nature of this translation, we could hypothesize that the title-name order sprang from his own stylistic preference, and

---

[287] Twice the phrase has no equivalent in I Esd, yet there are also two cases in which the order x מלכא in I Esd has no equivalent in the MT.

[288] We may note here that it does not fit the norm in the Hebrew portions either, a fact that may have its consequences concerning the language of the *Vorlage* of the story.

reject any possibility of a variant (x מלכא), otherwise not attested in Ezr. The fact is, however, that this pattern appears six times in the Aramaic of the Book of Daniel. Hence, it is not impossible that it was present in I Esd's source to begin with. If this unusual order does indeed signal a later linguistic development, we can tentatively suggest that I Esd's *Vorlage* represents a later stage than the MT in this respect, since it already reveals the tendency demonstrated by the Aramaic in the Book of Daniel.[289]

(b) Verbal Clauses

In discussing the subject of verbal clauses, we stand on even shakier ground. Since Greek, Hebrew and Aramaic all tolerate variation in the order of the components in the verbal clause, it becomes increasingly difficult to determine the extent to which the translator changed the word-order of his *Vorlage*.[290]

In general, the natural tendencies of the languages can be neatly divided between Greek on the one hand, and Hebrew and Aramaic on the other. While the verb usually comes towards the beginning of the sentence in Semitic languages, this is not true of the Indo-European languages. Scholars of the New Testament have often commented on this striking difference between the two language groups, and in fact, see this as one of the clear-cut signs of a Semitic substratum behind the New Testament.[291] It is not that sentences beginning with verbs constitute improper Greek,

---

[289] Charles (1929), pp. c-ci, draws far-reaching conclusions concerning the date of the Book of Daniel on the basis of the discussed word-order: "The evidence of this order of words seems in itself conclusive as to the Book of Daniel being not earlier than the second century B.C.".

[290] For the Aramaic, which again turns out to be our main concern, see Bauer-Leander (1927), pp. 99a-c, 100p, 101. In the last section, the freedom of word-order in verbal sentences is illustrated through examples of various combinations of subject-verb-object.

[291] Black (1967), pp. 50-51.

but that the sheer frequency of their occurrence gives the text a Semitic flavor.[292] When the verb comes towards the beginning of the sentence, but not actually at its start, the distinction becomes even cloudier. One thing, however, does seem certain: It is hard to imagine the translator seeking to move the verb towards the beginning of the sentence.

Against this background, the relationship between I Esd, or LXX-Daniel for that matter, and the MT, is rather surprising. Had we found that the translation tended to place the verb later in the sentence, we would have seen this as a syntactic reformulation expected of any translator concerned with producing a flowing Greek style. The facts, however, prove different. Of the approximately 25 cases in which I Esd and the MT have the verbs in different places, only 5 appear later in I Esd than the MT. No less interesting is that out of the remaining 20 cases in which the verb occurs earlier in I Esd, 13 come in the Aramaic sections of the book. The ratio between the Hebrew and Aramaic is thus 2:1, which is highly disproportionate considering that the Aramaic comprises only one fourth of the text. Other differences, such as the order of noun-modifiers, or interchanges of parataxis/hypotaxis and active/passive, which definitely derive from the translator, are more equally distributed throughout the Hebrew and Aramaic sections – four cases in Hebrew versus one in Aramaic. Why, then, would the translator make most changes in verb placement in the Aramaic material? The immediate, and probably most logical, conclusion is that for at least part of the Aramaic material the translator found these changes already present in his *Vorlage*.

Indeed, the sources anticipate a shift in the position of the verb. Evidently, while in Old Aramaic the verb appears towards the beginning of the sentence, as in other Semitic languages,[293] in Official Aramaic, the

---

[292] Blass & Debrunner (1961), §472, point out that the verb can stand at the beginning of a sentence in 'non-biblical' Greek as well; although, this is usual only for verbs of speech.

[293] Degen (1969), p. 81: "Kennzeichend für den Verbalsatz ist das finite Verb, das den Satz eröffnet".

verb comes later, apparently under the influence of Akkadian. In addition, the location of the verb is instrumental in determining whether Biblical Aramaic belongs to the western or eastern branch. The tendency of Biblical Aramaic to place the verb later in the sentence seems a sure sign of eastern influence.[294] I Esd steers a middle course by reflecting a word-order which is less 'eastern' than the Aramaic of the MT and closer to that of the Genesis-Apocryphon and the Aramaic Targum of Job from Qumran. In these texts, the verb comes either at the start of the sentence or just before the subject, the object, and other parts of the sentence. If Biblical Aramaic shows the same eastern influence as Official Aramaic – and this is only to be expected in documents emanating from the court of Persia – we can also say that it became more westernized over the years with the verb gradually moving towards the beginning of the sentence. Moreover, it appears that later Aramaic indeed reverted to the norms of western practice.[295] We can probably assume that complex processes such as these account for at least some of the differences between I Esd and the MT. The situation in Daniel is much the same with 30 (!) cases in which the verb comes earlier in the LXX than in the MT, all occuring in the Aramaic material. As in I Esd, here too we find a great deal of latitude in the placement of the verb.[296]

---

[294] Baumgartner (1927), p. 128: "Die Wortstellung des BA... von der sonst im Westsemitischen herrschenden abweicht, indem Subject, Object oder adverbiale Bestimmung dem verbalen Prädikat ebensogut voransehen wie folgen können"; Kutscher (1977), p. 105: "The characteristics of the Eastern type of A are... (4) The object (often) precedes the infinitive, (5) The object (often) precedes the finite verb, (6) The subject (often) precedes the verb"; see also Kitchen (1965), p. 76.

[295] See Kutscher (1977), pp. 33-34, on the language of the Genesis Apocryphon: "The 'Semitic' type... is prevalent: 1. The subject generally follows the verb. 2. The accusative object generally follows the verb. 3. The accusative object always follows the infinitive".

[296] E.g., נחוא ~ ופשרא. (Dan 2:4), ובתיכון נולו ~ יתשמון (2:5), שאל ~ מלכא (די) (2:11), יתן (5:7). In ~ ארגונא ~ ילבש... ותלתי במלכותא ~ ישלט (5:1), חמרא ~ שתה (2:16), די) זמן ~ לה). In the Hebrew portion of Daniel, the verb changes position only twice and in both cases the Greek has it later in the sentence (10:13 נותרתי שם, 11:36 ידבר נפלאות).

Due to the complexity of the subject, it would be unwise to make definite conclusions concerning the nature of the Aramaic underlying I Esd. Some of the differences may reflect a Hellenistic Greek tendency. Just how different the syntax of Hellenistic was from its Classical model we can see in Polybius' practice of placing the verb towards the beginning of subordinate (especially relative) clauses, and of administrative language placing the verb before a proper-noun subject.[297] Therefore, in cases such as 6:17 (Ezr 5:14) די נבוכדנצר הנפק ≈ ἃ ἐξήνεγκεν Ναβουχοδονοσόρ, the wording of the relative clause could just as easily reflect a tendency in the Greek as a different Aramaic *Vorlage*. However, it is not easy to establish such a tendency with our translator in view of a case such as די שכן שמה ≈ οὗ τὸ ὄνομα αὐτοῦ ἐπικέκληται, 6:32 (6:12); in which, the verb in the relative clause is rather postponed in I Esd in comparison with the MT. Generally, there is good reason to think that the change occurred in the *Vorlage*: (1) In spite of the developments in the Greek language, the translator would have little reason to re-order his *Vorlage* when the Greek not only tolerates the order found in the MT, but actually prefers it; (2) The word-order presumably reflected in I Esd is as natural as the Aramaic of the MT, a fact which makes it reasonable to assume a development in the Aramaic.

(1) The Verb precedes the Subject

In the following subordinate clauses, the translator may have preferred to have the verb precede the subject, as noted above:

1-2. 6:17, 25 (Ezr 5:14; 6:5) די נבוכדנצר הנפק ≈
ἃ ἐξήνεγκεν Ναβουχοδονοσόρ.

---

[297] Blass & Debrunner (1961), §472.

3. 8:13 (7:15) די מלכא ויעטוהי התנדבו ≈ ἃ ηὐξάμην ἐγώ τε καὶ οἱ φίλοι.[298]

4. 6:14 (5:12) להן מן די הרגזו אבהתנא ≈ καὶ ἐπεὶ οἱ πατέρες ἡμῶν παραπικράναντες ἥμαρτον.

The Hebrew material affords this example:

5. 9:50 (Neh 8:9) כי בוכים כל העם ≈ καὶ πάντες ἔκλαιον.

(2) The Verb Precedes the Object and its other Complements

6. 2:24 (Ezr 4:21) וקריתא דך לא תתבנא ≈ τοῦ οἰκοδομῆσαι τὴν πόλιν.

7. 6:10 (5:9) ביתא דנה למבניה ≈ οἰκοδομεῖτε τὸν οἶκον τοῦτον.

8. 6:16 (5:13) בית אלהא דנה לבנא ≈ οἰκοδομῆσαι τὸν οἶκον τοῦτον.

9. 6:18 (5:15) אל מאניא שא ≈ ἀπενέγκαντι πάντα τὰ σκεύη ταῦτα.

10. 6:24 (6:4) מן בית מלכא תתיהב ≈ δοθῆναι ἐκ τοῦ οἴκου Κύρου τοῦ βασιλέως.

11. 8:11 (7:14) כל קבל די מן קדם מלכא ושבעת יעטהי שליח ≈ δέδοκται ἐμοί τε καὶ τοῖς ἑπτὰ φίλοις συμβουλευταῖς.

12. 8:16 (7:18) בשאר כספא ודהבה למעבד ≈ ποιῆσαι χρυσίῳ καὶ ἀργυρίῳ.

13. 8:16 (7:18) כרעות אלהכם תעבדון ≈ ἐπιτέλει κατὰ τὸ θέλημα τοῦ θεοῦ σου.

Two examples occur in the Hebrew material:

14. 8:69 (9:4) ואלי יאספו ≈ καὶ ἐπισυνήχθησαν πρός με.

It is important to note that in this case the LXX and the Peshitta agree with I Esd against the MT.

---

[298] The reformulation here also involves a shift to the first person.

15. 9:55 (Neh 8:13) וביום השני נאספו ≈ καὶ ἐπισυνήχθησαν...

Since I Esd ends with this verb, we can only conjecture that a parallel of ביום השני followed the verb.

Let us also take note of the following example which proves somewhat more complicated since it occurs in a *casus pendens*. It is possible that the equivalent chosen for נדב required the change of order:

16. 5:43 (Ezr 2:68) התנדבו לבית האלהים להעמידו ≈ εὔξαντο ἐγεῖραι τὸν οἶκον.

There are only three places in I Esd where the change occurs in the opposite direction, so that the complement precedes the verb, against the MT:

17. 2:24 (4:22) למעבד על דנה ≈ παρὰ ταῦτα γένηται.

18. 6:31 (6:11) וזקיף יתמחא עלוהי ≈ καὶ ἐπὶ τούτου κρεμασθῆναι.

And in Hebrew:

19. 1:53 (2 Chr 36:20) ויגל השארית ≈ καὶ τοὺς ἐπιλοίπους ἀπήγαγεν.

(3) The Verb at the Beginning of the Sentence

20. 2:22 (Ezr 4:18) נשתונא די שלחתון עלינא מפרש קרי קדמי ≈ Ἀνέγνων τὴν ἐπιστολήν ἣν πεπόμφατε πρός με.

21. 2:25 (4:23) אדין מן די פרשגן נשתונא די ארתחששת מלכא קרי קדם ≈ τότε ἀναγνωσθέντων τῶν παρὰ τοῦ βασιλέως Ἀρταξέρξου γραφέντων.

22-23. 1:7 (2 Chr 35:8) ושריו לנדבה לעם לכהנים וללוים הרימו חלקיה וזכריהו ויחיאל נגידי בית האלהים לכהנים נתנו ≈ ἐδόθη κατ' ἐπαγγελίαν τῷ λαῷ καὶ τοῖς ἱερεῦσιν καὶ Λευίταις καὶ ἔδωκεν Χελκίας καὶ Ζαχαρίας καὶ Ἠσύηλος οἱ ἐπιστάται τοῦ ἱεροῦ τοῖς ἱερευσιν.

24-25. 1:41-42 (36:9) בן שמונה שנים יהויכין במלכו ושלשה חדשים ועשרה ימים מלך ≈ ὅτε γὰρ ἀνεδείχθη, ἦν ἐτῶν δέκα ὀκτώ, βασιλεύει δὲ μῆνας τρεῖς καὶ ἡμέρας δέκα.

The two transpositions in this last example are probably related and may well have been made by the translator, given his tendency to rework the formulae. In fact, all the changes in word-order under this heading seem to be part of a larger reformulation. Such changes add weight to the assumption that the translator was responsible for other changes in word-order as well.

In conclusion, some of the changes in word-order which involve the verb are part of more extensive paraphrases by the translator, others may reflect the tendency of Hellenistic Greek. In the final analysis, however, it seems that we are still left with a number of cases which reflect a different *Vorlage* and attest to a later development in the Aramaic language.

(4) The Place of the Verbal Complements

The following examples do not seem to have any unifying feature which would explain the position of the verbal complements. Nor, in trying to determine whether the reformulation occurred in the *Vorlage* or the translation, is there anything to tilt the scales in one direction or the other.

(α) Subject ~ Complement

1. 5:40 (Ezr 2:63) התרשתא להם (ויאמר) ≈ αὐτοῖς Νεεμίας καὶ Ἀτθαρίας.

This first example is a good case in point. The change involves a minor syntactic reformulation which could easily be ascribed to the translator were it not for the fact that the Lucianic mss to both Ezr and Neh 7:65 and the Peshitta to Ezr agree with I Esd. In addition, neither the Vulgate to Ezr nor ms B to Neh reflect להם in any way, thus pointing to its instability in the text. Hence, the change in word-order must have occurred in the *Vorlage*.

2. 1:41 (2 Chr 36:8) וימלך) יהויכין בנו תחתיו) ≈ ἀντ' αὐτοῦ 'Ιωακεὶμ ὁ υἱὸς αὐτοῦ.

3. 1:26 (35:22) ולא הסב) יאשיהו פניו) ≈ ἑαυτὸν 'Ιωσίας.

4. 6:7 (Ezr 5:6) די שלח) תתני... על דריוש מלכא) ≈ Δαρείῳ... Σισίννης.

(β) Adverb ~ Object

5. 1:1 (2 Chr 35:1) ויעש יאשיהו) בירושלם פסח) ≈ τὸ πάσχα ἐν 'Ιερουσαλήμ.

6. 8:10 (Ezr 7:13) למהך) לירושלם עמך) ≈ σοι εἰς 'Ιερουσαλήμ.

And *vice versa*:

7. 5:53 (3:7) להביא) עצי ארזים מן הלבנון) ≈ ἐκ τοῦ Λιβάνου ξύλα κέδρινα.

8. 1:17 (2 Chr 35:17) ויעשו...) את הפסח בעת ההיא) ≈ ἐν τῷ καιρῷ τούτῳ τὸ πάσχα.

(γ) Transposing Adverbs of Time and Place

9. 8:28 (Ezr 8:1) העלים עמי) במלכות ארתחשסתא המלך מבבל) ≈ ἐκ Βαβυλῶνος ἐν τῇ βασιλείᾳ 'Αρταξέρξου τοῦ βασιλέως.

10. 9:5 (10:9) ויקבצו...) ירושלם לשלשת הימים) ≈ ἐν τρισὶν ἡμέραις εἰς 'Ιερουσαλήμ.

Unlike the question of verb placement, where the Aramaic examples are disproportionately high, only two of these ten examples come from the Aramaic material. There is no obvious pattern to these changes, all of which could have originated as easily in the *Vorlage* as the translation.

3. Probable Change of Word-Order in the *Vorlage*

Changes made at the level of *Vorlage* would not normally fall within the purview of a chapter dealing with translation technique. When so many areas remain open to doubt, however, it becomes less easy to draw the line. Even cases which do not bear the particular stamp of the translator could have originated with him, and we have already had ample opportunity to see that preserving the word-order of his *Vorlage* was not one of his top priorities. Whether he made changes in the word-order for absolutely no reason at all is another question. The above-noted cases have one thing in common: they all come from the realm of syntax and style, and may thus be reasonably ascribed to the sensitivity of the translator to the quality of his target language. In the following texts, we find other factors at work, ones which are characteristic of the process of transmission rather than translation. This is true even of the minor changes, as when כל precedes different nouns, and certainly of the more complex cases, in which entire clauses are moved around. The following examples, then, would seem to suggest a different text.

1. 1:19 (2 Chr 35:18) וכל יהודה וישראל ≈ καὶ οἱ Ἰουδαῖοι καὶ πᾶς Ἰσραήλ, possibly reflecting: ויהודה וכל ישראל.

2. 8:52 (Ezr 8:22) על כל מבקשיו לטובה ≈ μετὰ τῶν ἐπιζητούντων αὐτὸν εἰς πᾶσαν ἐπανόρθωσιν, which may represent: על מבקשיו לכל טובה.

3. 1:12-13 (2 Chr 35:14) (ואחר הכינו להם) ולכהנים כי הכהנים בני אהרן ≈ τε καὶ τοῖς ἱερεῦσιν ἀδελφοῖς αὐτῶν υἱοῖς Ἀαρών. οἱ γὰρ ἱερεῖς..., probably for: ...(ואחר הכינו להם) ולכהנים אחיהם בני אהרן. כי הכהנים.

4. 1:47 (36:14) שרי הכהנים והעם ≈ καὶ οἱ ἡγούμενοι δὲ τοῦ λαοῦ καὶ τῶν ἱερέων, probably reflecting: שרי העם והכהנים. The translator could easily have kept the MT's terminology had he had it in front of him. The phrase

שרי הכהנים disappears in the LXX as well; even though, the groups there are different.

5. 6:30 (Ezr 6:10) (די להון מהקרבין ניחוחין לאלה שמיא) ומצלין לחיי מלכא ובנוהי ≈ ὑπὲρ τοῦ βασιλέως καὶ τῶν παίδων καὶ προσεύχωνται περὶ τῆς αὐτῶν ζωῆς, probably representing: על מלכא ובנוהי ומצלין לחייהון.

6. 9:47 (Neh 8:6) ויקדו וישתחוו לה׳ אפים ארצה ≈ προσπεσόντες ἐπὶ τὴν γῆν προσεκύνησαν τῷ κυρίῳ, possibly for: ויקדו אפים ארצה וישתחוו לה׳.

The following examples involve changes besides word-order:

7. 1:10 (2 Chr 35:10) והלוים על מחלקותם כמצות המלך... לתתם למפלגות ≈ καὶ οἱ Λευῖται ἔχοντες τὰ ἄζυμα κατὰ τὰς φυλάς, possibly for: והלוים במצות על מחלקותם למפלגות. The words המלך... לתתם are not represented in I Esd.

8. 1:24 (35:21) וישלח אליו מלאכים ≈ καὶ διεπέμψατο βασιλεὺς Αἰγύπτου πρὸς αὐτόν, possibly for: וישלח מלך מצרים אליו.

9. 1:25 (35:21) ואלהים אמר לבהלני חדל לך מאלהים אשר עמי ≈ καὶ νῦν κύριος μετ᾽ ἐμοῦ ἐστιν, καὶ κύριος μετ᾽ ἐμοῦ ἐπισπεύδων ἐστίν ἀπόστηθι. The MT is difficult and calls for reformulation, but so is the text presumably read by our translator: ועתה אלהים עמי ואלהים עמי לבהלני חדל לך.

10. 5:56 (Ezr 3:9)

קדמיאל ובניו בני יהודה כאחד לנצח על עשה המלאכה בבית האלהים בני חנדד בניהם ואחיהם הלוים

καὶ Καδμιηλ ὁ ἀδελφὸς καὶ οἱ υἱοὶ Ἰησοῦ Ημαδαβουν καὶ οἱ υἱοὶ Ἰωδὰ τοῦ Ἰλιαδοὺν σὺν τοῖς υἱοῖς καὶ ἀδελφοῖς, πάντες οἱ Λευῖται, ὁμοθυμαδὸν ἐργοδιῶκται ποιοῦντες εἰς τὰ ἔργα ἐν τῷ οἴκῳ τοῦ θεοῦ.

On the whole, I Esd reflects a text in which בני חנדד בניהם ואחיהם הלוים precedes כאחד.

In the last two examples, two larger texts change places:

11. 5:42 (2:66-67)

גמליהם ארבע מאות שלשים וחמשה ~ סוסיהם שבע מאות שלשים וששה
פרדיהם מאתים ארבעים וחמשה.

12. 8:81 (9:12)   בנותיכם אל תתנו לבניהם ~ ובנתיהם אל תשאו לבניכם.

In sum, if we disregard the particles, we find some 165 cases of changed word-order, two-thirds of which undoubtedly originate with the translator. This is quite a large number, considering that I Esd only has 285 verses (not counting the lists).

The first and largest group of changes in word-order (some 100 cases) consists primarily of nominal phrases. These can conceivably be attributed to the translator, and show him as being uncommitted to the order in his *Vorlage*. This group makes it likely that the remaining changes of word-order also originated with the translator; although, it is not impossible that they occurred already in the *Vorlage*. For this reason our second group of examples (some 50 cases), which consists mostly of verbal phrases, falls into the grey area of doubt; even though, the changes still pertain to sentence structure. The third and small group of changes, twelve in all, do not fall into the realm of syntax. They probably occurred already in the *Vorlage*, though here too we cannot rule out the possibility that the change occurred as a result of the translator's indifference to the original word-order.

e. Condensation and Expansion

Given the translator's tendency to devise his equivalents on the basis of logical units rather than the individual elements, it comes as no surprise to find that condensation occurs far more frequently than expansion. Indeed, our translator's tendency to condense two-word phrases into one single word is well-attested. Only rarely does he render one word with a compound idiom.

1. Condensation

Let us begin with the pronoun, which the translator probably regarded as redundant:

1. 2:4 (Ezr 1:2) והוא פקד ≈ καὶ ἐσήμηνεν.

2. 2:20 (4:16) מהודעין אנחנה ≈ ὑποδείκνυμεν.

3. 5:66 (4:2) אנחנו זבחים ≈ ἐπιθύομεν.

Similarly, it is not surprising that he did not translate the auxiliary verb on several occasions:

4. 6:28 (Ezr 6:8) תהוא מתיהבא ≈ δίδοσθαι.

5. 6:29 (6:9) להוא מתיהב ≈ ἀναλίσκεσθαι.

6. 6:30 (6:10) להון מהקרבין ≈ προσφέρωνται.

7. 5:69 (4:4) ויהי... מרפים ≈ ἐπικοιμώμενα.

8. 1:31 (2 Chr 35:27) הנם כתבים ≈ ἱστόρηται.

9. 1:40 (36:8) הנם כתבים ≈ ἀναγέγραπται.

His tendency to condense the text becomes readily apparent in the following standard equivalents:

10-12. 9:16, 17 (Ezr 10:16, 17), 9:40 (Neh 8:2) ביום אחד ≈ τῇ νουμηνίᾳ.

13. 9:41 (Neh 8:3) מחצית היום ≈ μεσημβρινός.

14. 8:86 (Ezr 9:15) כהיום הזה ≈ ἐν τῇ σήμερον.

15. 9:38 (Neh 8:1) כאיש אחד ≈ ὁμοθυμαδόν.

16-19. 8:1, 68, 92; 9:11 (Ezr 7:1; 9:3; 10:5, 13) הדברים האלה, הדבר הזה ≈ τούτοι, ταῦτα.

He easily condensed constructs into one term:

20-22. 1:4, 5, 10 (2 Chr 35:4, 5, 12) בית אבות ≈ πατριά, πατρική, πατέρες.

23. 1:7 (35:7) בני עזים ≈ ἔριφοι.

24. 7:8 (Ezr 6:17) צפירי עזים ≈ χίμαροι.

25. 2:9 (1:7) בבית אלהיו ≈ εἰδωλεῖον.

26. 8:50 (8:21) דרך ישרה ≈ εὐοδία.

27. 8:74 (9:7) ובבשת פנים ≈ αἰσχύνη.

28. 9:13 (10:14) חרון אף ≈ ὀργή.

One particularly large group consists of a verb and its complement condensed into one Greek verb:

29-39. שים טעם ≈ προστάσσειν, ἐπιτάσσειν, συντάσσειν.

40. 2:2 (Ezr 1:1) ויעבר קול ≈ καὶ ἐκήρυξεν.

41. 2:8 (1:6) חזקו בידיהם ≈ ἐβοήθησαν.

42. 2:21 (4:17) פתגמא שלח ≈ ἀντέγραψεν.

43. 6:12 (5:11) פתגמא התיבונא ≈ ἀπεκρίθησαν ἡμῖν.

44. 6:6 (5:5) יתיבון נשתונא ≈ προσφωνηθῆναι.

45. 6:31 (6:11) וזקיף יתמחא ≈ κρεμασθῆναι.

46. 8:26 (7:28) הטה חסד ≈ ἐτίμησεν.

47. 9:54 (Neh 8:12) ולעשות שמחה ≈ εὐφρανθῆναι.

48. 1:49 (2 Chr 36:16) עלות חמת הי ≈ τοῦ θυμωθέντα αὐτόν.

Sometimes the condensed elements are not adjacent:

49. 1:30 (35:25) יאמרו... בקינותיהם ≈ ἐθρήνησεν.

50. 6:6 (5:5) טעמא... יהך ≈ τοῦ ὑποσημανθῆναι.

51. 6:22 (6:2) כתיב... דכרונה ≈ ὑπεμνημάτιστο.

Despite their condensed form, the equivalents are usually accurate enough to identify without problem. Sometimes, however, an element becomes so blurred that we wonder if it even formed part of the *Vorlage*. This is especially true when a given element seems redundant, or when the translator apparently misconstrued it and therefore chose to represent it only indirectly:

52. 2:25 (4:23) פרשגן נשתונא ≈ γραφέντων.

53. 8:56 (8:27) וכפרי זהב ≈ καὶ χρυσώματα.

The translator probably did not know the meaning of either נשתון or כפרי; thus, condensing them was an excellent way out of the difficulty.

The vagueness of his translation becomes especially apparent when different words are rendered by the same condensed equivalent:

54. 2:14 (1:11) עם העלות הגולה ≈ ἅμα τοῖς ἐκ τῆς αἰχμαλωσίας.

55. 7:13 (6:21) השבים מהגולה ≈ οἱ ἐκ τῆς αἰχμαλωσίας.

Not only do two different expressions turn into one, but, they are also indistinguishable from a third, בני הגולה, which is rendered in the same way.

56. 2:18 (1:14) שלחנא והודענא ≈ προσφωνῆσαι.

57. 5:62 (3:13) תרועה גדולה ≈ μεγαλωστί.

The *Vorlage* might have read קול גדול, as attested by the LXX and the Peshitta.

58. 1:14 (2 Chr 35:15) חוזה המלך ≈ οἱ παρὰ τοῦ βασιλέως.

59-63. 9:45-54 (Neh 8:5-12) כל העם ≈ πάντες.

64. 8:24 (Ezr 7:26) (דתא די אלהך) ודתא די מלכא ≈ καὶ τὸν βασιλικόν.

The following is typical of I Esd:

65. 1:7 (2 Chr 35:7, 8) מרכוש המלך. ושריו ≈ ἐκ τῶν βασιλικῶν.

66. 1:51 (2 Chr 36:18) ואצרות המלך ושריו ≈ καὶ τὰς βασιλικὰς ἀποθήκας.

Repeated verbs are sometimes rendered by only one verb:

67. 8:10 (7:13) ‏(כל מתנדב...) למהך לירושלם עמך יהך‏ ≈ συμπορεύεσθαί σοι εἰς Ἰερουσαλήμ.

68. 8:18 (7:20) ‏(די יפל לך) למנתן תנתן‏ ≈ δώσεις.

In these latter examples, the Aramaic requires two verbs while the Greek can make do with only one. The same is true for the condensation of the repeated ‏מלך‏ in the introductory formulae:

69. 1:33 (2 Chr 36:2) ‏מלך ...במלכו‏ ≈ καὶ ἐβασίλευσεν.

70. 1:44 (36:11) ‏מלך ...במלכו‏ ≈ βασιλεύει δέ.

The following condensation is particularly striking:

71. 2:23 (Ezr 4:20) ‏מדה בלו והלך מתיהב להון‏ ≈ φορολογοῦντες.

These examples amply illustrate our translator's tendency to streamline his text. Only rarely can we suggest a different, more condensed reading in the *Vorlage*. His technique should not be seen as an indicator of negligence or disrespect for the *Vorlage*; but, rather a desire to render his work in a more palatable and idiomatic language.

2. Expansion

1. 1:38 (2 Chr 36:6) ‏בנחשתים‏ ≈ ἐν χαλκείῳ δεσμῷ; also in the LXX.

2. 1:32, 35, 44 (36:1, 4, 10) ‏להמליך‏ ≈ ἀνέδειξαν βασιλέα.

3. 1:23 (35:20) ‏להלחם‏ ≈ πόλεμον ἐγεῖραι, cf. also v. 27 (35:20).

4. 1:29 (35:24) ‏וימת‏ ≈ μετήλλαξεν τὸν βίον αὐτοῦ.

5. 6:19 (Ezr 5:16) ‏ולא שלם‏ ≈ οὐκ ἔλαβεν συντέλειαν.

On some occasions nominal clauses are expanded with the auxiliary εἶναι. Other complementary elements are sometimes, though only rarely added: e.g., αὐτός is added in 8:55 (Ezr 8:25), and ἴδιος in 5:8 (2:1). The personal pronoun is added with the creation of the acc.c.inf. in 5:40, 53 (2:63; 3:7), and the sentence becomes better organized by preceding the sentences with αὐτοί and οὗτοι in 1:49, 50 (2 Chr 36:16, 17). It is difficult to know whether it was the translator who reorganized the sentence by providing the conjunctive ὁμοίως δέ in 6:29 (6:9) and 8:20 (7:22), or by specifying the subject: καὶ οἱ Ἰουδαῖοι in 2:19 (4:15) and καὶ οἱ ἄνθρωποι in 2:23 (4:20). Whether more significant expansions also come from the hand of the translator, we have no way of knowing;[299] though, it seems quite unlikely. We treated these cases as possible expansions in I Esd's *Vorlage*. There are, however, dozens of double translations which served our translator as an interpretive device and as such contribute to the expansive quality of the translation.

II. Double Translations

We approach here the complicated subject of 'double translations', namely, cases in which one unit in the *Vorlage* is paralleled by two alternative units in the translation.[300] Two preliminary criteria are in order.[301] The self-evident rule would be that 'double translation' is a phenomenon within the target language. Therefore, it must first be determined whether a disparity between a text and its translation actually originates in the Greek or whether it is a rendering of an expanded *Vorlage* and, more specifically, of a 'double reading'.[302] Secondly, a distinction should be made between 'double

---

[299] E.g., the addition of the adjective where Ezra's vestment is concerned, 8:68, 70 (Ezr 9:3, 5) בגדי ומעילי ≈ τὰ ἱμάτια καὶ τὴν ἱερὰν ἐσθῆτα.

[300] 'Double translations' is a major problem in other books of the LXX as well; e.g., in the Book of Samuel, for which see Driver (1913), pp. lv-lvii; Pisano (1984); also in the Book of Judges, cf. Talshir (1986), pp. 47-56.

[301] For further definitions and examples from the LXX see Talshir (1986).

[302] See Talmon (1960), pp. 144-184; (1961), pp. 335-383.

translations' and other expanded renderings that serve the translator in his exegetical efforts to match his *Vorlage*. The term specifies that alternate renderings are meant, that is, each of the two renderings now joined in a 'double translation' could have been independent equivalents of the item in question.[303] Bearing these reservations in mind, we may submit that a minimum of thirty cases of double translations are to be found in I Esd.[304]

The major problem in the evaluation of the phenomenon lies in the difficulty to distinguish between double translations which originated in compilatory activity in the process of transmission, and those which are an exegetical means used by one and the same translator as part of his translation technique.[305]

---

[303] However, there should be a difference between the components of the 'double translation' in order to justify the use of the term. Frankel (1841), pp. 171-172, speaks of 'doppelte Uebersetzung' under the heading of 'Hermeneutik und Exegese', referring to the practice of rendering the same word twice in order to solve a syntactical problem, similar to the hermeneutic rule מקרא נדרש לפניו ולאחריו. While formally one word is represented twice, the two equivalents are not meant as semantic alternatives and indeed do not differ from each other apart from their syntactic role in the context; cf. the double representation of עבדיהם ואמהתיהם in I Esd 5:41 (Ezr 2:64); see p. 171.

[304] Klein (1966), pp. 227-247, counts 72 cases of "double translations and the use of hendiadys". Even if we sift out the cases of hendiadys there still remain many cases that are not acceptable as real double translations. Reluctant as he is to recognize the possibility of a wider text in the *Vorlage*, Klein expands the range of double translations; thus, the importance of the omissions increases, and his basic assumption about the 'shorter text' represented in I Esd is justified.

[305] Conflation of extant renderings is characteristic of revisions such as Lucian's. The problem is raised regarding the Targumim. Sperber (1973), vol. IV-B, p. 3, concludes on the basis of doublets containing a literal and a non-literal rendering that there were two schools of translators: "How else shall we account for the existence of such doublets but by assuming that in these passages the translations originating in each one of the two schools were fused together"; cf. his examples on p. 191. Klein (1982), pp. 145-151, argues against him, claiming that most of the material is from one and the same translator.

Establishing criteria for this kind of evaluation is not easy. There are times when the components of a double translation have the same meaning and are placed one beside the other, without any link between them, or linked by a simple conjunction, and, in addition, assume the same syntactical position in the sentence. In such cases, the two components are mutually exclusive in respect of content and form, and are best interpreted as a technical fusion of translation traditions, and not as part of the translator's interpretive process. But together with this, even when the source lies in the different translation traditions, the very fact of fusing them is an interpretive process, and could have been used in the same manner that the translator employed the 'double translation' as an interpretive means.

The large number of double translations in I Esd makes it reasonable to suppose that at least some of them are the result of the history of the translation. Even though I Esd also has a few examples of mechanical fusion of two mutually exclusive equivalents, the overall impression, however, is that we are talking about a deliberate and creative interpretive process.

The first group of examples will prove beyond all doubt that our translator indeed employed double translations as part of his translation technique. In these cases, the translator used two verbs expressing different aspects of the *Vorlage* in order to render one verb, and connected them in a hypotactical construction; he clearly perceived the combined verbs as one equivalent, not as two alternatives.[306] These verbs in all likelihood originated with the translator himself and are not a result of having fused two existing translation traditions.

---

[306] In this respect they may not fall under a strict definition of 'double translations'. Klein (1966) named this kind of translation 'hendiadys', a term which I believe should be restricted to well-established pairs of words.

(1) 1:39 (2 Chr 36:7) הביא ≈ λαβών... καὶ ἀπενέγκας.

(2) 1:51 (36:18) הביא ≈ ἀναλαβόντες ἀπήνεγκαν.[307]

(3) 5:69 (Ezr 4:4) ומבלהים (כת: ומבלהים) ≈ καὶ πολιορκοῦντες εἶργον.

(4) 6:14 (5:12) הרגזו ≈ παραπικράντες ἥμαρτον.

(5) 6:15 (5:21) סתרה ≈ καθελόντες ἐνεπύρισαν.

The syntactical structure reveals that we are dealing with the translator's activity; however, the following examples are not essentially different even though the two verbs are joined simply by a connecting particle.

(6) 2:14 (1:11) העלה ≈ διεκομίσθη... ἀνηνέχθη δέ.

(7) 6:8 (5:8) אזלנא ≈ παραγενόμενοι... καὶ ἐλθόντες.

(8) 5:57 (3:10) להלל ≈ ὑμνοῦντες... καὶ εὐλογοῦντες.[308]

(9) 5:59 (3:11) הריעו ≈ ἐσάλπισαν καὶ ἐβόησαν.

The last example clearly demonstrates the translator's thought process: in his expanded rendering, or double translation, he expresses two shades of meaning comprised in the single item of his *Vorlage*.[309] The same goes for his double representation of the following nouns and adjectives:

(10) 9:46 (Neh 8:6) צבאות (אלהי) ≈ σαβαώθ παντοκράτορι.

(11) 9:8 (Ezr 10:11) תודה ≈ ὁμολογίαν δόξαν.

---

[307] Cf. the examples adduced by Frankel (1841), p. 166: Exod 3:8 ולהעלותו ≈ ἐξαγαγεῖν... καὶ εἰσαγαγεῖν; 2 Kgs 2:20 ויקח ≈ καὶ ἔλαβον καὶ ἤνεγκαν.

[308] One cannot rule out the possibility that he actually had an expanded *Vorlage* להלל ולהודות; cf. 5:58 (3:11) בהלל ובהודת ≈ δι᾽ ὕμνων ὁμολογοῦντες.

[309] In fact, this practice of attributing two meanings to one word is not confined to double translations. He achieves the same effect by rendering an unusual word such as אשתדור once by πολιορκία and once by πόλεμος in two close verses, 2:19, 23 (Ezr 4:15, 19); see Leiter (1985), pp. 79-95. Onkelos features a similar device; cf. Komlosh (1973), pp. 242-243.

(12) 6:26 (6:6) אפרסכיא ≈ ἀποτεταγμένοις … ἡγεμόσιν.

(13) 2:23 (4:20) תקיפין ≈ ἰσχυροὶ καὶ σκληροί.[310]

(14) 8:10 (7:13) כל מתנדב ≈ τοὺς βουλομένους … αἱρετίζοντας

(15) 6:8 (5:8) גלל ≈ ξυστῶν πολυτελῶν.

Later in the chapter, 6:24 (6:4), ξυστῶν alone matches גלל.

(16) 8:68 (9:3) משומם ≈ σύννους καὶ περίλυπος.

The latter is a telling example of the translator's search for the right shade of meaning.[311] Notably, in the following verse, περίλυπος alone is left over.

The last two examples involve an additional aspect of the discussion; since alongside the doublet, in the near context, only one of the components of the doublet is used. In view of the following examples, it becomes clear that we are not dealing with incidental doublets.

(17) 8:11 (Ezr 7:14): יעטהי ≈ φίλοις συμβουλευταῖς.

Φίλοι is a common term in the administration of the Hellenistic period,[312] while the stem συμβουλ- is a literal rendering. Interestingly enough, in 8:13 (7:15), יעטוהי is rendered by οἱ φίλοι; whereas, ויועציו in 8:26 (7:28) is rendered by καὶ τῶν συμβουλευόντων,[313] and in 8:55 (8:25) by οἱ συμβούλοι αὐτοῦ. It seems clear that the doublet is a conflation of

---

[310] Both Greek words are established equivalents of תקף. However, it may also reflect a conjectured Aramaic pair, תקיפין וחסינין, suggested by the pair תקף/חסן in the Book of Daniel, e.g., 2:37, 4:27.

[311] It is interesting that the II Esd^{Luc} also has a doublet here, though one that is completely different: ἠρέμων καὶ θαυμάζων, introducing the verb's connotation of desolation as well as of astonishment.

[312] See Talshir (1984*), p. 142.

[313] In this verse the φίλοι appear as well, but they seem to stand for שרים, thus: ויועציו ולכל שרי המלך הגברים = καὶ τῶν συμβουλευόντων καὶ πάντων τῶν φίλων καὶ μεγιστάντων αὐτοῦ. Indeed, in Esther φίλοι is, *inter alia*, the equivalent of שרים; see 3:1; 6:9, also 1:3; 2:18.

two possible renderings which are actually used separately in the same
chapter. The doublet may be the result of the translator's indecisiveness;[314]
although, one cannot rule out the possibility that he may have used an
existing translation, or that he was aware of an existing traditional equivalent.
It is not likely that we are dealing here with the work of a redactor who set
out to replace one term with another, e.g., who endeavored to replace the
technical term with a literal equivalent: we would have to say then that he
twice removed φίλοι altogether, overlooked it in one case, and provided it
with an alternative in another.

(18) 2:21 (Ezr 4:17) בעל טעם ≈ τῷ γράφοντι τὰ προσπίπτοντα καὶ
Βεελτεέμῳ.

The first equivalent is an explanation filling the title with a given
content. Rehum is believed to be in charge of writing down the things that
came to pass.[315] The second is the title transliterated. This is proven beyond
any doubt by the equivalents of בעל טעם in its previous occurrences in the
chapter. In 2:15 (4:8), בעל טעם is paralleled by Βεελτέεμος; while in 2:16
(4:9), it is rendered by ὁ τὰ προσπίπτοντα. This variety of equivalents in
three verses so close to one another makes it quite difficult to suppose that
someone manipulated an original translation, being eager to insert one
equivalent or the other. It rather reflects the efforts invested by the translator
in the transmission of an unfamiliar term. Admittedly, the conjunction καί
is quite strange.

Applying Lagarde's 'axiome' to double translations, one may argue
that the servile equivalents, or those in agreement with the MT, are later

---

[314] His indecisiveness expresses itself as well in the three different uses of the stem
συμβουλ-: he presents two different nouns – συμβουλευτής (only here in the LXX)
and σύμβουλος, and a participium – συμβουλεύων. In II Esd it is always σύμβουλοι.

[315] The verb προσπίπτειν is used with similar shades of meaning in the papyri of the
second and third centuries B.C.E., cf. further its use in 8:8 (Ezr 7:11) to designate the
arrival of an official letter. This reminds us of Rehum's position in our text as the
writer of such a letter.

insertions.[316] To be sure, the free equivalents are those characteristic of
I Esd and there is hardly any evidence to support a later revision of I Esd
towards the MT-form.

The almost Midrash-like use of double translation is well-attested in
the following examples, in which neither form nor content reveals at first
sight the procedure that is responsible for the state of the text. The disguise
is provided by the ingenuity of the translator who had two solutions for
the same word and chose to weave them together.

(19) 6:8 (Ezr 5:8) {השכחנא לשבי יהודיא} ≈ κατελάβομεν τῆς αἰχμαλωσίας
τοὺς πρεσβυτέρους τῶν Ἰουδαίων.

This is a conjecture, with no *Vorlage* to account for it. We assume
that the addition includes a double translation which resulted from two
different vocalizations of the word שבי, rendered by both αἰχμαλωσία and
πρεσβύτεροι. Indeed, in 6:27 (Ezr 6:8), the translator must have read שבי
as שְׁבִי, rendering it by αἰχμαλωσία; whereas, in 6:26, 7:2 (6:7, 14), he
read שָׂבֵי (=MT) and rendered it by πρεσβύτεροι. The two renderings are
combined in 6:8. The words are of different meaning ('captivity', 'elders')
and of different syntactical function. Moreover, they are related to each
other: the text speaks of 'the elders of the Jews of the captivity'.

The same double translation occurs in the following example:

(20) 6:5 (5:5) ועין אלההם הות על שבי יהודיא ≈ καὶ ἔσχοσαν χάριν ἐπισκοπῆς
γενομένης παρὰ τοῦ Κυρίου ἐπὶ τὴν αἰχμαλωσίαν οἱ πρεσβύτεροι
τῶν Ἰουδαίων.

In this complicated case, the translation presumably holds two
interconnected double translations for two phrases joined into a compound
construction, the components of which are no longer separable: ועין ... הות
was rendered by both καὶ ἔσχοσαν χάριν (possibly reflecting וחן for ועין)
and by the gen. abs. ἐπισκοπῆς γενομένης, and שבי – by both αἰχμαλωσία

---

[316] Lagarde (1863), p. 3.

and πρεσβύτεροι. Moreover, οἱ πρεσβύτεροι functions as the subject of
καὶ ἔσχοσαν χάριν; whereas, ἐπὶ τὴν αἰχμαλωσίαν complements the
gen. abs. ἐπισκοπῆς γενομένης. This well-planned doublet is credited to
the translator who created the text. Yet, one must keep in mind that it may
not have been entirely his own creation. He could well have borrowed
some of the equivalents from another work at his disposal.

In the following examples, the translator renders the genitival attribute
in two ways, 1) literally, by a noun in the genitive, and 2) by an adjective.

(22) 5:39 (Ezr 2:62) כתבם המתיחשים ≈ τῆς γενικῆς γραφῆς ἐν τῷ
καταλοχισμῷ.

(23) 6:20 (5:17) בבית גנזיא די מלכא ≈ ἐν τοῖς βασιλικοῖς βιβλιοφυλακίοις
τοῦ κυρίου βασιλέως.

Both the adjective βασιλικός and the expanded title κύριος βασιλεύς
are common terms used by this translator when designating something as
royal.

(24) 6:25 (6:5) מאני בית אלהא ≈ τὰ ἱερὰ σκεύη τοῦ οἴκου Κυρίου.

(25) 8:55 (8:25) ואת הכלים תרומת בית אלהינו ≈ καὶ τὰ ἱερὰ σκεύη τοῦ
οἴκου Κυρίου ἡμῶν.

The same pattern is used for the phrase כלי בית ה' or מאני בית אלהא.
Usually (7 times), it is rendered in I Esd by τὰ ἱερὰ σκεύη τοῦ Κυρίου. It
seems probable that τὰ... σκεύη represents כלי or מאני; τοῦ Κυρίου stands
for ה' or אלהא, and the adjective ἱερὰ fills the place of בית; this is
supported by the standard equivalent in I Esd (והי) בית = τὸ ἱερόν. In two
cases, we find this rendering expanded by a double representation of בית:
τὰ ἱερὰ σκεύη τοῦ οἴκου Κυρίου. Again, it is not reasonable to assume
that out of a total of nine cases somebody interfered in two of them in
order to do justice to the word בית.

(26-27) 8:66, 67 (9:1, 2) עמי הארצות ≈ τὰ ἀλλογενῆ ἔθνη τῆς γῆς.

In 8:89; 9:9 (10:2, 11), he renders the phrase literally, by τὰ ἔθνη τῆς γῆς, as in those verses where the foreign wives are explicitly mentioned and ἀλλογενεῖς is used for נכריות. Cf. also 8:80 (9:11) עמי הארצות ≈ ἀλλογενῶν τῆς γῆς.

In several cases, the unit represented twice is not a single word but a phrase or even an entire sentence.

(28) 5:49 (3:3) כי באימה עליהם ≈ καὶ ἐπισυνήχθησαν αὐτοῖς... ὅτι ἐν ἔχθρα ἦσαν αὐτοῖς καὶ κατίσχυσαν αὐτούς.

(29) 6:9 (5:8) ועבידתא דך אספרנא מתעבדא ומצלח בידהם ≈ καὶ τὰ ἔργα ἐκεῖνα ἐπὶ σπουδῆς γιγνόμενα καὶ εὐοδούμενον τὸ ἔργον ἐν ταῖς χερσίν αὐτῶν καὶ ἐν πάσῃ δόξῃ καὶ ἐπιμελείᾳ συντελούμενα.

(30) 6:31 (6:11) די יהשנא פתגמא דנה ≈ παραβῶσιν τι τῶν προειρημένων καὶ τῶν προσγεγραμμένων ἢ καὶ ἀκυρώσωσιν.

(31) 8:8 (7:11) וזה פרשגן הנשתון אשר נתן ≈ προσπεσόντος δὲ τοῦ γραφέντος προστάγματος... οὗ ἐστιν ἀντίγραφον τὸ ὑποκείμενον.

It is obvious that 'double translation' is a device manipulated by our translator to the point where the two components are deliberately interconnected and are no longer separable.[317] In these cases, it is difficult to count the double translations. If we count, unwisely, the words paralleled by a doublet, and not the sentences, we come closer to forty cases of double translation, rather than the thirty stated earlier.

---

[317] See Weiss (1979), pp. 191-197. He defines this phenomenon as following: There are cases in which the sentence is meaningful only when the two components of the double translation are joined together. They are neither the result of the work of two different translators nor later additions; they were written by one and the same translator, and deliberately so. E.g., Job 36:10 כי ישובו מאון ≈ די יתובון מן עובדיהון אין 'nothingness'); און 'sinful', אין בישיא דדמיין ללמא (און 'sinful', קרתא דבית ≈ עיר ההרס 18:19 Isa ;('nothingness' חרס 'sun', הרס 'destruction'). שמש דעתיד למיחרב (חרס)

There are a few other cases which may come under the definition of double translation, but they are too problematic to be introduced as definitive cases of this phenomenon.

In conclusion, it is impossible to exclude the possibility that behind the relatively large number of double translations in I Esd looms an editorial fusing of an existing translation, or of an accepted translation tradition, with a new translation by the present translator or revisor, as obviously occurred in the case of Lucian. But, primarily speaking, this is indeed a means of expression used by our translator, whose philosophy of translation made him perceive double translations as a legitimate means in translating a text.

III. The Linguistic Milieu of I Esd

Our examination of the translation technique employed in I Esd shows that we are dealing with a creative translator who sought to adapt the language of his *Vorlage* to the structure of the target-language, and who endeavored to present the 'Greek' reader with a pleasant and lucid reading experience. Let us now proceed one step beyond the questions of translation technique and attempt to evaluate his distinctive vocabulary in comparison with the LXX.[318]

The examination of a group of expressions peculiar to a certain work – in this case a translation – which in turn belongs to a larger corpus, clearly requires great caution. Firstly, a literary work is not characterized only by its peculiarities. Secondly, the group of words peculiar to a given translation may well be rooted in the nature of the original work being

---

[318] The data encompasses both the undoubtedly translated parts of I Esd and the Story of the Three Youths, which in our view is part and parcel of the rest of the translation. It should be noted that the story in no way alters the overall picture of the book as a whole, and that in this respect at least, there is no justification for viewing it separately.

translated rather than the individuality of a specific translator. Finally, the peculiarity may simply be the result of coincidence; a word is not necessarily characteristic of a book when it appears there but nowhere else, nor does it cease to be characteristic when one finds it in other books. Due to these and similar qualifications, it would seem unwise to describe the vocabulary in terms of precise distribution, reduced to mere numbers and percentages. Below we shall seek only to indicate the orientation of the translator in selecting the equivalents that characterize his work. This orientation is best studied through groups of words rather than individual ones because this narrows the danger of alighting on trends that are more apparent than real.

I Esd is an integral part of the LXX and closely akin to such books as LXX-Esther and LXX-Daniel. Similar to these two books, if only because of the large additions *vis-à-vis* the MT, I Esd functions as a bridge between the canonical books and the Apocrypha, whether translations or original compositions in Greek. The midway position of our translator's language will emerge time and again in the discussion below. There is no doubt, however, that the language of I Esd is rooted in that of the LXX and is widely shared with this corpus.

The affinity between I Esd and the LXX is conspicuous in the translator's use of terms which entered the Greek language by means of the LXX, such as θυσιαστήριον 'altar' (5 times in I Esd, including once in the epilogue to the Story of the Three Youths, 4:52), ὁλοκαύτωμα, ὁλοκαύτωσις 'burnt offering' (3 times), ἄζυμα 'unleavened bread' (3 times), and κιβωτός 'ark of the Lord' (2 times).[319]

Another type of translation, which may be loosely defined as 'contextal translation', points even more strongly in the same direction. In Ezr, for example, the Temple vessels restored by Cyrus king of Persia are called

---

[319] Cf. Tov (1978), p. 123.

אגרטלים, מחלפים,[320] and כפורים (Ezr 1:9-10). The words are either *hapax legomena* (אגרטל, מחלף), or rare (כפור, again in Ezr 8:27 and 1 Chr 28:17). In I Esd, these terms are rendered respectively by σπονδεῖα (LXX ≈ קשות, 3 times); θυίσκαι (in the LXX usually ≈ כף), and φιάλαι (usually ≈ מזרק); all are terms which also occur in the lists of Temple vessels in the LXX. I Esd thus borrowed terms from the context of Temple vessels in the LXX in order to render related terms with which he was apparently unfamiliar. Evidence of this can be seen in his different treatment of כפורים in its subsequent reoccurrence in 8:56 (Ezr 8:27). There he rendered כפרי זהב with an inexact χρυσώματα, since, on the one hand, he did not know the actual meaning of כפור and, on the other, he could not here employ the technical terms used in the LXX for the Temple vessels, seeing that the context now concerned the contributions of the king, his ministers and all Israel.[321]

As a final example of I Esd's close relationship with the rest of the LXX, let us mention the translation of אורים ותמים in 5:40 (2:63) עד עמד כהן לאורים ולתמים ≈ ἕως ἀναστῇ ἀρχιερεὺς ἐνδεδυμένος τὴν δήλωσιν καὶ τὴν ἀλήθειαν. This translation is obviously based on the LXX.[322] If we did not know the original phrase or its standard LXX equivalent, we would surely have difficulty in making sense of the Greek here. While such translational oddities are not uncommon in the LXX, they are seldom found in I Esd.

a. *Sancta*

Admittedly, the above-quoted examples all relate to the area of the cult, where consistency and even stereotyping might be expected in

---

[320] Whether or not מחלפים is actually a type of vessel, the translator understood it as such.

[321] Cf. in the Story of the Three Youths, 3:6 καὶ ἐν χρυσώμασιν πίνειν.

[322] Exod 28:26 (30); Lev 8:8; Num 27:21; Deut 33:8 (in changed order); 1 Sam 28:6.

translation. However, it is precisely in matters pertaining to the cult that we discover the translator's independence. He does not hesitate to break away from the conventions used in the LXX. He delights in introducing terminology drawn from his own environment, and even in airing his own views in matters apparently close to his heart.

1. The translator's treatment of the center of the cult, viz. the Temple, deserves particular attention. In the Books of Chr-Ezr-Neh, the Temple is known primarily as בית הי, בית אלהים, בית אלהא 'the House of the Lord'. In the LXX, this term is rendered literally by ὁ οἶκος τοῦ κυρίου. I Esd too makes use of this equivalent (17 times),[323] but equally employs another one: τὸ ἱερόν, either for בית alone (12 times),[324] or for the entire term (6 times).[325] It can hardly be assumed that in all these instances the translator had a text in which בית or בית הי had been replaced by מקדש. Derivations of קדש would normally be translated in I Esd by derivations of ἁγι-,[326] as in the LXX.[327] This becomes even clearer when considering his way of rendering another common term: כלי בית הי/אלהים ≈ τὰ ἱερὰ σκεύη τοῦ κυρίου (7 times). Here, too, we are certainly not dealing with variants, e.g., similar to 1 Chr 22:19 וכלי קדש האלהים. The latter, again, would rather involve the use of ἅγιος; cf. 8:57 (8:28) והכלים קדש ≈ καὶ τὰ σκεύη ἅγια. It should thus be stated: just as τὸ ἱερόν frequently represents בית in the term בית הי, so does the adjective ἱερός repeatedly stand for בית in the phrase כלי בית הי. A similar translation is found in LXX-Dan 1:2 ומקצת כלי בית האלהים ≈ καὶ μέρος τι τῶν ἱερῶν σκευῶν τοῦ κυρίου.

---

[323] Strangely enough, בית without the attribute הי or אלהים, but unquestionably indicating the 'House of the Lord', is always rendered simply by οἶκος.

[324] Cf. the Aramaic translation of בית הי ≈ בית מקדשא דהי.

[325] See also 5:44 (Ezr 2:69), and 8:18 (7:20) ms A.

[326] Thus, e.g., 1:3 (twice), 1:5, 1:50 (2 Chr 35:3, 5; 36:17). This last verse is particularly instructive: בית מקדשם ≈ τοῦ ἁγίου αὐτῶν ἱεροῦ, i.e., בית ≈ τὸ ἱερόν, מקדש ≈ ἅγιος.

[327] See Hanhart (1974*), p. 62.

In sum, the translator of I Esd introduces into his work the term τὸ ἱερόν, which was probably part of his linguistic milieu. This term is rare in the canonical books, appearing some six times altogether, but is quite common in 1-4 Macc. In fact, the LXX to the canonical books refrains from employing ἱερός completely. Matters pertaining to sanctity, to God, and his Temple above all, are described by ἅγιος.[328] I Esd, in contrast, abounds in ἱερο-, as we shall see below.

In concluding this point, let us take note of the translator's sensitivity to this matter which finds expression in his translation of בית אלהים, when it refers to the gods of the Babylonian king: בבית אלהיו ≈ ἐν τῷ ἑαυτοῦ εἰδωλείῳ, 2:9 (Ezr 1:7). Εἰδωλεῖον, based on εἴδωλον – the preferred rendering in the LXX for such words as שקוץ, פסל, גלולים, אליל,[329] appears in the LXX of the canonical books only in Dan 1:2 ואת הכלים הביא בית אלהיו אוצר ≈ καὶ ἀπηρείσατο αὐτὰ ἐν τῷ εἰδωλείῳ αὐτοῦ. Once again, we are witness to a striking affinity between LXX-Dan and I Esd;[330] see also Bel 10 and 1 Macc 1:47, 83.

2. Let us now move on to matters related to the Temple (in the spirit of I Esd: τὰ κατὰ τὸν ἱερόν).[331] First of all, we mention ὁ ἀρχιερεύς 'the high priest'. The term appears only four times in the LXX of the canonical books, randomly distributed and not attested in all MSS.[332] It is frequently used in 1-4 Macc alongside some of its derivatives (ἀρχιερᾶσθαι,

---

[328] See Seeligmann (1948), p. 102: "...ἅγιος is also the exalted God... in the midst of His Heavenly throng, while, on earth, the circle of His worshippers, humbly and in fear, seeks to approach His sanctuary. It is not, indeed, mere accident that the Temple is always called ἅγιον, never ἱερόν".

[329] Seeligmann (1948), p. 99.

[330] See Torrey (1910), p. 84.

[331] See his paraphrase, precipitated by a misunderstanding of מלח היכלא מלחנא in 2:18 (Ezr 4:14) ἐνεργεῖται τὰ κατὰ τὸν ἱερόν "as the things pertaining to the temple are now underway".

[332] See Lev 4:3 for הכהן המשיח, Josh 22:13 regarding Eleazar son of Aaron, 1 Kgs 1:25 referring to Eviatar; also 1 Chr 15:14 (in the plural).

ἀρχιερατεύειν, and ἀρχιερωσύνη). In I Esd, it occurs four times. It is introduced for כהן in 5:40 (Ezr 2:63), since the priest in question is a priest with Urim and Thummim (cf. Exod 28). Otherwise, ἀρχιερεύς is reserved for Ezra.[333] Accordingly, Ezra's garments also receive special attention. Thus, for בגדי ומעילי I Esd reads τὰ ἱμάτια καὶ τὴν ἱερὰν ἐσθῆτα in 8:68, 70 (3:3, 5).[334] In the same connection, the adjective ἱερατικός deserves special notice. It appears in 5:44 (2:69) וכתנות כהנים ≈ καὶ στολὰς ἱερατικάς, and again in exactly the same expression in the epilogue to the Story of the Three Youths in 4:54; similarly in 2 Macc 3:15. It does not appear elsewhere in the LXX.

We further note the collective noun ἱερωσυνή 5:38 (2:62 ≈ כהנה 'priesthood'), which appears besides our text only once in LXX-Chr, once in Sirach and more frequently in 1 Macc (4 times) and 4 Macc (twice). The stem ἱερ- is also used for words other than derivatives of כהן: ἀνιεροῦν 9:4 (10:8 ≈ יחרם), elsewhere only in 3 Macc 3:20; and ἱερατεύειν, a verb common in the LXX for כהן, which is aptly used in I Esd for משרתים (לבית אלהיו, 8:45 (8:17).

3. Against this background of diversity in using the stem ἱερ-, it is not surprising to find groups of Temple officials bearing titles that incorporate this element. First of all, mention should be made of a compound unique to I Esd, viz. the ἱεροστάται, 7:2 (Ezr 6:13-14; the Hebrew equivalent

---

[333] 9:39, 40, 49 (Neh 8:1, 2, 9), even though he is not consistent – in three other cases Ezra is simply ὁ ἱερεύς, 8:8; 9:16, 42 (Ezr 7:11; 10:16; Neh 8:4). It is interesting to note that אהרן הכהן הראש is rendered Ἀαρὼν τοῦ πρώτου ἱερέως in 8:2 (Ezr 7:5). Note that the title ἀρχιερεύς is held by certain *strategoi* in the Seleucid administration; cf. Bagnall (1976), pp. 15, 48.

[334] The reference to the priestly garb found in 5:57 (Ezr 3:10) ויעמידו הכהנים מלבשים ≈ καὶ ἔστησαν οἱ ἱερεῖς ἐστολισμένοι, is further repeated in I Esd without a corresponding מלבשים in the MT; see 1:2 (2 Chr 35:2); 7:9 (Ezr 6:18). This, again, is due to the emphasis on the official priestly attire in Exod 28 and 39. These changes, to be sure, may well have occurred in the *Vorlage*.

is not clear), which might be translated 'those appointed over the Temple'. Of interest is the definition of this term which is given at the beginning of the verse and is apparently part of a double translation: ἐπεστάτουν τῶν ἱερῶν ἔργων.[335] Similarly, there appear two other terms for the Temple-singers and Temple-servants. I Esd renders משוררים 'singers' once by ψάλτης in a passage where the connection with the Temple is not wholly clear, 5:41 (2:65). The singers of the Temple, however, are referred to as ἱερο-ψάλται in all six cases. Neither ψάλτης nor ἱεροψάλτης appears elsewhere in the LXX.[336] The latter does appear in an inscription from the 2nd century B.C.E.

The picture is similar regarding נתינים, rendered in I Esd as ἱερόδουλοι (6 times), a term which does not occur elsewhere in the LXX.[337] The Greek term is well documented in the papyri and inscriptions of the last three centuries B.C.E. referring to servants of the sanctuaries.

We mention in passing I Esd's equivalent for שוערים 'gate-keepers', though not derived from ἱερο-, viz. θυρωροί (7 times).[338] Again, θυρωροί is attested in papyri and inscriptions of the 2nd-1st centuries B.C.E, albeit not specifically in reference to gate-keepers of a sanctuary.

The translator's choice of equivalents for 'singers', 'temple-servants' and 'gate-keepers' illustrates the way he drew on his own linguistic milieu, selecting words current in the cultic language of his immediate surroundings. He was aware of the technical status of the terms in his *Vorlage*, and that

---

[335] A similar redundancy is found in another title appearing in the Story of the Three Youths: οἱ σωματοφύλακες οἱ φυλάσσοντες τὸ σῶμα, 3:4; see p. 88.

[336] In the LXX, the singers are simply οἱ ᾄδοντες (3 times in Chr; 21 times in Ezr-Neh) or οἱ ψάλτῳδοί (9 times in Chr).

[337] In Ezr-Neh, נתינים is transliterated; in its single appearance in 1 Chr 9:2, it is derived from נתן and rendered by διδόναι.

[338] The word occurs at random in the LXX (3 times), but the gate-keepers *par excellence*, namely, the group which plays a specific part in the Temple maintenance, are usually termed πυλωροί in the LXX (28 times in Ezr-Neh and Chr).

they demanded suitable technical parallels. Moreover, he used them with remarkable consistency, inasmuch as consistency is not one of his characteristics. However, in respect of his independence within the tradition of the LXX, one must proceed cautiously, taking the following points into account: (1) The three terms discussed above function as technical terms for the first time in Ezr-Neh-Chr. (2) The translator of I Esd apparently did not know of or at least did not make use of the known Greek translations to Ezr-Neh (whether LXX or not) and Chr. (3) Consequently, the translator of I Esd worked in a vacuum in regard to these terms. He cannot be said to have deviated from an existing translation-tradition but only to have been unacquainted with any such tradition, and was thus obliged to fall back on his own experience in seeking the appropriate solutions.

4. One additional technical term is that of the priestly and Levitical מחלקות 'divisions'. This is rendered in LXX-Chr mostly by διαίρεσις (17 times) and ἐφημερία (10 times). The translator of I Esd is not aware of these equivalents. When he encountered the term, he rather chose φυλή, the well-known equivalent of שבט 'tribe' in the LXX; 1:4, 10 (2 Chr 35:4, 10); 7:9 (Ezr 6:18). Why did the translator choose to describe the priestly and Levitical divisions as φυλαί? He might have adhered to φυλή since he was acquainted with a meaning known from Egyptian epigraphic sources of the 3rd century B.C.E., in which φυλή indicates a sub-division of priests in Egyptian sanctuaries. Another term used by our translator points in the same direction: שרי הכהנים 'the chiefs of the priests' he consistently renders with οἱ φυλάρχοι τῶν ἱερῶν; 8:54, 58, 92 (8:24, 29; 10:5). For him, then, the 'chiefs of the priests' are the chiefs of the φυλαί, the divisions of the priests.[339]

---

[339] A text from Canopus, Egypt (3rd century B.C.E, the reign of Ptolemy Euergetes), reveals both the use of φυλή as a priestly division and the use of φυλάρχος as the head of such a division. The writer specifies that in addition to the four priestly divisions (φυλαί) found in every sanctuary, an extra fifth division was added, over

It should be emphasized, however, that our translator seems to have combined the different uses of φυλή and φυλάρχος. He may well have been familiar with the technical use of the terms surrounding the sanctuaries in his day, but he also adopted their non-cultic meaning as used in the LXX. Thus, he employs φυλή to denote Judah and Benjamin, 2:7; 5:63; 9:5 (without parallel in the MT, Ezr 1:5; 4:1; 10:9), and φυλάρχοι for the heads of tribes of Israel, 7:8 (6:17).[340] He may have understood that the priests and Levites were divided according to the divisions of the people, that is the tribes.[341] Indeed, the related מפלגות is rendered by μεριδαρχία, a sort of 'district-governorship'. In this case, the terms lie beyond the domain of *sancta*.

b. Governmental Administration

The distance between the sphere of the Temple and that of the Government need not be great; some of the terms mentioned above in reference to the Temple infringe on the realm of administration. It is here, more than any other realm of activity, that the equivalents of the translator are best explained as having come from his own linguistic environment. It

---

which a division-head (φυλάρχος) was appointed, as with the other four: Προσαποδειχθῆναι δὲ πρὸς ταῖς νῦν ὑπαρχούσαις τέσσαρσι φυλαῖς τοῦ πλήθους τῶν ἱερέων τῶν ἐν ἑκάστωι ἱερῶι καὶ ἄλλην ἢ προσονομασθήσεται πέμπτη φυλὴ τῶν Εὐεργετῶν θεῶν... μετέχειν δὲ καὶ τοὺς ἐκ τῆς πέμπτης φυλῆς τῶν Εὐεργετῶν θεῶν τῶν ἀγνειῶν καὶ τῶν ἄλλων ἁπάντων τῶν ἐν τοῖς ἱεροῖς, καὶ φύλαρχον αὐτῆς εἶναι, καθὰ καὶ ἐπὶ τῶν ἄλλων τεσσάρων φυλῶν ὑπάρχει. See Dittenberger (1903), 56:20-30.

[340] Cf. LXX Deut 31:28; Josh 11:23 ויתנה יהושע לנחלה לישראל כמחלקתם לשבטיהם "and Joshua assigned it to Israel to share according to their tribal divisions", also Josh 12:7; 18:10.

[341] Indeed in Chr itself מחלקות may indicate the divisions of both the people and the Temple personnel; cf. Japhet (1968), pp. 344ff, who, however, classifies our verses with those indicating the divisions of Temple personnel.

would be incorrect, however, to infer from this that I Esd should be treated as a reliable historical document. In fact, at times the opposite is true, as when contemporary concepts are used anachronistically. The translator's sources left room for interpretation and elaboration, and it is interesting to observe his skill in an area where other translators might remain stilted and obscure.

1. The translator's skill is especially apparent in regard to official correspondence. Instead of the confused and disorderly text of Ezr 4:6-11, we find in I Esd 2:15-16 a well-organized opening.[342] The credit for the exemplary arrangement does not necessarily belong to the translator since his source text may have differed from the MT; his formulation, however, is outstanding, especially the conclusion in 2:15 ...κατέγραψεν... τὴν ὑπογεγραμμένα ἐπιστολήν. Also worthy of note is the response of the king in 2:21 (4:17): ...ἀντέγραψεν... τὴν ὑπογεγραμμένα. The verb which gives a certain grace to the presentation of the following letter, ὑπογράφειν, is found in a perfectly parallel use in Esth 8:12 (Addition E 1): ὧν ἐστιν ἀντίγραφον τῆς ἐπιστολῆς τὰ ὑπογεγραμμένα; also in 2 Macc 9:18 ἔγραψε... τὴν ὑπογεγραμμένην ἐπιστολήν and elsewhere in 1-3 Macc. Needless to say, this use is formulaic in inscriptions and papyri, used to indicate 'that which is written below'.

One particular use of a formula occurs in 8:8 (Ezr 7:11) προσπεσόντος δὲ τοῦ γραφέντος προστάγματος οὗ ἐστί ἀντίγραφον τὸ ὑποκείμενον "Now the edict reached Ezra..., of which the following is a copy". Again we are not concerned with the precise relationship between the source and the translation because even if the translator's *Vorlage* differed in details, the particular manner of expression is entirely his own. The verb προσ-πίπτειν which in the LXX has a different meaning (e.g., 'to bow', 'to fall'), appears in documents with the meaning 'to reach somebody, to come into one's hands'. One might compare LXX-Esth 9:4 προσέπεσεν

---

[342] Cf. Ezr 7:11-12, and the discussion on pp. 41-43.

γὰρ τὸ πρόσταγμα τοῦ βασιλέως; 3 Macc 3:25 ἅμα τῷ προσπεσεῖν τὴν ἐπιστολήν; 3 Macc 4:1 ὅπου προσέπιπτε τοῦτο τὸ πρόσταγμα, and further in a papyrus from the 2nd century B.C.E.: προσπεσούσης μοι τῆς ἐπιστολῆς, and others like it. Similarly, the last verb in 8:8 – ὑποκείσθαι 'to be given below in the text' – finds a parallel only in 1 Macc 12:7 ὡς τὸ ἀντίγραφον ὑπόκειται. This usage is especially common in the papyri, e.g., in the Zenon Papyri 355, 122: κατὰ τὴν... συγγραφήν, ἧς τὸ ἀντίγραφον ὑπόκειται.

In addition to ὑποκείσθαι, ὑπογράφειν and προσπίπτειν, we find a number of other verbs belonging to the realm of reports, official writings and proclamations: ἱστορεῖν (3 times), ὑπομνηματίζεσθαι, ἀντιγράφειν, ἀπογράφειν, προερεῖν, προσφωνεῖν (3 times), ἀποσημαίνειν, διαγορύειν, ὑπαγορεύειν. These verbs, appearing either in I Esd alone or in I Esd and 1-3 Macc, are attested in epigraphic sources from the last centuries B.C.E. with similar meanings and in similar contexts. The use of all these terms gives I Esd a distinctive character within the LXX.

Also belonging to this group of terms are words such as τόμος 'roll of papyrus' 6:2 (Ezr 6:21 ≈ מגלה), found also in LXX-Isa 8:1 for גליון; ἀντίγραφον (2 times), and further in LXX-Esth, Ep.-Jer and 1 Macc; ὀνοματογραφία – a word unique to I Esd within the LXX and virtually first attested in the Greek – for שמות 'names', 6:11 and 8:48 (5:10; 8:20). Thus, a simple word like שמות becomes in the translator's hands something of a technical term.

2. Several other 'official' words point to the translator's linguistic individuality: the act of subverting an order is referred to by ἀκυροῦν in 6:31 (6:11), a word which recurs only in 4 Macc. Someone who violates an order and becomes liable to punishment is threatened with κολάζειν in 8:24 (7:26), a term which appears once in LXX-Dan 6:12(13) with no parallel in the MT, in Wisdom (12 times) and 1-4 Macc (8 times). One who accepts responsibility on himself is said to ἐπιδέχεσθαι ≈ עמד על

9:14 (10:15), elsewhere limited to Sirach and 1-3 Macc. The action of one who assists him is described as συμβοαβεύειν ≈ עזר (*ibid*), which is unique to I Esd. Especially noteworthy is his use of ἐμποιεῖν ≈ בקש 5:38 (2:61), with the meaning attested in epigraphic sources 'to lay claim'. If these particular words, and others, had not been familiar to the translator, he would presumably have made use of the standard equivalents of the LXX.

In the official realm proper, we find that the translator's terminology for taxation, though akin to that of the LXX, is nonetheless morphologically distinct. Three times he uses φορολογία which elsewhere occurs once in 1 Macc. Especially noteworthy is his paraphrase in 2:18 (4:13) מנדה בלו והלך לא ינתנון ≈ φορολογίαν οὐ μὴ ὑπομείνωσιν δοῦναι. In addition, the adjective ἀφορολόγητος appears in the epilogue of the Story of the Three Youths, 4:50, in describing the special privileges of those exempt from the royal tax; cf. 1 Macc 11:28 ποιῆσαι τὴν Ἰουδαίαν ἀφορολόγητον. Both terms are well-attested in papyri and inscriptions from the 3rd-2nd centuries B.C.E.

3. Even more interesting are the translator's administrative concepts as reflected in a number of Hebrew-Greek equivalents. The first is actually an avoidance of the simple equivalent עיר ≈ πόλις, in a number of places where it might have been expected. Πόλις is reserved in I Esd almost exclusively for Jerusalem – some twelve times. Other cities are referred to in various ways: ἰδίοις, κατοικίαι (2 times), κώμαι.[343] An exception is 5:8 (Ezr 2:1) איש לעירו ≈ ἕκαστος εἰς τὴν ἰδίαν πόλιν; this verse, however, is different from the others in that the word עיר is in the singular. In spite of this verse, we may surmise that for the translator of I Esd Jerusalem was ἡ πόλις and the rest of the country ἡ χώρα, just as Alexandria was for a considerable time ἡ πόλις and Egypt ἡ χώρα. Indeed, twice, 5:45 (2:70) and 9:37 (Neh 7:72), we find ἐν Ἱερουσαλὴμ καὶ ἐν τῇ χώρᾳ

---

[343] Κώμαι serves in the LXX to translate ערים a number of times, quite appropriately, e.g., Josh 10:39.

corresponding to בעריהם; the Greek phrase speaks for itself, regardless of its exact *Vorlage*.[344]

A more inclusive concept of administrative division is indicated by a pair of words already mentioned above: φυλή / μεριδαρχία. If φυλή is not, for the translator, a division exclusively of priests but also of the people in general, the pairing of these two terms is interesting in that it combines ethnic and geographic criteria, a division which must be attributed to a person knowledgeable in such matters. Μεριδαρχία itself is a technical term, even if we do not know for certain whether the translator was familiar in his time with the division of the province into meridarchies. While μεριδαρχία is not found at all in the LXX, I Esd makes use of it four times: 1:5 (2 Chr 35:5, apparently for פלגה or חלקה), 1:10 (35:12, for מפלגה), 8:28 (Ezr 8:1 התיחשם; it is questionable whether this was in the translator's text), and 5:4, towards the end of the epilogue of the Story of the Three Youths. We read in 1 Macc that Jonathan was appointed μεριδάρχης (and strategos) and the same title appears in a papyrus from the 2nd century B.C.E.[345] It is doubtful whether the regional connotation of the term is appropriate for the Hebrew terms it substitutes in Ezr; in fact, it is possible to argue that the translator of I Esd added an element foreign to the context. Nevertheless, the very use of such terms is worthy of note.

The translator's skillful use of technical terms is most obvious in his treatment of the term 'Abar Nahra. In the LXX, עבר נהרא/ה, עבר הנהר is rendered literally by πέραν τοῦ ποταμοῦ; in I Esd, it has one of two equivalents: Συρία καὶ Φοινίκη (7 times) or κοίλη Συρία καὶ Φοινίκη (6 times). We find the latter also in the epilogue to the Story of the Three Youths, 4:48. There are no apparent conditions which render the appearance

---

[344] Cf. Pelletier (1962), pp. 54-56. He shows how the idiomatic expression regarding the status of Alexandria in the Letter of Aristeas (22): εἴς τε τὴν πόλιν καὶ τὴν χώραν becomes εἴς τε τὰς πόλεις ἡμῶν καὶ τὴν χώραν in the hands of Josephus (Ant. XII, §28), who was no longer aware of the special status of the city.

[345] Cf. also Josephus, Ant. XV, §216.

of one or the other predictable. The translator interprets rather than translates literally the term he found before him; in his view, 'Abar Nahra was nothing other than 'Coele-Syria and Phoenicia' or 'Syria and Phoenicia'. We cannot know for certain to what extent the translator's use of these phrases is anachronistic. Our sources are few and less than definitive, and the problem of 'Syria and Phoenicia' has received different solutions. We can probably say that I Esd uses later terminology to describe an earlier period. 'Coele-Syria' does appear already in the 4th century B.C.E, but it is doubtful whether the term is an administrative one.[346] 'Syria and Phoenicia' becomes a standard administrative term in the days of Ptolemaic rule in the area, and 'Coele-Syria and Phoenicia' under that of the Seleucids.[347] It is also questionable whether these terms indicated the fifth satrapy as described by Herodotus 3, 91, corresponding to 'Abar Nahra. More likely, I Esd uses terms indicating the reduced satrapy (ἡ κάτω Συρία) in order to render a term with a much wider sense. It is tempting to date I Esd precisely on the basis of these terms but this is no easy task, and perhaps impossible. Schalit has suggested the 3rd century B.C.E. [348] Bikerman held that I Esd, as well as 1-3 Macc and the Letter of Aristeas, were written in

---

[346] See Leuze (1935), p. 366 (210): "Auch ist zu betonen, dass Συρία wie κοίλη Συρία im Periplus nur als geographische Landschaftsbezeichnungen aufzufassen sind, nicht als politische oder adminstrative Einheiten..."; also Bickerman (1947*), pp. 256-268, who clearly distinguishes the literary sources from the official ones. See further Schalit (1954), p. 64.

[347] Bengston (1952), pp. 166ff.

[348] Schalit (1954), p. 77, is very precise: "I incline to the supposition that the book of I Esd was written during the 3rd century B.C., in the days of Ptolemaic rule in southern Syria, and that the author inserted into it the 'Ptolemaic' interpretation of κοίλη Συρία καὶ Φοινίκη, in other words, the meaning given to it by Ptolemy Lagus when he wished to carry out the conquest of Syria in its full extent". In order to accept this, we should at least be able to produce evidence that Ptolemy Lagus himself made use of the term 'Coele-Syria and Phoenicia' to indicate 'Abar Nahra, or that it was an accepted Ptolemaic term for the region.

the 2nd century B.C.E due to their use of 'Coele-Syria', the common administrative term of the time.[349] We may further suggest that the translator's indiscriminate use of both terms points to a date in the transition period from Ptolemaic to Seleucid rule, between the 3ʳᵈ to 2ⁿᵈ centuries. Thus in the Hephzibah inscription, from about 195 B.C.E, the governor is designated strategos of 'Syria and Phoenicia'; whereas, in a somewhat later inscription from Soloi in Cilicia, the same governor is called strategos of 'Coele-Syria and Phoenicia'.[350] It might still be argued that the mixing of terminology in I Esd reflects an earlier period and that the available documents simply offer no assistance.

4. Due to the nature of the book, I Esd introduces a number of personages in official capacity, designated by titles characteristic of the translator. We shall mention here only a few which point out his individuality. Most prominent are the φίλοι, a term which appears in I Esd not as a literal equivalent of a parallel title, such as רֵעַ 'friend', but with reference to the king's advisors יועצים/יעטין, 8:11, 13, 26 (Ezr 7:14, 15, 28).[351] Φίλοι as an official title is common in LXX-Esth (≈ חכמים, שרים, אהבים), LXX-Dan (≈ רברבנין, הדברין) and 1-4 Macc; cf. also Prov 25:1, [חזקיה] אנשי ≈ οἱ φίλοι. It is doubtful whether the translators, including I Esd's, considered the terms essentialy equivalent, identifying the character of the administrative institution in their source with that of the φίλοι.[352] It is more reasonable to assume that they selected a common title – and φίλοι is indeed very common, especially in the Ptolemaic period – from the

---

[349] Bickerman (1947*), pp. 264, 256.

[350] Stern (1981), pp. 65-68.

[351] In the first and last verses, the word occurs alongside the customary LXX title συμβουλεύτης, συμβουλεύων; see p. 242-243.

[352] See Donner (1961), pp. 270-271. See in particular LXX-1 Kgs 4:5 (המלך) רעה ≈ σύμβουλος. See also the comments of Bar-Kochva (1980), pp. 182, 184, 232-233, on the possible *Vorlage* of 1 Macc 3:38, 6:28. Had he considered the above series of equivalents, he might have refrained from simply retroverting φίλος to רֵעַ.

political life of their own day, in order to render a broadly comparable
term.

A title unique to I Esd is the translator's equivalent for סופר: Ezra the
scribe is always ὁ ἀναγνώστης. It may be that the translator found a title
which perfectly matched his conception of Ezra, since the meaning of the
Greek word is both 'reader' and 'secretary': Ἀναγνώστης 'reader'
characterizes Ezra as the 'reader of the Torah' in the account of Neh 8,
which forms part of the translated material in I Esd, while, ἀναγνώστης
'secretary', which appears in inscriptions for the secretary of the city or
Gerousia, corresponds to the Hebrew title סופר (cf. its regular translation
in the LXX by γραμματεύς).

It appears that the translator of I Esd was not altogether sure of how
to deal with the title בעל טעם.[353] He did, however, make an attempt by
rendering it ὁ τὰ προσπίπτοντα in 2:16 (Ezr 4:8), or the somewhat
clearer ὁ γράφων τὰ προσπίπτοντα in 2:21 (4:17). We may recall that
he used the verb προσπίπτειν with reference to letters; here he seems to
refer to the person in charge of recording events.

Let us note two additional curiosities in the translation which further
demonstrate the translator's interest in official matters and his efforts to
carefully select his terminology. In 1:30 (2 Chr 35:25), the translator read
instead of the MT's השרים והשרות "singers, male and female", השרים
והשרות "the ministers and the lady-ministers", and translated it by οἱ προκαθήμενοι σὺν γυναιξίν "the ministers with their wives"! In 1:14 (35:15)
he renders חוזה המלך (which he apparently construed in the plural) by οἱ
παρὰ τοῦ βασιλέως, 'the king's men', exactly like the expression of
1 Macc 2:15. The translator took the phrase to mean 'those who see the
king' (cf. the phrase ראי פני המלך 2 Kgs 25:19; Esth 1:14), and rendered it
by a parallel, though not literal term. Such a translation may derive from
the difficulty of accounting for the title חוזה 'seer' in this context; in any

---

[353] See pp. 243-244.

case, the translator integrated his solution into a scene most familiar to
him: the retinue of the king.

c. The King

Finally, we come to the king himself. As expected, we find the
translator's particular touch in this area as well.

1. To crown a king, להמליך, is rendered in I Esd three times by an
expanded expression, quite in contrast to his usual conciseness:
ἀναδεικνύειν βασιλέα, 1:32, 35, 44 (2 Chr 36:1, 4, 10), cf. as well 1:41
(36:9), 2:3 (Ezr 1:2), instead of the LXX's usual βασιλεύειν. The verb is
used in similar contexts in LXX-Dan and in 2-3 Macc. The entire expression
is found in 2 Macc 9:25. It can be said that both stylistic considerations
and a particular interest account for this rendering. The same factors account
for the translator's use of βασιλικός to indicate that which belongs to the
king. This adjective replaces expressions with מלך in the construct state in
Num 20:17; 21:22; 2 Sam 14:26, but is best attested in LXX-Esth (6
times) and LXX-Dan (8 times) and especially in 1-4 Macc. We are hardly
surprised to find I Esd making ample use of the word (8 times). The use of
this adjective is not simply a matter of literary style: the translator is fully
aware of its meaning. Thus, he renders ואצרות המלך ושריו by καὶ τὰς
βασιλικὰς ἀποθήκας in 1:51 (2 Chr 36:18); and ...ושריו המלך. מרכוש by ἐκ
τῶν βασιλικῶν in 1:7 (35:7-8). Finally, we find it in a passage in which it
is not strictly required by the *Vorlage*: וביתה נולי יתעבד ≈ καὶ τὰ ὑπάρχοντα
αὐτοῦ εἶναι βασιλικά, 6:31 (Ezr 6:11), that is, he who disobeys the word
of the king forfeits his property to the crown. The parallel from Dan 2:5
speaks for itself: ובתיכון נולי יתשמון ≈ καὶ ἀναληφθήσεται ὑμῶν τὰ
ὑπάρχοντα εἰς τὸ βασιλικόν.[354]

---

[354] Cf. also LXX Ezr 6:11 and Dan 3:29.

We will briefly mention here an additional phrase; even though, it is unclear whether it comes from the hands of the translator or from a variant Hebrew text: seven times we find in I Esd, corresponding to the title מלכא 'the king', the expanded κύριος βασιλεύς, a customary expression of deference to (gods and) kings in Greek sources; see also Dan 4:21 מרי (מראי) מלכא, and pp. 221-223.

2. While there are other such details indicating the translator's proximity to and reverence for the king, none of them is quite as expressive as τὰ φιλάνθρωπα. I Esd 8:10 opens with the words καὶ τὰ φιλάνθρωπα ἐγὼ κρίνας. These words have no parallel in Ezr 7:13.[355] The Greek term serves to characterize the benevolent rule of the king and is especially appropriate for the Persian kings. Thus, Esth 8:13 (Addition E 11): ἔτυχεν ἧς ἔχομεν πρὸς πᾶν ἔθνος φιλανθρωπίας ἐπὶ τοσοῦτον "he enjoyed the benevolence which we have for every nation". It is similarly used in the papyri and other works of the last centuries B.C.E.[356]

Φιλανθρωπία is a good example of a key-word embodying the values of a society, and one that characterizes the orientation of our translator, no matter what source lay before him. It is integral to I Esd, whose *raison d'être* is the Story of the Three Youths, a story which serves as a paradigm of royal benevolence and good will.

---

[355] One doubts whether this is merely an unexpected flourish on the part of the translator, or is somehow connected with the last two words of the preceding verse in the MT, which have no equivalent in I Esd: גמיר וכענת. It is possible that the translator read ורעות instead of וכענת. The word רעות appears twice in the book; 8:16 (Ezr 7:18) (ו)רעות (מלכא על דנה ישלח) (5:17) 6:21 and ,as expected ,θέλημα ≈ (כ)רעות (האלהים) עלינא) ≈ κρίνηται. The latter supports the possibility that we have here a double or expanded translation of רעות.

[356] In a papyrus adduced by Dittenberger (139), we read: ...στήλην, ἐν ἧι ἀναγράψομεν τὴν γεγονυῖαν ἡμῖν ὑφ' ὑμῶν περὶ τούτων φιλανθρωπίαν, ἵνα ἡ ὑμετέρα χάρις ἀείμνηστος ὑπάρχει. Similarly, Hecataeus of Abdera proclaims φιλανθρωπία to be the outstanding virtue of Ptolemy I (*Ag Ap* 1, 186).

d. God

1. The translator's view of man's relationship with God finds expression in a pair of concepts, which, though not common in the book, nevertheless leaves an undeniable impression: εὐσέβεια – δυσσέβεια.[357] I Esd is not strikingly different from the LXX in its use of these words; yet, a certain individuality can be detected. The stem σεβ-, and especially with the privative prefix, is common in the LXX: thus we find the verb ἀσεβεῖν, which appears twice in I Esd, ἀσέβημα and ἀσεβής. The positive form with εὐ (εὐσέβεια, εὐσεβής) also appears in the LXX; although, it is less common in the canonical books. Thus, יראה, יראת ה׳, is rendered as εὐσέβεια four times in Prov and Isa, but dozens of times in 4 Macc, with five occurrences in 2-3 Macc. The word also appears in I Esd 1:21, a passage without parallel in the MT. On the other hand, δυσσέβεια, along with δυσσέβημα, δυσσεβής, are found only in 2-3 Macc, and twice in I Esd 1:40, 49 (2 Chr 36:8, 16), without a parallel in the MT that would explain the translator's choice of words. The fact that the Greek words have no direct source in the MT may cause them to assume an undue importance in the thought-world of the translator, yet together with this, they surely must indicate that in his eyes at least, the relations between man and God navigate the poles of εὐσέβεια and δυσσέβεια.

2. Divine epithets further reflect the translator's concept of God and the individuality with which he expressed it. Let us describe his approach in two points. His treatment of אלה שמיא/אלהי השמים is outstanding. He consistently avoided the common epithet. It is never rendered literally, to

---

[357] These are fundamental concepts in Greek religion. See the chapter devoted to 'Eusebeia' in Kern (1926), pp. 273-290, which begins: "Durch das Wort σέβεσθαι bezeichnet der Hellene das Verhältnis des Menschen zu den überirdischen Gewalten. Es ist die Scheu, die er ihnen gegenüber empfindet, die Ehrfurcht, die er ihnen schuldet... So ist die εὐσέβεια so alt wie die Religion...".

define, as it were, God's sphere of influence.[358] Sometimes, שמיא is simply not represented (3 times), and in those instances, one might argue that this element was lacking in the *Vorlage*. On one occasion, the epithet is broken up by the insertion of an adjective: אלה שמיא וארעא ≈ τοῦ κυρίου τοῦ κτίσαντος τὸν οὐρανὸν καὶ τὴν γῆν, 6:12 (Ezr 5:11). Here too, however, an argument can be made for a variant in a more expansive text: אלה עבד שמיא וארעא. The assumption of a variant is much less likely when אלה שמיא is rendered by ὁ θεὸς ὁ ὕψιστος, as in 6:30; 8;19, 21 (6:10; 7:21, 23); see however, the repeated אלהא עלאה in Dan 3:26, 32; 5:18, 21 etc.[359] Two instances are particularly interesting: 2:3 (1:2) הי אלהי השמים ≈ ὁ κύριος τοῦ 'Ισραὴλ κύριος ὁ ὕψιστος, and 6:14 (5:12) לאלה שמיא ≈ εἰς τὸν κύριον τοῦ 'Ισραὴλ τὸν οὐράνιον. We will not go into all the problems these verses present, and suffice with three comments. Firstly, in the latter case the translation is closest to the source when it renders שמיא by the adjective οὐράνιος; only, it also causes the original connotation to recede. Secondly, the whole import of the epithet is entirely changed through the additional ὁ κύριος τοῦ 'Ισραὴλ which precedes it. Finally, we find the translator employing κύριος instead of θεὸς. LXX-Dan also renders אלה שמיא by ὁ κύριος ὁ ὕψιστος, twice, Dan 2:18, 19.[360]

The second point which we wish to discuss is that of the translator's use of κύριος. 'Ο κύριος in I Esd is no longer, as in the LXX, a sort of

---

[358] Baudissin (1929), p. 378: "Der Autor vermeidet es, von einem spiritualisierenden Gottesbegriff ausgehend, Gott unter irgendeinem Namen in eine unmittelbare Bezeihung zum Himmel zu setzen".

[359] Grinz (1963), p. 144, sees the divine epithet ὁ θεὸς ὁ ὕψιστος in connection with the title adopted by the High Priest Yohanan: וכשגברה מלכות חשמונאי ונצחום התקינו שיהו מזכירין שם שמים אפילו בשטרות וכך היו כותבים בשנת כך וכך ליוחנן כהן גדול לאל עליון "and when the government of the Hasmoneans became strong and defeated them, they ordained that they should mention the name of God even on bonds and they used to write thus: In the year so and so of Johanan, High Priest to the most High God" (Babylonian Talmud, Rosh ha-Shana 18b).

[360] In LXX-Dan we find also a literal translation of אלה שמיא in 2:37; cf. v. 28.

proper name, a parallel to the tetragrammaton, but a title which retains the content of the Greek word – and of the Masoretic reading for יהוה, i.e., אדני. Accordingly, it can govern the genitival case of 'Israel' as well as other modifiers.[361] These expressions in Greek give no cause at all for assuming a Hebrew variant with the tetragrammaton and must therefore derive from the translator. The use of κύριος reveals yet another similarity with the translators of Esther and Daniel,[362] and thus represents a later stratum of the LXX.[363]

---

[361] Ὁ κύριος αὐτοῦ, αὐτῶν, etc., ὁ κύριος τῶν πατέρων; see Baudissin (1929), p. 370: "Daneben hat 1 Esra ein κύριος in deutlich appellativem Wert, das mit Genetiven verbunden wird".

[362] Baudissin, *ibid*, pp. 284-285, 308, 371.

[363] Hanhart (1977), pp. 201, 221. For further discussion of this point see especially pp. 209-211 and Hanhart's conclusion on p. 212: "Innerhalb der gesamten Überlieferung der LXX aber stellt es nach Sprachgebrauch und Aussage ein Stadium letzter Reife dar, das sich am deutlichsten manifestiert in dem 1. Esrabuch eigentümlichen Begriff des 'Herren Israels' (κύριος᾽Ισραήλ)".

Conclusion

The translation preserved in I Esd' is thus highly distinct within the corpus of the LXX. The various ways in which the translator avoids manacling the Greek to the language of his source are in themselves enough to distinguish him from many other translators. Beyond the general literary orientation of the translator, we find that there were certain matters which engaged his particular interest. In matters related to the Temple, government administration, the monarchy and the divinity, he is at his creative best, borrowing terms from his milieu, selecting and discarding particular words and searching out the ever-elusive *mot juste* for his translation. It is very difficult to reach definite conclusions concerning the world of any translator since his work is necessarily aimed at representing the world of his source rather than his own. The milieu of the translator is further obscured by the fact that he operates on the basis of an established and even sacred tradition of translation. Nevertheless, an examination of the terminology peculiar to a certain translator and which reflects his own interest in certain areas, may also bear fruit for the study of his milieu. In this particular case, we are dealing with a translator who drew heavily from his official linguistic milieu, which would seem to date him to the second century B.C.E.

SUMMARY

The author of I Esd composed his work on the basis of 2 Chr 35-36, Ezra and Neh 8, with the addition of the apocryphal Story of the Youths, unparalleled in the canonical books. Our study of I Esd analyzed this book from three different perspectives which together depict the overall process of its creation: the composition of the book, its *Vorlage*, and the nature of its translation.

The book in its present form is a vibrant translation into Greek of a Hebrew-Aramaic work. The translator of I Esd does not belong to the main stream of LXX-translators, but is rather a unique and creative translator, best compared with the LXX-translator of Daniel. He expends great efforts in presenting a fluent Greek composition, often allowing his target language and his cultural milieu to interfere with an accurate and faithful translation of the original. Only a close investigation of his translation technique, made possible by comparing the parallel sections in the MT, gives us a glimpse of the original text now concealed by the veil of translation.

The relationship between the *Vorlage* of I Esd and the parallel parts in the MT provides an outstanding case for textual criticism. Both the text crystallized in the MT and the text preserved in I Esd underwent a massive amount of changes after the texts took their different courses. Nevertheless, the variance between the texts seems to be due to the natural course of their transmission. Our technical / syntactical outline of the differences between the texts clearly shows that similar phenomena characterize the development of both texts, except for a few changes which are particularly characteristic of the revision of I Esd.

In our view, I Esd is indeed a revision of parts of Chr-Ezr-Neh, the sole purpose of which is the interpolation of the Story of the Youths. Most of the differences between the structure and sequence of the events in I Esd and the canonical books derive from the need to create an appropriate setting for the Story of the Youths. The Story of the Youths is thus the *raison d'être* of I Esd. The book has no independent literary or ideological existence without it. The Story of the Youths was added in order to provide Zerubbabel, the scion of the House of David, with a more prominent role in the narrative of the Return. This goal, however, is not achieved by a programmatic, ideological statement, but rather by a 'story'. This story presents an artificial admixture of genres; on the one hand, it elaborates on a common literary motif – a wisdom debate concerning the most powerful factor in the universe, on the other hand, it borrows many themes from the stories of the Return in the canonical books, especially that of Nehemiah who has no role in I Esd. The interpolation of the Story of the Youths results in an impossible combination of two different accounts of the same event: the Return of Zerubbabel is related both in the version of the Story of the Youths and in the version of the canonical books. I Esd thus presents an unreasonable course of events and is therefore, in the final analysis, a rather incoherent composition.

ABBREVIATIONS

AB	Anchor Bible
AJSL	American Journal of Semitic Languages and Literatures
BZ	Biblische Zeitschrift
BZAW	Beihefte zur Zeitschrift für die alttestamentliche Wissenschaft
CBQ	Catholic Biblical Quarterly
FRLANT	Forschungen zur Religion und Literatur des Alten und Neuen Testaments
HAT	Handbuch zum Alten Testament
HSM	Harvard Semitic Monographs
HSS	Harvard Semitic Studies
HTR	Harvard Theological Review
ICC	International Critical Commentary
JBL	Journal for Biblical Literature
JJS	Journal of Jewish Studies
JQR	Jewish Qurterly Review
JSOR	Journal of the Society of Oriental Research
JThSt	Journal of Theological Studies
KHAT	Kommentar zum Alten Testament
MGWJ	Monatschrift zur Geschichte undWissenschaft des Judentums
OBO	Orbis Biblicus et Orientalis
OLZ	Orientalische Literaturzeitung
OTL	Old Testament Library
SCS	Septuagint and Cognate Studies
SVT	Supplements Vetus Testamentum
ThQ	Theological Quarterly
VT	Vetus Testamentum
ZAW	Zeitschrift für die alttestamentliche Wissenschaft

BIBLIOGRAPHY OF CITED WORKS

Aejmelaeus, A.

1982   *Parataxis in the Septuagint,* Helsinki.

Allen, L.C.

1974   *The Greek Chronicles,* I-II (SVT 25, 27), Leiden.

Allgeier, A.

1941   Beobachtungen am Septuagintatext der Bücher Esdras und Nehemias, *Biblica* 22, pp. 227-251.

Allrik, H.L.

1954   1Esdras according to Codex B and A as Appearing in Zerubabel's List in 1Esdras 5, 8-23, *ZAW* 66, pp. 272-292.

Attridge, H.W.

1984   I Esdras, in: *Jewish Writings of the Second Temple Period* (ed. M.E. Stone), Assen-Philadelphia, pp. 157-160.

Avishur, Y.

1974   *Pairs of Words in Biblical Literature and their Parallels in Semitic Literature of the Ancient Near East,* Diss., Jerusalem [Hebrew]

Baars, W. & J.C.H. Lebram, eds.,

1972   *I (3) Esdras,* The Old Testament in Syriac (The Peshitta Institute, IV), Leiden.

Bagnall, R.S.

1976   *The Administration of the Ptolemaic Possessions Outside Egypt*, Leiden.

Bar-Kochva, B.

1980   *The Battles of the Hasmonaeans*, Jerusalem [Hebrew].

Barr, J.

1979   *The Typology of Literalism in Ancient Biblical Translations*, Göttingen.

1989   Hebrew, Aramaic and Greek in the Hellenistic Age, *The Cambridge History of Judaism*, II, Cambridge, pp. 79-114

Barthélemy, D.

1982   *Critique Textuelle de l'Ancien Testament* (OBO 51/1), Fribourg-Göttingen.

Batten, L.W.

1913   *The Books of Ezra and Nehemiah* (ICC), Edinburgh.

Baudissin, W.W.

1929   *Kyrios*, I, Giessen, pp. 359-405.

Bauer, H. and P. Leander,

1927   *Grammatik des Biblisch-Aramäischen*, Tübingen.

Baumgartner, W.

1927   Das Aramäische im Buche Daniel, *ZAW* 4, pp. 81-133.

Bayer, P.E.

1911   *Das dritte Buch Esdras*, Freiburg.

Bengston, H.
1952   *Die Strategie in der hellenistischen Zeit*, III, München.

Bertholdt, L.
1813   *Historisch- kritische Einleitung in sammtliche kanonische und apokryphische Schriften des Alten und Neuen Testaments*, III, Erlangen, pp. 1005-1013.

Bertholet, A.
1902   *Die Bücher Esra und Nehemia* (KHAT), Tübingen-Leipzig.

Bewer, J.A.
1919-20 The Gap between Ezra Chapter 1 and 2, *AJSL* 36, pp. 18-26.
1922   *Der Text des Buches Ezra* (FRLANT 31), Göttingen.

Beyer, K.
1984-94 *Die aramäischen Texte vom Toten Meer*, I-II, Göttingen.

Bickerman, E.J.
1946   The Edict of Cyrus in Ezra 1, *JBL* 65, pp. 249-275.
1947   *From Ezra to the Last of the Maccabees*, New York.
1947*   La Coelé-Syrie, *RB* 54, pp. 256-268.

Black, M.
1967   *An Aramaic Approach to the Gospels and Acts*,[3] Oxford.

Blass, F. & A. Debrunner
1961   *A Greek Grammar of the New Testament* (tr. and revised by R.W. Funk), Chicago & London.

Böhler, D.

1997   *Die heilige Stadt in Esdras α und Esra-Nehemia*, Göttingen.

Brooke, A.E. & N. McLean, eds.,

1935   *IEsdras, Ezra-Nehemiah*, The Old Testament in Greek, IV, Cambridge.

Büchler, A.

1897   Das apokryphische Esrabuch, *MGWJ* 41, pp. 1-16, 49-66, 97-103.

Burney, C.F.

1922   *The Aramaic Origin of the Fourth Gospel*, Oxford.

Charles, R.H.

1913   *The Apocrypha and Pseudoepigrapha of the Old Testament in English*, I-II, Oxford.

1929   *A Critical and Exegetical Commentary on the Book of Daniel*, Oxford.

Coggins, R.G. & M.A. Knibb

1979   *The First and Second Books of Esdras* (The Cambridge Bible Commentary), Cambridge.

Cook, S.A.

1913   I Esdras, in: R.H. Charles, *The Apocrypha and Pseudo-epigrapha of the Old Testament*, I, Oxford, pp. 1-58.

Cowley, A.

1923   *Aramaic Papyri of the Fifth Century B.C.*, Oxford.

Crenshaw, J.L.

1981　The Contest of Darius' Guards, in: *Images of Man and God* (ed. B.O. Long), Sheffield, pp. 74-88; 119-120.

Cross, F.M.

1975　The Evolution of a Theory of Local Texts, in: F.M. Cross and Sh. Talmon eds., *Qumran and the History of the Biblical Text*, Cambridge Mass.-London, pp. 306-320.

Dähne, A.F.

1834　*Geschichtliche Darstellung der jüdisch-alexandrinischen Religions Philosophie*, Halle, pp. 116-125.

Degen, R.

1969　*Altaramäische Grammatik der Inschriften des 10.-8. JH.V.CHR.*, Wiesbaden.

Denter, P.Th.

1962　*Die Stellung der Bücher Esdras im Kanon des Alten Testaments*, Diss., Freiburg.

Dittenberger, W.

1903　*Orientis Graeci Inscriptiones Selectae*, Leipzig.

Donner, H.

1961　Der Freund des Königs, *ZAW* 73, pp. 269-277.

Driver, G.R.

1957　*Aramaic Documents of the Fifth Century B.C.*,[2] Oxford.

Driver, S.R.

1913   *Notes on the Hebrew Text and Topography of the Books of Samuel*, Oxford.

Eichhorn, J.G.

1795   Über den apokryphischen Esras, in: *Einleitung in die Apokryphischen Schriften*, Leipzig, pp. 335-377.

Eskenazi, T.C.

1986   The Chronicler and the Composition of 1 Esdras, *CBQ* 48, pp. 39-61.

Fischer, J.

1904   Das apokryphe und das kanonische Esrabuch, *BZ* 2, pp. 351-364.

Flusser, D.

1978-80 *The Jossipon* [Josephus Gorionides], I-II, Jerusalem [Hebrew].

Frankel, Z.

1841   *Vorstudien zu der Septuaginta*, Leipzig.

Fritzsche, O.F.

1851   *Kurzgefasstes exegetisches Handbuch zu den Apokryphen des Alten Testament*, I, Leipzig, pp. 1-66.

Gardner, A.E.

1986   The Purpose and Date of I Esdras, *JJS* 37, pp. 18-27.

Gelston, A.

1966   The Foundations of the Second Temple, *VT* 16, pp. 232-235.

Gerleman, G.

1948   *Synoptic Studies in the Old Testament*, Lund.

Glatt, D.A.

1991   *Chronological Displacement in Biblical and Related Literatures*, Diss., Philadelphia, pp. 179-222.

Goodman, W.R.

1972   *A Study of I Esdras 3:1-5:6*, Diss., Duke.

Göttsberger, J.

1926   Über das III. Kapitel des Esrabuches, *JSOR* 10, pp. 270-280.

Grintz, Y.M.

1963   Hebrew Literature in the Persian Period, *Ch. Albeck Jubilee Volume*, Jerusalem, pp. 123-151 [Hebrew].

Guthe, H.

1900   *Das dritte Buch Esra*, in: E. Kautzsch, Die Apokryphen und Pseudepigraphen des Alten Testament, I, Tübingen, pp. 1-23.

Hanhart, R.

1974   *Esdrae liber I* (Septuaginta Vetus Testamentum Graecum VIII, 1), Göttingen.

1974*   *Text und Textgeschichte des 1. Esrabuches*, Göttingen.

1977   Zu Text und Textgeschichte des ersten Esrabuches, *Proceedings of the Sixth World Congress of Jewish Studies*, I, Jerusalem, pp. 201-212.

1993   *Esdrae Liber II* (Septuaginta Vetus Testamentum Graecum VIII, 2), Göttingen.

1995   Ein unbekannter Text zur griechischen Esra-Überlieferung, *Mitteilungen des Septuaginta-Unternehmens* XXII, pp. 111-132.

Haran, M.

> 1986   Explaining the Identical Lines at the End of Chronicles and the Beginning of Ezra, *Bible Review* 2, pp. 18-20.

Heinemann, Y.

> 1950   *The Ways of the Aggada*, Jerusalem [Hebrew].

Heltzer, M.

> 1977   Ein epigraphischer Blick auf das III. Esrabuch, *Biblica* 58, pp. 62-72.
>
> 1980   The Greek Text of I Esdras III 1-2; Its Date and Subordination at the Achaemenian Court, *Henoch* 2, pp. 150-155.

Heltzer, M. & M. Ohana

> 1978   *The Extra-Biblical Tradition of Hebrew Personal Names*, Haifa [Hebrew].

Höffken, P.

> 1975   Warum schwieg Jesus Sirach über Esra?, *ZAW* 87, pp. 184-202.

Holladay, C. R.

> 1983   *Fragments from Hellenistic Jewish Authors*, I, Chico.

Howorth, H.H.

> 1893   A Criticism of the Sources and the Relative Importance and Value of the Canonical Book of Ezra and the Apocryphal Book Known as Esdras I, *Transactions of the Ninth International Congress of Orientalists*, II, London, pp. 68-85.
>
> 1893*   The Real Character and the Importance of the First Book of Esdras, I-IV, *The Academy* 43, pp. 13-14, 60, 106, 174-175, 326-327, 524; *ibid*, 44, pp. 233-234, 73-74, 295, 549-550.

Howorth, H.H.

1901 Some Unconvencional Views on the Text of the Bible, *Proceedings of the Society of Biblical Archaeology* 23, pp. 147-159, 305-325.

1902 *ibid*, 24, pp. 147-172, 332-340.

1903 *ibid*, 25, pp. 15-22, 90-96.

1904 *ibid*, 26, pp. 25-31, 63-69, 94-100.

1905 *ibid*, 27, pp. 267-278.

1907 *ibid*, 29, pp. 31-38, 61-69.

Humbert, P.

1928 Magna est Veritas et Praevalet (3 Esra 4, 35), *OLZ* 31, pp. 148-150.

1967 Note sur YASAD et ses dérivés, in: *Hebräische Wortforschung, Festschrift zum 80. Geburtstag von W. Baumgartner* (SVT 16), Leiden, pp. 135-142.

Hurvitz, A.

1971 "Diachronic Chiasm" in Biblical Hebrew, in: *Bible and Jewish History – Studies dedicated to the Memory of J. Liver* (ed. B. Uffenheimer), Tel Aviv, pp. 248-255 [Hebrew].

1972 *The Transition Period in Biblical Hebrew*, Jerusalem [Hebrew].

In der Smitten, W.Th.

1967 *Esra, Quellen, Überlieferung und Geschichte* (BZAW 102), Berlin.

1971 Review of K.F. Pohlmann, *BO* 28, pp. 381-382.

1972 Zur Pagenerzählung im III.Esra, *VT* 22, pp. 492-495.

Jacob, A.

   1912   *Septuagintastudien zu Ezra*, Diss., Breslau.

Jahn, G.

   1909   *Die Bücher Esra (A und B) und Nehemja*, Leiden.

Japhet, S.

   1968   The Supposed Common Authorship of Chronicles and Ezra-
           Nehemiah Investigated Anew, *VT* 18, pp. 330-371.
   1982   Sheshbazzar and Zerubbabel, *ZAW* 94, pp. 66-98.
   1991   The Relationship between Chronicles and Ezra-Nehemiah,
           SVT 43, pp. 298-313.
   1993   *I & II Chronicles* (OTL), Lewisville.

Jellinek, A.

   1938   *Bet ha-Midrasch*, I-VI^2, Jerusalem.

Kahana, A. (ed.)

   1930   *The Apocrypha* I-II, Jerusalem [Hebrew].

Kaufmann, Y.

   1956   I Esdras, *Beit Miqra* 1, pp. 103-107 [Hebrew].
   1967   *Israel's Religion (Toledot ha-Emuna ha-Yisre'elit)*, IV,
           Jerusalem and Tel Aviv [Hebrew].

Kellermann, U.

   1967   *Nehemia, Quellen, Überlieferung und Geschichte* (BZAW
           102), Berlin.

Kern, O.

   1926   *Die Religion der Griechen*, I, Berlin.

Kitchen, K.A.

    1965   The Aramaic of Daniel, in: *Notes on Some Problems in the Book of Daniel*, London.

Klein, M.L.

    1982   *Anthropomorphisms and anthropopathisms in the Targumim of the Pentateuch*, Jerusalem.

    1986   *Genizah Manuscripts of Palestinian Targum to the Pentateuch*, I, Cincinnati.

Klein, R.W.

    1966   *Studies in the Greek Texts of the Chronicler*, Harvard diss., Cambridge.

    1969   Old Readings in IEsd; the List of Returnees from Babylon, *HTR* 62, pp. 99-107.

Komlosh, Y.

    1973   *The Bible in the Light of the Aramaic Translations*, Tel Aviv [Hebrew].

Kooij, A. van der

    1991   On the Ending of the Book of 1 Esdras, Proceedings of the XVII Congress of the IOSCS 1989, Atlanta, pp. 37-49.

    1991*   Zur Frage des Anfangs des 1. Esrabuches, *ZAW* 103, pp. 239-252.

Kraeling, E.G.

    1953   *The Brooklyn Museum Aramaic Papyri*, New Haven.

Kropat, A.

    1909   *Die Syntax des Autors der Chronik* (BZAW 16), Giessen.

Kutscher, E.Y.
   1974   *The Language and Linguistic Background of the Isaiah Scroll*
          (1QIsaᵃ), Leiden.
   1977   Hebrew and Aramaic Studies, Jerusalem [Hebrew].
   1982   *A History of the Hebrew Language*, Leiden.

Lagarde, P. de
   1863   *Anmerkungen zur griechischen Übersetzung der Proverbien,*
          Leipzig.

Lammert, F.
   1927   Σωματοφύλακες, *BW* 2, 5, p. 991-992.

Laqueur, R.
   1911   Ephoros, *Hermes* 46, pp. 171-173 (note).

Leiter, N.
   1985   Assimilation and Dissimilation Techniques in the LXX of the
          Book of Balaam, *Textus* 12, pp. 79-95.

Leuze, O.
   1935   *Die Satrapieneinteilung in Syrien*, Halle.

Liver, J.
   1964   The Sequence of Persian Kings in Ezra and Nehemiah, *M.H.*
          Segal Volume, Jerusalem, pp. 127-138 [Hebrew].

Marquart, J.
   1896   *Fundamente israelitischer und jüdischer Gesch-ichte,*
          Göttingen, pp. 44-47.

Marquis, G.

    1986   Word Order as a Criterion for the Evaluation of Translation Technique in the LXX and the Evaluation of Word-Order Variants as Exemplified in LXX-Ezekiel, *Textus* XIII, pp. 59-94

Martin, R.A.

    1974   *Syntactical Evidence of Semitic Sources in Greek Documents* (SCS 3), Missoula.

Mayser, E.

    1934   *Grammatik der griechischen Papyri aus der Ptolemaerzeit*, Berlin and Leipzig.

Meyer, E.

    1896   *Die Entstehung des Judenthums*, Halle a. S.

Milik, J.T.

    1976   *The Books of Enoch*, Oxford.

Min, Y.J.

    1970   *The Minuses and Pluses of the LXX Translation of Jeremiah*, diss. Jerusalem

Mosis, R.

    1973   *Untersuchungen zur Theologie des chronistischen Geschichtswerkes*, Freiburg im Breisgau.

Moulton, W.J.

    1899   Über die Überlieferung und den textkritischen Werth des dritten Esrabuches, *ZAW* 19, pp. 209-258.

    1900   *ibid*, 20, pp. 1-35.

Mowinckel, S.

1964   *Studien zu dem Buche Ezra-Nehemia*, I, Oslo, pp. 7-28.

Muraoka, T.

1972   Notes on the Aramaic of the Genesis Apocryphon, *RB* 8.

1984   *A Greek-Hebrew/Aramaic Index to I Esdras* (SCS 16), Chico, California.

1986   A Computer-generated 'Perfect' Concordance?, *Biblica* 67, pp. 565-567.

Myers, J.M.

1965   *Ezra-Nehemiah* (AB), New York.

1974   *I&II Esdras* (AB), New York.

Nestle, E.

1893   *Marginalien und Materialien*, Tübingen, pp. 23-31.

Neuman, A.A.

1952   Josippon and the Apokrypha, *JQR* 43, pp. 1-26.

Panchatantra

1949   *The Panchatantra*, translated from Sanskrit by A. W. Ryder, Bombay.

Payne Smith, R.

1901   *Thesaurus Syriacus* II, Oxford.

Pelletier, A.

1962   *Flavius Josèphe adaptateur de la Lettre d'Aristée*, Paris.

Peretz, Y.

1968   Juxtaposition of Proper Noun and Adjective, *Fourth World Congress of Jewish Studies* II, Jerusalem, pp. 129-133 [Hebrew].

Pfeifer, G.

1967   *Ursprung und Wesen der Hypostasenvorstellungen im Judentum*, Stuttgart.

Pfeiffer, R.H.

1949   *History of New Testament Times with an Introduction to the Apocrypha*, Chapter I: I Esdras (The Greek Ezra), New York, pp. 233-257.

Pisano, S.

1984   *Additions or Omissions in the Books of Samuel* (OBO 57), Göttingen.

Pohlmann, A.A.

1859   Über das Ansehen des apokryphischen dritten Buches Esdras, *ThQ* 41, pp. 257-275.

Pohlmann, K.F.

1970   *Studien im dritten Esra*, Göttingen.

Pohlmann, K.F.

1980   *3. Esra-Buch* (Jüdische Schriften aus hellenistisch-römischer Zeit I, 5), Gütersloh.

Polzin, R.

1976   *Late Biblical Hebrew* (HSM 12), Missoula.

Pope, H.

    1907   The Third Book of Esdras and the Tridentine Canon, *JThSt* 8, pp. 218-232.

Qimron, E.

    1986   *The Hebrew of the Dead Sea Scrolls* (HSS 29), Atlanta, Georgia.

Rabin, C.

    1962   The Ancient Versions and the Indefinite Subject, *Textus* 2, pp. 60-76.

Rainey, A.F.

    1969   The Satrapy "Beyond the River", *Australian Journal of Biblical Archaeology* I, pp. 51-78.

Riessler, P.

    1899   *Das Buch Daniel*, Stuttgart.

    1907   Der textkritische Wert des dritten Esrabuches, *BZ* 5, pp. 146-158.

Rosenthal, F.

    1963   *A Grammar of Biblical Aramaic*, Wiesbaden.

Rudolph, W.

    1945/48 Der Wettstreit der Leibwächter des Darius, *ZAW* 61, pp. 176-190.

    1949   *Esra und Nehemia* (HAT), Tübingen.

    1955   *Chronikbücher* (HAT), Tübingen.

Rundgren, F.

1957   Zur Bedeutung von οἰκογενής in 3 Esra 3, 1, *Eranos* 55, pp. 145-152.

Ryan, J.K.

1956   Magna est Veritas et praevalebit (3 Ezra), *AER* 135, pp. 116-124.

Sarfatti, G.B.

1987   The Use of the Syntagm נמצא עושה in Mishnaic Hebrew, *Language Studies* II-III, Jerusalem, pp. 225-243.

Schaeder, H.H.

1930   *Esra der Schreiber*, Halle a. S.

Shaked, Sh.

1984   From Iran to Islam; Notes on Some Themes in Transmission, *Jerusalem Studies in Arabic and Islam* 4, pp. 31-67.

Schalit, A.

1947   The Date and Place of the Story about the Three Bodyguards of the King in the Apocryphal Book of Ezra, *Bulletin of the Jewish Palestine Exploration Society* 13, pp. 119-128 [Hebrew].

1954   Κοίλη Συρία from the Mid-Fourth Century to the Beginning of the Third Century B.C., *Scripta Hierosolymitana* 1, pp. 64-77.

1969   *König Herodes*, Berlin, pp. 705-708.

Schürer, E.

1986   *The History of the Jewish People in the Age of Jesus Christ
        (175 b.c.-a.d. 135)* (eds. G. Vermes; F. Millar, M. Goodman),
        III, Edinburgh.

Seeligmann, I.L.

1948   *The Septuagint Version of Isaiah*, Leiden.

Segal, M.H.

1943   The Books of Ezra-Nehemiah, *Tarbiz* 14, pp. 81-103 [Hebrew].

Segert, S.

1975   *Altaramäische Grammatik*, Leipzig.

Smith, M.

1971   *Palestinian Parties and Politics that Shaped the Old Testament*,
        New York.

Sollamo, R.

1979   *Renderings of Hebrew Semiprepositions in the Septuagint*,
        Helsinki.

Sperber, A.

1959-73 *The Bible in Aramaic*, I-IV, Leiden.

Stern, M.

1981   The Hellenistic Period, in: *The History of Eretz Israel*, III,
        Jerusalem, pp. 9-190 [Hebrew].

Talmon, Sh.

1960   Double Readings in the MT, *Textus* 1 (1960), pp. 144-184.

Talmon, Sh.

1961   Synonymous Readings in the Textual Traditions of the Old
        Testament, *Scripta Hierosolymitana* 8, pp. 335-383.

1975   The Textual Study of the Bible – A New Outlook, in: F.M.
        Cross, and Sh. Talmon, eds., *Qumran and the History of the
        Biblical Text*, Cambridge Mass.-London, pp. 321-400.

1976   Ezra and Nehemiah, *IDB Suppl. Vol.*, Nashville, pp. 317-328.

Talshir, D.

1988   A Reinvestigation of the Linguistic Relationship between
        Chronicles and Ezra-Nehemiah, *VT* 38, pp. 165-193.

1988*   The References to Ezra and the Books of Chronicles in
        B. Baba Bathra 15a, *VT* 38, pp. 358-360.

Talshir, Z.

1982   I Esdras – A Portrait of a Literal Translation, Proceedings of
        the Eighth Congress for Jewish Studies, I, Jerusalem,
        pp. 47-52.

1983   The Transmission of the Second Temple Founding Tradition,
        *I. L. Seeligmann Volume – Essays on the Bible and the Ancient
        East* (eds. A. Rofé and Y. Zakovitch), I, Jerusalem, pp. 347-359
        [Hebrew].

1984   *First Esdras – Origin and Translation*, Diss. Jerusalem
        [Hebrew].

1984*   The Milieu of 1 Esdras in the light of its Vocabulary, *De
        Septuaginta – Studies in honour of J.W. Wevers*, Mississauga,
        pp. 129-147.

1985   Review of T. Muraoka, A Greek-Hebrew/Aramaic Index to
        I Esdras (SCS 16), Chico, California 1984, *Biblica* 66, pp.
        438-440.

Talshir, Z.

1986   Double Translations in the Septuagint, *VI Congress of the International Organization for Septuagint and Cognate Studies* (SCS 23), Jerusalem, pp. 21-63.

1986*   Linguistic Development and the Evaluation of Translation Technique in the Septuagint, *Scripta Hierosolymitana* 33, pp. 301-320.

1995   The Story of the Three Youths (I Esdras 3-4) – towards the Question of the Language of its Vorlage, *Textus* XVIII, pp. 135-155 (in collaboration with D. Talshir).

1996   The Three Deaths of Josiah and the Strata of Biblical Historiography, *VT* XLVI, pp. 213-236.

Tedesche, S.S.

1938   *A Critical Edition of I Esdras*, Diss, New Haven.

Thackeray, H.J.

1898   Esdras, *HDB*, I, New York, pp. 758-763.

1909   *A Grammar of the Old Testament in Greek*, Cambridge.

Theis, J.

1910   *Geschichtliche und literarkritische Fragen in Esra 1-6*, Münster.

Torrey, C.C.

1910   *Ezra Studies*, Chicago.

1945   A Revised View of First Esdras, *Louis Ginzberg Jubilee Volume*, New York, pp. 395-410.

Tov, E.

1978   Studies in the Vocabulary of the Septuagint, *Tarbiz* 47,
        pp. 120-138 [Hebrew]

1981   *The Text-Critical Use of the Septuagint in Biblical Research,*
        Jerusalem.

1982   The Representation of the Causative Aspects of the Hiphᶜil
        in the LXX, *Biblica* 63, pp. 417-424.

1992   *Textual Criticism of the Hebrew Bible,* Minneapolis-Assen /
        Maastricht, pp. 187-197.

Treuenfels, A.

1850   Über das apocryphische Buch Esra, *Literaturblatt des Orients,*
        15, pp. 231-235; 16, pp. 245-250; 17, pp. 257-262; 18, pp.
        281-287; 40, pp. 633-636; 41, pp. 650-655; 42, pp. 663-677;
        43, pp. 682-685; 44, pp. 693-697; 45, pp. 713-718; 48, pp.
        762-765; 49, pp. 774-777.

Turner, N.

1976   *A Grammar of New Testament Greek* (by J.H. Moulton), *IV:
        Style,* Edinburgh.

Walde, B.

1913   *Die Esrabücher der Septuaginta,* Freiburg.

Wasserstein, A.

1983   Greek Elements in Ancient Jewish Literature, *I.L. Seeligmann
        Volume – Essays on the Bible and the Ancient East* (eds.
        A. Rofé and Y. Zakovitch), II, Jerusalem, pp. 483-498
        [Hebrew].

Weiss, R.

1979   *The Aramaic Targum of Job*, Tel Aviv [Hebrew].

Widengren, G.

1957   Quelques rapports entre Juifs et Iraniens à l'Époque des Parthes,
        Volume du Congres Strasbourg 1956 (SVT 4), pp. 197-241.

Willi, Th.

1972   *Die Chronik als Ausleung*, Göttingen.

Williamson, H.G.M.

1977   *Israel in the Book of Chronicles*, Cambridge, esp. pp. 12-36.

1982   *1 and 2 Chronicles* (New Century Bible), London.

1987   Did the Author of Chronicles Also Write the Books of Ezra
        and Nehemiah?, *Bible Review* 3, pp. 56-59.

York, H.C.

1909-10 The Latin Versions of First Esdras, *AJSL* 26, pp. 253-302.

Zakovich, Y.

1978   *The Literary Pattern of Three-Four in the Bible*, Dissertation,
        Jerusalem [Hebrew].

Zimmermann, F.

1963-64 The Story of the Three Guardsmen, *JQR* ns 54, pp. 179-200.

Zunz, L.

1832   Dibre Hajamim oder die Bücher der Chronik, in: *Die gottes-
        dienstlichen Vorträge der Juden historisch entwickelt*, Berlin,
        pp. 12-34.

Other Titles in the Septuagint and Cognate Studies Series

ROBERT A. KRAFT (editor)
Septuagintal Lexicography (1975)
Code: 06 04 01
Not Available

ROBERT A KRAFT (editor)
1972 Proceedings: Septuagint and Pseudepigrapha Seminars (1973)
Code: 06 04 02
Not Available

RAYMOND A. MARTIN
Syntactical Evidence of Semitic Studies in Greek Documents (1974)
Code: 06 04 03
Not Available

GEORGE W. E. NICKELSBURG, JR. (editor)
Studies on the *Testament of Moses* (1973)
Code: 06 04 04
Not Available

GEORGE W.E. NICKELSBURG, JR. (editor)
Studies on the *Testament of Joseph* (1975)
Code: 06 04 05
Not Available

GEORGE W.E. NICKELSBURG, JR. (editor)
Studies on the *Testament of Abraham* (1976)
Code: 06 04 06
Not Available

JAMES H. CHARLESWORTH
Pseudepigrapha and Modern Research (1976)
Code: 06 04 07
Not Available

JAMES H. CHARLESWORTH
Pseudepigrapha and Modern Research with a Supplement (1981)
Code: 06 04 07 S

JOHN W. OLLEY
"Righteousness" in the Septuagint of Isaiah: A Contextual Study (1979)
Code: 06 04 08

MELVIN K. H. PETERS
An Analysis of the Textual Character of the Bohairic of Deuteronomy (1980)
Code: 06 04 09
Not Available

DAVID G. BURKE
The Poetry of Baruch (1982)
Code: 06 04 10

JOSEPH L. TRAFTON
Syriac Version of the Psalms of Solomon (1985)
Code: 06 04 11

JOHN COLLINS, GEORGE NICKELSBURG
Ideal Figures in Ancient Judaism: Profiles and Paradigms (1980)
Code: 06 04 12

ROBERT HANN
The Manuscript History of the Psalms of Solomon (1982)
Code: 06 04 13

J.A.L. LEE
A Lexical Study of the Septuagint Version of the Pentateuch (1983)
Code: 06 04 14

MELVIN K. H. PETERS
A Critical Edition of the Coptic (Bohairic) Pentateuch Vol. 5: Deuteronomy (1983)
Code: 06 04 15

T. MURAOKA
A Greek-Hebrew/Aramaic Index to I Esdras (1984)
Code: 06 04 16

JOHN RUSSIANO MILES
Retroversion and Text Criticism:
The Predictability of Syntax in An Ancient Translation
from Greek to Ethiopic (1985)
Code: 06 04 17

LESLIE J. MCGREGOR
The Greek Text of Ezekiel (1985)
Code: 06 04 18

MELVIN K.H. PETERS
A Critical Edition of the Coptic (Bohairic) Pentateuch,
Vol. 1: Genesis (1985)
Code: 06 04 19

ROBERT A. KRAFT AND EMANUEL TOV (project directors)
Computer Assisted Tools for Septuagint Studies
Vol 1: Ruth (1986)
Code: 06 04 20

CLAUDE E. COX
Hexaplaric Materials Preserved in the Armenian Version (1986)
Code: 06 04 21

MELVIN K.H. PETERS
A Critical Edition of the Coptic (Bohairic) Pentateuch
Vol. 2: Exodus (1986)
Code: 06 04 22

Order from:
Scholars Press Customer Services
P.O. Box133089
Atlanta, GA 30333-3089
1-888-747-2354 or 404-727-2354